YEARBOOK

2000

Volume 4

INTERNATIONAL TRIBUNAL FOR THE LAW OF THE SEA

Hamburg, Germany

YEARBOOK 2000

Volume 4

KLUWER LAW INTERNATIONAL
THE HAGUE / LONDON / NEW YORK

Library of Congress Cataloging-in Publication Data

ISBN-90-411-1762-8

International Tribunal for the Law of the Sea
Tribunal international du droit de la mer
Am Internationalen Seegerichtshof 1
22609 Hamburg, Germany.

Published by Kluwer Law International,
P.O. Box 85889, 2508 CN The Hague, The Netherlands.

Sold and distributed in North, Central and South America
by Kluwer Law International,
101 Philip Drive, Norwell, MA 02061, USA.

In all other countries, sold and distributed
by Kluwer Law International, Distribution Centre,
P.O. Box 322, 3300 AH Dordrecht, The Netherlands.

Printed on acid-free paper

Printed and bound in Great Britain by Antony Rowe Limited.

PREFACE

The Yearbook provides general information on the organization, jurisdiction, activities and administration of the Tribunal.

Each volume of the Yearbook covers the period from 1 January to 31 December of the year for which it is published. The present volume, which is the fourth in the series to date, covers the 2000 calendar year.

The Yearbook is prepared and published by the Registry and in no way involves the responsibility of the Tribunal; in particular, information on Judgments and Orders contained in Chapter IV cannot be quoted against the actual texts of those Judgments and Orders and does not constitute an interpretation thereof.

Throughout the Yearbook, the following abbreviations have been used:

"Convention" for the United Nations Convention on the Law of the Sea;
"Statute" for the Statute of the International Tribunal for the Law of the Sea;
"Rules" for the Rules of the Tribunal;
"Resolution" for the Resolution on the Internal Judicial Practice of the Tribunal; and
"Guidelines" for the Guidelines concerning the Preparation and Presentation of Cases before the Tribunal.

Philippe Gautier
Registrar
(October 2001)

TABLE OF CONTENTS

INTRODUCTION

The International Tribunal for the Law of the Sea is the central judicial forum in the comprehensive system for the settlement of disputes established under the United Nations Convention on the Law of the Sea of 10 December 1982.[1/] The historical background of the adoption of the Convention and of the establishment of the Tribunal is elaborated in the Introduction of the Tribunal's *Yearbook 1996–1997*.

The Tribunal is composed of 21 judges who are elected by the States Parties to the Convention. The first election took place on 1 August 1996 and the Tribunal began its work on 1 October 1996. On 28 October 1997 the Tribunal adopted its Rules and on 13 November 1997 it received its first case.

In 2000, the Tribunal dealt with two prompt release proceedings: on 7 February 2000, the Tribunal delivered its Judgment in the "*Camouco*" *Case (Panama* v. *France)* and on 18 December 2000, it delivered its Judgment in the "*Monte Confurco*" *Case (Seychelles* v. *France)*. In addition, by Order dated 20 December 2000, the Tribunal, pursuant to the request of Chile and the European Community, formed a special chamber of five judges in accordance with article 15, paragraph 2, of the Statute to deal with the *Case concerning the Conservation and Sustainable Exploitation of Swordfish Stocks in the South-Eastern Pacific Ocean (Chile/European Community)*.

The Tribunal held two sessions devoted to administrative matters in 2000. The Ninth Session took place from 6 to 17 March 2000. The Tenth Session was held from 18 to 29 September 2000.

[1/] The Convention entered into force on 16 November 1994.

CHAPTER I

ORGANIZATION AND FUNCTIONING OF THE TRIBUNAL

I. Members of the Tribunal

1. Composition of the Tribunal

The Tribunal is composed of 21 independent members (Statute, article 2, paragraph 1) elected by secret ballot (Statute, article 4, paragraph 4) by the States Parties to the Convention. Each State Party may nominate up to two candidates from among persons enjoying the highest reputation for fairness and integrity and of recognized competence in the field of the law of the sea (Statute, article 2, paragraph 1). The persons elected to the Tribunal are those nominees who obtain the largest number of votes and a two-thirds majority of the States Parties present and voting. The two-thirds majority must also be an absolute majority of all States Parties (Statute, article 4, paragraph 4).

No two members may be nationals of the same State and in the Tribunal as a whole it is necessary to assure the representation of the principal legal systems of the world and equitable geographical distribution; there shall be no fewer than three members from each geographical group as established by the General Assembly of the United Nations (African States, Asian States, Eastern European States, Latin American and Caribbean States and Western European and Other States). The geographical distribution within the Tribunal was decided at the fifth Meeting of States Parties in 1996.[2]

Members are elected for nine years and may be re-elected, the terms of one third of the members expiring every three years (Statute, article 5, paragraph 1).

On 10 October 2000, Judge Lihai Zhao (China), who had been elected as a member for a term of six years commencing 1 October 1996, passed away. Allowing for this change, on 31 December 2000, the composition of the Tribunal was as follows:

	Name (order of precedence)	*Country*	*Date of expiry of term of office*
President	P. Chandrasekhara Rao	India	30 September 2008
Vice-President	L. Dolliver M. Nelson	Grenada	30 September 2005

[2] See SPLOS/L.3/Rev.1.

Judges	Hugo Caminos	Argentina	30 September 2002
	Vicente Marotta Rangel	Brazil	30 September 2008
	Alexander Yankov	Bulgaria	30 September 2002
	Soji Yamamoto	Japan	30 September 2005
	Anatoly Lazarevich Kolodkin	Russian Federation	30 September 2008
	Choon-Ho Park	Republic of Korea	30 September 2005
	Paul Bamela Engo	Cameroon	30 September 2008
	Thomas A. Mensah	Ghana	30 September 2005
	Joseph Akl	Lebanon	30 September 2008
	David Anderson	United Kingdom	30 September 2005
	Budislav Vukas	Croatia	30 September 2005
	Rüdiger Wolfrum	Germany	30 September 2008
	Edward Arthur Laing	Belize	30 September 2002
	Tullio Treves	Italy	30 September 2002
	Mohamed Mouldi Marsit	Tunisia	30 September 2005
	Gudmundur Eiriksson	Iceland	30 September 2002
	Tafsir Malick Ndiaye	Senegal	30 September 2002
	José Luis Jesus	Cape Verde	30 September 2008

The biographies of the members of the Tribunal are contained in Chapter VIII.

2. Changes in the Composition of the Tribunal in 2000

Acting pursuant to article 6, paragraph 1, of the Statute, the Registrar, in a note verbale dated 8 November 2000, informed States Parties to the Convention of the vacancy which had occurred in the Tribunal due to the death of Judge Lihai Zhao and invited Governments of States Parties to submit by 9 January 2001 the names of candidates they might wish to nominate for election as member of the Tribunal. In the note verbale, the Registrar informed States Parties that the member elected to replace Judge Lihai Zhao would serve until 30 September 2002.

By a note verbale dated 12 December 2000, the Registrar informed States Parties to the Convention that the President, after consultation with the President of the Meeting of States Parties, Mr. Peter Donigi, considered it advisable to have the election held during the Eleventh Meeting of States Parties, which was to take place from 14 to 18 May 2001, and requested States Parties to send their comments in this regard no later than 8 January 2001.

3. Former President and Vice-President and Former Members of the Tribunal

The following Judges have served as President or Vice-President before the current holders of those offices:

Thomas A. Mensah as President, and Rüdiger Wolfrum as Vice-President, from October 1996 to September 1999.

Apart from the present Judges, the following have been members of the Tribunal (the names of deceased Judges are preceded by an asterisk):

Name	*Country*	*Period of office*
Joseph Sinde Warioba	United Republic of Tanzania	1996–1999
*Lihai Zhao	China	1996–2000

II. Judges *Ad Hoc*

If the Tribunal, or a chamber, does not include a judge of the nationality of a party to the dispute, that party may choose a person to sit as a judge (Statute, article 17, paragraphs 2 and 3). Should there be several parties in the same interest, they are considered for this purpose as one party only (Statute, article 17, paragraph 5). Judges *ad hoc* need to fulfil the conditions applying to members, as set out in articles 2, 8 and 11 of the Statute, and participate in the case for which they are chosen on terms of complete equality with the other judges (Statute, article 17, paragraph 6). They take precedence after the members of the Tribunal and in order of seniority of age. The selection procedure is laid down in articles 19 to 21 of the Rules. Article 22 of the Rules deals with the particular case of a judge *ad hoc* chosen by an entity other than a State Party (international organization, natural or juridical person, or State enterprise).

Since the institution of the Tribunal, judges *ad hoc* have been chosen in the following cases:

Southern Bluefin Tuna Cases (New Zealand v. *Japan; Australia* v. *Japan), Provisional Measures* (1999). Mr. Ivan Shearer (Australia) was jointly nominated by Australia and New Zealand.

Case concerning the Conservation and Sustainable Exploitation of Swordfish Stocks in the South-Eastern Pacific Ocean (Chile/European Community). Mr. Francisco Orrego Vicuña (Chile) was chosen by Chile. The biography of Mr. Orrego Vicuña is contained in Chapter VIII.

III. The Presidency

1. Functions of the Presidency

The President directs the work and supervises the administration of the Tribunal; he represents the Tribunal in its relations with States and other entities (Rules, article 12).

2. The President and the Vice-President

The President and Vice-President are elected by secret ballot by a majority of the members (Rules, article 11, paragraphs 2 and 3). They serve for a period of three years and may be re-elected (Statute, article 12, paragraph 1). The terms of office of the President and Vice-President begin to run from the date on which the term of office of the members elected at a triennial election begins (Rules, article 10, paragraph 1).

The President presides at all meetings of the Tribunal (Rules, article 12). In the event of an equality of votes, the President has a casting vote (Statute, article 29, paragraph 2). The President is also an *ex officio* member of the Chamber of Summary Procedure (Rules, article 28, paragraph 1). The President presides over any special chamber of which he or she is a member (Rules, article 31, paragraph 1).

The Vice-President exercises the functions of the presidency in the event of a vacancy in the presidency or of the inability of the President to exercise the functions of the presidency (Rules, article 13, paragraph 1). The Vice-President is an *ex officio* member of the Chamber of Summary Procedure (Rules, article 28, paragraph 1) and presides over any special chamber of which he or she is a member when the chamber does not include the President (Rules, article 31, paragraph 1).

On 1 October 1999, the Tribunal elected Judge Chandrasekhara Rao as President of the Tribunal for the period 1999–2002, commencing on 1 October 1999. On 4 October 1999, the Tribunal elected Judge Nelson as Vice-President of the Tribunal for the period 1999–2002, commencing on 1 October 1999.

IV. Chambers of the Tribunal

1. Seabed Disputes Chamber and *Ad Hoc* Chambers of the Seabed Disputes Chamber

The Seabed Disputes Chamber is established in accordance with Part XI, section 5, of the Convention and article 14 of the Statute. The Chamber deals with disputes arising out of the exploration and exploitation of the International Seabed Area and has exclusive jurisdiction over such disputes. The jurisdiction of the Seabed Disputes Chamber is set out in Chapter II.

The Chamber is composed of 11 judges (Statute, article 35, paragraph 1). A quorum of seven members is required to constitute the Chamber (Statute, article 35, paragraph 7). Members of the Chamber are selected by the members of the Tribunal every three years and may be selected for a second term (Statute, article 35, paragraphs 1 and 3). The term of office of members of the Chamber selected at the first selection expired on 30 September 1999; the term of office of members selected at subsequent triennial selections expires on 30 September every three years thereafter (Rules, article 23). The selection process ensures the representation of the principal legal systems of the world, as well as equitable geographical distribution.

The Chamber elects its President from among its members (Statute, article 35, paragraph 4).

On 4 October 1999, the Tribunal selected the members of the Seabed Disputes Chamber. The members of the Chamber entered upon their duties forthwith and elected Judge Treves to be President of the Chamber. Due to the death of Judge Lihai Zhao, who was a member of the Chamber, the composition of the Chamber on 31 December 2000 was as follows:

	Name (Order of precedence)
President	Tullio Treves
Judges	Vicente Marotta Rangel
	Soji Yamamoto
	Anatoly Lazarevich Kolodkin
	Choon-Ho Park
	Paul Bamela Engo
	Budislav Vukas
	Rüdiger Wolfrum
	Edward Arthur Laing
	Mohamed Mouldi Marsit

The terms of office of the members of the Chamber expire on 30 September 2002.

Any party to a dispute over which the Seabed Disputes Chamber has jurisdiction may request the Seabed Disputes Chamber to form an *ad hoc* chamber (Convention, article 187, subparagraph (a), and article 188, paragraph 1(b)). An *ad hoc* chamber is composed of three members of the Seabed Disputes Chamber (Statute, article 36, paragraph 1). The composition of the *ad hoc* chamber is determined by the Seabed Disputes Chamber with the approval of the parties to the dispute (Statute, article 36, paragraph 1). Members of the *ad hoc* chamber may not be in the service of, or nationals of, any of the parties (Statute, article 36, paragraph 3).

2. Special Chambers

(a) Chamber of Summary Procedure

In accordance with article 15, paragraphs 3 and 4, of the Statute, the Chamber of Summary Procedure may hear and determine a case by summary procedure if the parties so request. In addition, the Chamber may prescribe provisional measures if the Tribunal is not in session or a sufficient number of members is not available to constitute a quorum (Statute, article 25, paragraph 2; Rules, article 91, paragraph 1).

The Chamber of Summary Procedure, constituted annually, is composed of five members and two alternates, as provided for by the Statute (Statute, article 15, paragraph 3). The President and the Vice-President of the Tribunal are members *ex officio* of the Chamber; the President of the Tribunal serves as President of the Chamber (Rules, article 31).

For the period ending 30 September 2000, the composition of the Chamber was as follows:

	Name (Order of precedence)
President	P. Chandrasekhara Rao
Judges	L. Dolliver M. Nelson
	Budislav Vukas
	Gudmundur Eiriksson
	Tafsir Malick Ndiaye
Alternates	Vicente Marotta Rangel
	Soji Yamamoto

On 27 September 2000, the Chamber was constituted for the period ending 30 September 2001. Its composition is as follows:

	Name (Order of precedence)
President	P. Chandrasekhara Rao
Judges	L. Dolliver M. Nelson
	Anatoly Lazarevich Kolodkin
	Paul Bamela Engo
	David Anderson
Alternates	Alexander Yankov
	Mohamed Mouldi Marsit

(b) Chamber for Fisheries Disputes

The Chamber for Fisheries Disputes, established in accordance with article 15, paragraph 1, of the Statute, is available to deal with disputes concerning the conservation and management of marine living resources, which parties may agree to submit to it. The Chamber consists of seven members.

On 4 October 1999, the Tribunal selected the members of the Chamber for Fisheries Disputes. The members of the Chamber entered upon their duties forthwith and elected Judge Eiriksson to be President of the Chamber. The composition of the Chamber is as follows:

	Name (Order of precedence)
President	Gudmundur Eiriksson
Judges	Hugo Caminos
	Soji Yamamoto
	Anatoly Lazarevich Kolodkin
	Choon-Ho Park
	Tafsir Malick Ndiaye
	José Luis Jesus

The terms of office of the members of the Chamber expire on 30 September 2002.

(c) Chamber for Marine Environment Disputes

The Chamber for Marine Environment Disputes, established in accordance with article 15, paragraph 1, of the Statute, is available to deal with disputes relating to the protection and preservation of the marine environment, which parties may agree to submit to it. The Chamber consists of seven members.

On 4 October 1999, the Tribunal selected the members of the Chamber for Marine Environment Disputes. The members of the Chamber entered upon their duties forthwith and elected Judge Yankov to be President of the Chamber. The composition of the Chamber is as follows:

	Name *(Order of precedence)*
President	Alexander Yankov
Judges	Vicente Marotta Rangel
	Paul Bamela Engo
	Thomas A. Mensah
	Joseph Akl
	David Anderson
	Budislav Vukas

The terms of office of the members of the Chamber expire on 30 September 2002.

(d) Chambers under article 15, paragraph 2, of the Statute

Pursuant to article 15, paragraph 2, of the Statute, the Tribunal shall form a chamber for dealing with a particular dispute if the parties so request. The composition of such a chamber is determined by the Tribunal with the approval of the parties, as provided for in article 30 of the Rules.

By exchange of letters dated 18 and 19 December 2000, Chile and the European Community informed the Tribunal that further to a recent exchange of views, including through the good offices of the President, they had agreed that the dispute between Chile and the European Community concerning the conservation and sustainable exploitation of swordfish stocks in the South-Eastern Pacific Ocean should not be proceeded with in accordance with the arbitral procedure instituted by Chile under article 287, paragraph 3, of the Convention but should be submitted to a special chamber of the Tribunal to be formed in accordance with article 15, paragraph 2, of the Statute. Chile and the European Community requested the Tribunal to determine the composition of a special chamber with their approval to hear the dispute. By separate letters dated 19 December 2000, Chile, in exercise of its right under article 17 of the Statute, nominated Mr. Orrego Vicuña as judge *ad hoc* and the European Community confirmed this nomination.

By Order dated 20 December 2000, the Tribunal decided to accede to the request of Chile and the European Community to form a special chamber of five judges to deal with the case. This is the first time that a case has been submitted to a special chamber of the Tribunal. The issues to be decided by the Special Chamber are set out in Chapter IV.

The composition of the Special Chamber to deal with the case is as follows:

	Name *(Order of precedence)*
President	P. Chandrasekhara Rao
Judges	Hugo Caminos
	Alexander Yankov
	Rüdiger Wolfrum
Judge *ad hoc*	Francisco Orrego Vicuña

V. Committees and Working Group of the Tribunal

On 27 September 2000, the Tribunal extended until 30 September 2001 the terms of office of the members of the committees who had been selected to serve for the period ending 30 September 1999.

The committees, as well as a newly established working group, are as follows:

1. Committee on Rules and Judicial Practice

The Committee on Rules and Judicial Practice is entrusted with the function of reviewing the Rules of the Tribunal and their application, the Resolution on the Internal Judicial Practice of the Tribunal and the Guidelines concerning the Preparation and Presentation of Cases before the Tribunal. The Committee is responsible for proposing any modification which it may determine to be necessary or appropriate for the consideration of the Tribunal. The Committee is presided over by the President of the Tribunal, Judge Chandrasekhara Rao; its other members are Vice-President Nelson and Judges Caminos, Yankov, Mensah, Akl, Anderson, Vukas, Laing, Treves (member *ex officio*), Eiriksson and Ndiaye.

2. Committee on Budget and Finance

The Committee on Budget and Finance makes proposals to the Tribunal on budgetary and financial matters. In particular, the Committee is responsible for considering and making recommendations on draft budget proposals and financial regulations, as prepared by the Registrar, and on management of the finances and accounts of the Tribunal. It also reviews the accounting and financial reports of the Tribunal and makes recommendations, as necessary. Judge Wolfrum is the Chairman of the Committee; the other members of the Committee are Judges Yankov, Mensah, Akl, Anderson and Jesus.

3. Committee on Staff and Administration

The Committee on Staff and Administration is mandated to make recommendations to the Tribunal on matters concerning the administration and the staffing of the Registry, with special reference to the terms and conditions of service and the procedures for recruitment, discipline and separation from service. The Chairman of the Committee is Judge Mensah; the other members of the Committee are Judges Yamamoto, Kolodkin, Bamela Engo, Laing, Marsit and Eiriksson.

4. Committee on Library and Publications

The Committee on Library and Publications advises on the organization, requirements and functioning of the Library including, in particular, policy and procedures for the development of the collections. The Committee also makes recommendations concerning publications, with special reference to the nature and format of publications to be issued. The Chairman of the Committee is Judge Park; the other members of the Committee are Judges Caminos, Marotta Rangel, Anderson, Vukas, Wolfrum, Treves, Marsit and Ndiaye.

5. Committee on Buildings and Electronic Systems

The Committee on Buildings and Electronic Systems makes recommendations with respect to the permanent premises of the Tribunal, including associated electronic systems and services. In addition, its mandate encompasses the works of art, information systems and electronic equipment for the premises. The Chairman of the Committee is Judge Laing; the other members of the Committee are Judges Yankov, Mensah, Akl, Wolfrum, Marsit and Eiriksson.

6. Working Group on Bonds and Other Financial Security

On 15 March 2000, the Tribunal constituted a working group to deal with the question of bonds and other financial security in prompt release proceedings. The Chairman of the Working Group is Judge Laing; the other members of the Working Group are Judges Akl, Vukas, Eiriksson and Ndiaye. On 27 September 2000, the Tribunal extended the terms of office of the members of the Working Group until 30 September 2001.

VI. Experts under Article 289 of the Convention

Pursuant to article 289 of the Convention, in any dispute involving scientific or technical matters, the Tribunal may, at the request of a party or *proprio motu*, select no fewer than two scientific or technical experts. The selection is made in consultation with the parties and should preferably be based on the relevant list prepared according to article 2 of Annex VIII to the Convention. Further provisions concerning the selection of such experts are contained in article 15 of the Rules.

Experts appointed under article 289 of the Convention sit with the Tribunal but without the right to vote. They take part in the judicial deliberations of the Tribunal (Rules, article 42, paragraph 2).

VII. The Registry

The Registry is the administrative organ of the Tribunal. Its role is defined by articles 32 to 39 of the Rules. Instructions for the Registry are drawn up by the Registrar and approved by the Tribunal (Rules, article 38, paragraph 3). Instructions for the Registry as adopted by the Tribunal on 17 March 2000 are contained in Annex IV.

1. The Registrar

The general functions of the Registrar are set out in article 36 of the Rules. The Registrar is responsible for all legal work, both substantive and procedural, for all administrative arrangements and support, for the assessment and collection of contributions, and for the administration of the accounts and finances of the Tribunal. The Registrar is the regular channel of communications to and from the Tribunal, keeps a List of cases, and keeps copies of communications and agreements as required by the Rules.

The Registrar is assisted by the Deputy Registrar, who acts as Registrar in the absence of the Registrar (Rules, article 37).

The Tribunal elects its Registrar for a term of seven years. The Tribunal elects a Deputy Registrar for a term of seven years; it may also elect an Assistant Registrar. The Tribunal may provide for the appointment of such other officers as may be necessary (Statute, article 12; Rules, article 32).

The other staff members of the Registry are appointed by the Tribunal on proposals submitted by the Registrar; however, for such posts as the Tribunal may determine, the appointment is made by the Registrar with the approval of the President (Rules, article 35, paragraph 1).

On 31 December 2000, the Registrar was Mr. Gritakumar E. Chitty (Sri Lanka). He was elected as Registrar of the Tribunal on 23 October 1996.

On 31 December 2000, the Deputy Registrar was Mr. Philippe Gautier (Belgium). He was elected as Deputy Registrar of the Tribunal on 25 October 1996.

2. Composition of the Registry

On 31 December 2000 the Registry was composed as follows:

Function	Name	Country
Registrar	Gritakumar E. Chitty	Sri Lanka
Deputy Registrar	Philippe H. Gautier	Belgium
Chief of Administration	Garry M. Slark	United Kingdom
Head of Conference and Linguistic Services	James Nolan	United States
Translator/Revisor	Edaly Gassama	Senegal
Librarian	Ellen Schaffer	United States
Budget and Finance Officer	Gurpreet S. Sodhi	United States
Systems Adminstrator	Sami Dimassi	Lebanon
Legal Officer	Robert van Dijk	The Netherlands
Associate Legal Officer	Ximena Hinrichs	Chile
Associate Administrative Officer (Transport/Building Management)	Kafui Gaba-Kpayedo	Togo
Associate Administrative Officer (Contributions/Benefits)	Christoph Schwarte	Germany
Computer Systems Assistant	Luis Prieto-Vales	Spain
Press Assistant	Julia Pope	United Kingdom
Library Assistant	Laure Boschmans	France
Secretary to the President	Ellen Nas	The Netherlands
Secretary to the Registrar	Antje Vorbeck	Germany
Secretary to the Deputy Registrar	Anke Egert	Germany
Finance Assistant	Valia Dikova	Bulgaria
Administration Assistant	Irene Kamps	Germany
Secretaries to Judges	Berit Albiez	Germany
	Martine Becker	France

Secretary	Gerardine Sadler	Singapore
Finance Assistant	Roman Ritter	Germany
Administrative Assistant (Contributions/Accounts Travel)	Jacqueline Winkelmann	Germany
Personnel Assistant	Emma Bartlett	United Kingdom
Conference Assistant	Elizabeth Roth	Kenya
Receptionist	Inga Marzahn	Germany
Security /Driver	Iheanyi Chuks Ntinugwa	Nigeria

For assistance at meetings and in the servicing of the legal and administrative work of the Tribunal, recourse was had to temporary assistance. Those serving on a short-term basis during this period were:

Function	Name	Country
Driver/Security Assistance	Kenan Aydin	Turkey
	Boniface Aziamble	Togo
	Andreas Bothe	Germany
	Stephan Haag	Germany
	Volker Haak	Germany
	Michael Manns	Germany
	Nils Westphal	Germany
	Mario Woerner	Germany
	Kurt Zschiegner	Germany
Secretarial Assistance	Adeline Boyko	Canada
	Lana Gyimah	Ghana
	Gemma Juvanteny Sanglas	Spain
	Sonia Khoudja	Germany/Tunisia
	Shiraz Kutar	Germany
	Petra Meyer	Germany
	Valerie O'Connor	Ireland
	Regine Sullivan	Belgium
	Imke Voss	Germany
	Wendy Swaby	United Kingdom
General Temporary Assistance	Sven Duddek	Germany
	Mathias Kircher	Germany
	Anne Katrin Escher	Germany
	Monika Frank	Germany
Computer Systems Assistance	Alfred Gbadoe	Togo
Legal Assistance	Maurice Kamga	Cameroon
Translation	Jean-Luc Rostan	France
	Lazhar Slimane	Tunisia
Interpretation	Danielle Bolhuis Zerner	France
	Christiane Driesen	France
	George Drummond	United Kingdom
	Susan Fergusson-Guenther	United Kingdom
	Annick Halsband-Leguen	Germany
	Hugh Thirlway	United Kingdom
	Patricia Vanderelst	United Kingdom

Verbatim Reporters	Lindsay Bickers	United Kingdom
	Mady Martinelli	France
	Evelyn Medves	France
	Sylvie Portrait	France
	Ian Sinclair	United Kingdom
	Sandra Smith	United Kingdom
Consultants	Naved Husain	USA
	Donald Rogers	United Kingdom
	Ian Williams	United Kingdom

3. Library

Building upon the basic collection of donated monographs and serials, the Tribunal continued its efforts to develop its specialized Library in keeping with the decision of the fourth Meeting of States Parties.[3/] The Library currently subscribes to, or receives via donation, over 110 periodical publications. Its monograph collection contains approximately 2000 monographs. The seventh Meeting of States Parties approved in principle the ongoing need, during the first five years, to appropriate a budget for the procurement of books and for start-up costs of the Library and to continue to include provisions to this effect in the Tribunal's budgets. Specific budgetary provisions were included for this purpose in the budgets for 2000 and 2001, as adopted by the ninth and tenth Meetings of States Parties.

In 2000, the Library received donations of monographs and periodicals from various persons and entities. According to its decision of 6 October 1998, the Tribunal may also accept appropriate cash donations to fund the purchase of books and other materials for the Library. A list of donors to the Library in 2000 is contained in Annex IX.

In 2000, the Library began to prepare for the installation of an integrated online library system for the Tribunal. Training was initiated and the process will continue in the coming year.

The Librarian and the Library Assistant also planned and organized the move of the Library's collections to the new premises building.

A monthly "List of New Monographs and Serials" received in the Library is prepared and circulated to all judges and staff members of the Registry.

4. Archives

The Registrar is responsible for the archives of the Tribunal (Rules, article 36, paragraph 1(p)). The archives of the Tribunal are not open to the public.

[3/] SPLOS/WP.3/Rev.1, para. 12.

5. Staff Regulations and Rules of the Registry

The Staff Regulations of the Registry, approved by the Tribunal on 8 October 1998, were submitted to the ninth Meeting of States Parties. The Meeting took note of the Staff Regulations. On 29 September 2000, the Tribunal approved the Staff Rules reported by the Registrar with provisional effect from 1 October 2000. In accordance with Staff Regulation 12.4, the Staff Rules were to enter into force on 1 January 2001.

VIII. Seat

The seat of the Tribunal is in the Free and Hanseatic City of Hamburg in the Federal Republic of Germany (Statute, article 1, paragraph 2); the Tribunal may, however, sit and exercise its functions elsewhere whenever it considers this desirable (Statute, article 1, paragraph 3).

Pending the completion of the permanent premises, the host country provided the Tribunal with temporary premises located at Wexstraße 4 in the centre of Hamburg.

Since 27 November 2000, the Tribunal has occupied the permanent premises located at Am Internationalen Seegerichtshof 1, in the district of Nienstedten, Hamburg, built at the expense of the Free and Hanseatic City of Hamburg and the Federal Republic of Germany. The permanent premises were officially opened on 3 July 2000, in a ceremony attended by the Secretary-General of the United Nations, Mr. Kofi Annan, the President of the Tribunal, Mr. P. Chandrasekhara Rao, the Federal Minister of Justice of the Federal Republic of Germany, Mrs. Herta Däubler-Gmelin, the First Mayor of Hamburg, Mr. Ortwin Runde, and the Registrar of the Tribunal, Mr. Gritakumar E. Chitty. The ceremony was attended by other high dignitaries including the Vice-President and Judges of the Tribunal, the President of the Meeting of States Parties, Mr. Peter Donigi, the Legal Counsel of the United Nations, Mr. Hans Corell, Ministers of States, Government representatives and representatives of international organizations. The statements delivered at the ceremony are contained in Annex X.

The relations between the Tribunal and the host country concerning the premises will be regulated by a headquarters agreement which, *inter alia*, will define the headquarters district, spell out the mutual obligations of the parties and cover such matters as law and authority in, and the inviolability and protection of, the headquarters district. It will also include provisions relating to public services and communications. The headquarters agreement is supplemented by an additional agreement concerning the occupancy and use of the premises.

The Agreement between the International Tribunal for the Law of the Sea and the Government of the Federal Republic of Germany on the Occupancy and Use of the Premises of the International Tribunal for the Law of the Sea in the Free and Hanseatic City of Hamburg (Additional Agreement) of 18 October 2000 establishes the terms and conditions under which the premises are made available to the Tribunal by the Government. It regulates matters such as the transfer and use, operation, maintenance, repairs and alterations to, damage to and destruction of, access to, and vacation of the premises. It also provides for public services in the premises, a consultative mechanism for resolving issues and a dispute settlement procedure.

IX. Relations with the Public

1. Correspondence

The Registrar is the regular channel of communications, notifications and transmission of documents required by the Convention, the Statute, the Rules or any other relevant international agreement (Rules, article 36, paragraph 1(a)).

Correspondence should be addressed to:

The Registrar
International Tribunal for the Law of the Sea
Am Internationalen Seegerichtshof 1
22609 Hamburg
Germany

Alternative means of communicating with the Tribunal include:
Telegraphic address: International Tribunal for the Law of the Sea
Tel.: (49) (40) 356070
Fax: (49) (40) 35607-245, -275
e-mail: itlos@itlos.org

2. Information

The Registrar deals with inquiries and provides information concerning the Tribunal and its work (Rules, article 36, paragraph 1(m) and (o)).

The Tribunal publicized its work by means of press releases and press notices and by distribution of its judgments and orders and publications such as the *Yearbook*. Addresses and publications by the judges and staff members of the Registry also helped to publicize the work of the Tribunal. Press releases and press notices, issued separately in English and French, are available free of charge on application to the Registry.

Background information about the Tribunal and the texts of its judgments and orders are also available on the United Nations website: http://www.un.org/Depts/los. In the future, the information will also be available on the Tribunal's own website: http://www.itlos.org in English and http://www.tiddm.org in French.

X. Publications of the Tribunal

1. *Yearbook*

The *Yearbook* gives an account of the work of the Tribunal during the calendar year. It presents information about the judges, organization, jurisdiction, procedure, practice, finances, privileges and immunities, and activities of the Tribunal. A select bibliography of articles and books on the settlement of disputes concerning the law of the sea is also included.

There is a French edition of this publication, the *Annuaire*. The present *Yearbook* is the fourth in the series, which started with *ITLOS Yearbook 1996–1997*. Unlike subsequent yearbooks, the first volume covered a period of 17 months, from 1 August 1996 to 31 December 1997, and includes the preparatory work that preceded the constitution of the Tribunal on 1 October 1996.

Abbreviated reference: *ITLOS Yearbook*, with an indication of the year covered by the volume, e.g.: *ITLOS Yearbook 1998*.

2. *Reports of Judgments, Advisory Opinions and Orders*

This annual publication contains the Judgments, Orders and Advisory Opinions given in cases submitted to the Tribunal, both in English and French.

Abbreviated reference: *ITLOS Reports*, with an indication of the year covered by the volume, e.g.: *ITLOS Reports 1998.*

3. *Pleadings, Minutes of Public Sittings and Documents*

This publication reproduces the pleadings in cases before the Tribunal as well as the minutes of the hearings and other relevant documents. The documents are reproduced only in the official language(s) of the Tribunal in which they have been submitted to the Tribunal.

Abbreviated reference: *ITLOS Pleadings, Minutes and Documents*, with an indication of the year covered by the volume and the abbreviated title of the case, e.g.: *ITLOS Pleadings, Minutes and Documents 1997, M/V "SAIGA" (Saint Vincent and the Grenadines* v. *Guinea), Prompt Release.*

4. *Basic Texts*

The *Basic Texts*, a bilingual publication in English and French, reproduces the text of the United Nations Convention on the Law of the Sea of 10 December 1982, the Agreement relating to the Implementation of Part XI of the United Nations Convention on the Law of the Sea of 10 December 1982, the Statute of the Tribunal, the Rules of the Tribunal, the Resolution on the Internal Judicial Practice of the Tribunal, the Guidelines concerning the Preparation and Presentation of Cases before the Tribunal and the Agreement on the Privileges and Immunities of the International Tribunal for the Law of the Sea.

CHAPTER II

COMPETENCE

I. Access to the Tribunal

1. States Parties to the Convention

The Tribunal is open to States Parties to the Convention (Convention, article 291, paragraph 1; Statute, article 20, paragraph 1). The entities referred to in article 305, paragraph 1(c) to (f), of the Convention may also become parties.

As of 31 December 2000, 135 States and other entities referred to in article 305 of the Convention had become States Parties to the Convention. They are listed in Annex I.

2. Entities other than States Parties

The Tribunal is open to entities other than States Parties in any case expressly provided for in Part XI of the Convention or in any case submitted pursuant to any other agreement conferring jurisdiction on the Tribunal which is accepted by all the parties to that case (Convention, article 291; Statute, article 20, paragraph 2).

II. Jurisdiction of the Tribunal

1. Contentious Cases

(a) Jurisdiction over any dispute concerning the interpretation or application of the Convention

The Tribunal has jurisdiction over any dispute which is submitted to it in accordance with Part XV of the Convention concerning the interpretation or application of the Convention (Convention, article 288, paragraph 1; Statute, article 21) and the Agreement relating to the Implementation of Part XI of the Convention.

Limitations and exceptions to applicability of the compulsory procedures entailing binding decisions (Convention, Part XV, section 2) are contained in articles 297 and 298 of the Convention. The texts of declarations made pursuant to article 298 are reproduced in Annex II. Any dispute belonging to the categories referred to in articles 297 and 298 of the Convention may, nevertheless, be submitted to the Tribunal if the parties to the dispute so agree.

(b) Jurisdiction over any dispute concerning the interpretation or application of other agreements

Under article 288, paragraph 2, of the Convention, the Tribunal has jurisdiction over any dispute concerning the interpretation or application of an international agreement related to the purposes of the Convention which is submitted to it in accordance with the agreement. Under article 21 of the Statute, the jurisdiction of the Tribunal includes all matters specifically provided for in any agreement, other than the Convention, which confers jurisdiction on the Tribunal.

Three multilateral agreements have been concluded which confer jurisdiction on the Tribunal. The relevant provisions of these agreements are reproduced in Annex III.

Pursuant to article 22 of the Statute, any disputes concerning the interpretation or application of a treaty or convention already in force and relating to the subject-matter covered by the Convention may, if all the parties to such agreement so agree, be submitted to the Tribunal in accordance with the agreement.

(c) Jurisdiction of the Seabed Disputes Chamber

The Seabed Disputes Chamber has jurisdiction over disputes with respect to activities in the Area, as defined in article 1 of the Convention, falling within the categories referred to in article 187, subparagraphs (a) to (f), of the Convention. Parties to such disputes may be States Parties, the International Seabed Authority, the Enterprise, state enterprises and natural or juridical persons referred to in article 153, paragraph 2(b), of the Convention.

Disputes between States Parties concerning the interpretation or application of Part XI of the Convention and the Annexes thereto may be submitted to a special chamber of the Tribunal at the request of the parties, or to an *ad hoc* chamber of the Seabed Disputes Chamber at the request of any party (Convention, article 188, paragraph 1). Disputes concerning the interpretation or application of a contract referred to in article 187, subparagraph (c) (i), of the Convention are required to be submitted, at the request of a party, to binding commercial arbitration, unless the parties otherwise agree. However, a commercial arbitral tribunal has no jurisdiction to decide any questions of interpretation of Part XI and the Annexes relating thereto, and such questions are to be referred to the Seabed Disputes Chamber for a ruling (Convention, article 188, paragraph 2).

The Seabed Disputes Chamber has no jurisdiction with regard to the exercise by the International Seabed Authority of its discretionary powers and it has no competence to pronounce itself on the question of whether any rules, regulations and procedures of the International Seabed Authority are in conformity with the Convention, or to declare them invalid (Convention, article 189).

(d) The Tribunal itself decides any question as to its jurisdiction

In the event of a dispute as to whether the Tribunal has jurisdiction, the matter shall be settled by decision of the Tribunal (Convention, article 288, paragraph 4; Rules, article 58).

(e) Provisional measures

If a dispute has been duly submitted to the Tribunal and if the Tribunal considers that *prima facie* it has jurisdiction under Part XV or Part XI, section 5, of the Convention, the Tribunal may prescribe any provisional measures which it considers appropriate under the circumstances to preserve the respective rights of the parties to the dispute or to prevent serious harm to the marine environment, pending the final decision (Convention, article 290, paragraph 1; Statute, article 25, paragraph 1).

The Tribunal may also prescribe provisional measures in the case covered by article 290, paragraph 5, of the Convention. Under this provision, pending the constitution of an arbitral tribunal to which a dispute is being submitted and if, within two weeks from the date of a request for provisional measures, the parties do not agree to submit the request to another court or tribunal, the Tribunal may prescribe provisional measures if it considers that *prima facie* the arbitral tribunal to be constituted would have jurisdiction and that the urgency of the situation so requires.

(f) Prompt release of vessels and crews

The Tribunal has jurisdiction to entertain an application for the prompt release of a detained vessel or its crew in accordance with the provisions of article 292 of the Convention. This article provides that where the authorities of a State Party have detained a vessel flying the flag of another State Party and it is alleged that the detaining State has not complied with the provisions of the Convention for the prompt release of the vessel or its crew upon the posting of a reasonable bond or other financial security, the question of release from detention may be submitted to the Tribunal if, within 10 days from the time of detention, the parties have not agreed to submit it to another court or tribunal (Convention, article 292, paragraph 1). The application for release may be made only by or on behalf of the flag State of the vessel (Convention, article 292, paragraph 2).

2. Advisory Opinions

(a) Advisory opinions under the Convention

The Seabed Disputes Chamber has jurisdiction to give advisory opinions at the request of the Assembly or the Council of the International Seabed Authority (Convention, articles 159, paragraph 10, and 191).

(b) Advisory opinions on the basis of other international agreements

The Tribunal may also give an advisory opinion on a legal question if an international agreement related to the purposes of the Convention specifically provides for the submission to the Tribunal of a request for such an opinion (Rules, article 138, paragraph 1).

CHAPTER III

PROCEDURE

I. General Provisions

1. Basic Texts

The procedural rules and guidelines concerning the conduct of cases before the Tribunal[4/] are contained in the Convention, the Statute of the Tribunal (Annex VI to the Convention), the Rules of the Tribunal, adopted on 28 October 1997, the Resolution on the Internal Judicial Practice of the Tribunal, adopted on 31 October 1997, and the Guidelines concerning the Preparation and Presentation of Cases before the Tribunal, adopted on 28 October 1997.

2. Proceedings

The proceedings consist of two stages: written and oral. They are to be conducted without unnecessary delay or expense (Rules, articles 44, paragraph 1, and 49).

3. Official Languages

The official languages of the Tribunal are English and French (Rules, article 43).

4. Official Communications and Means of Communication

In all cases submitted to the Tribunal, communications, notifications and documents are addressed to the Registrar, who is the regular channel of communications to and from the Tribunal (Rules, articles 36, paragraph 1(a), and 51).

All communications to the parties are sent to their agents, who shall have an address in Hamburg or Berlin (Rules, articles 52, paragraph 1, 53, paragraph 1, and 56, paragraph 1).

All documents, pleadings and other communications may be delivered to the Tribunal directly, by courier or by regular mail. They may also be sent by facsimile or other electronic means; in such a case the date on which the Tribunal receives them is regarded as the

---

[4/] For more detailed commentary on the procedures before the Tribunal, see *Yearbook 1996–1997.*

material date provided that the paper originals are received without unreasonable delay (Guidelines, paragraph 10).

5. List of Cases

The Registrar keeps a List of cases submitted to the Tribunal. Extracts from the List of cases are supplied by the Registrar on request (Rules, article 36, paragraph 1(b)).

II. Contentious Cases

1. Proceedings before the Tribunal

(a) Institution of proceedings and representation of parties

(i) Application or special agreement

Proceedings before the Tribunal are instituted by the submission of an application or by notification of a special agreement. Any application or special agreement is to be filed with the Registry in one (or both) of the official languages of the Tribunal. If it is filed in another language, it has to be accompanied by a translation into one of the official languages. When proceedings are instituted on the basis of an agreement other than the Convention, a certified copy of the agreement must accompany the application or notification (Rules, article 57, paragraph 1).

When proceedings are instituted by means of an application, the original of the application has to be signed by the agent of the party concerned or by the diplomatic representative of that party in Germany or by some other duly authorized person. Except when the application is signed by a diplomatic representative, the signature must be authenticated by the diplomatic representative or by the competent governmental authority (Rules, article 54, paragraph 3).

The notification of a special agreement may be effected by the parties jointly or by one or more of them (Rules, article 55, paragraph 1). An original or certified copy of the special agreement must accompany the notification (Rules, article 55, paragraph 2).

(ii) Transmission of documents

When the proceedings are instituted by means of an application, the Registrar transmits forthwith to the respondent a certified copy thereof (Rules, article 54, paragraph 4). In the case of the notification of a special agreement by one or more of the parties, the Registrar transmits forthwith a certified copy thereof to any other party to the dispute (Rules, article 55, paragraph 1).

After the proceedings have been instituted, the application or the special agreement is notified by the Registrar to all concerned and to all States Parties to the Convention (Statute, article 24, paragraphs 2 and 3).

(iii) Representation of the parties

The party which institutes proceedings informs the Tribunal at the same time of the name and address of its agent. The other party informs the Tribunal of the name and address of its agent as soon as possible thereafter (Rules, article 56, paragraphs 2 and 3).

Except in the case where the party against which the application is made has not yet expressed its consent to the jurisdiction of the Tribunal, all steps on behalf of the parties after proceedings have been instituted are taken by agents. The parties may also appoint a co-agent or a deputy agent and they may have the assistance of counsel, advocates or advisers.

(iv) Consultations with the parties

The President ascertains the views of the parties with regard to questions of procedure. For this purpose, he may summon the agents to meet him or use other appropriate means of communication such as telephone, facsimile, video-conference, etc. (Rules, article 45).

(v) Additional information concerning the competence of international organizations

An international organization which is a party to a dispute may be requested by the Tribunal, at the request of any other party or *proprio motu*, to provide information as to which, as between the organization and its member States, has competence in respect of any specific question which has arisen. The proceedings may be suspended until such information is received (Rules, article 57, paragraph 2).

(b) Written proceedings

(i) Filing of pleadings and formal requirements

The written proceedings consist of the communication of pleadings to the Tribunal and to the parties. The pleadings consist of a memorial and a counter-memorial, and, if the Tribunal so authorizes, a reply and a rejoinder, as well as all documents in support (Rules, articles 44, paragraph 2, 60 and 61, paragraph 3).

The original of each pleading is signed by the agent, who supplies the Registry with the documents required under articles 63 to 65 of the Rules and paragraph 9 of the Guidelines. Every pleading must be dated. When a pleading has to be filed by a certain date, the date of its receipt in the Registry is regarded by the Tribunal as the material date (Rules, article 65, paragraphs 1 and 2).

If a pleading does not satisfy the formal requirements of the Rules, the Registrar will return it to the party concerned for rectification. After rectification, the pleading is properly filed and the Registrar endorses it on the date of its receipt in the Registry (Guidelines, paragraphs 10 and 11).

Upon receipt of a pleading, a certified copy of the pleading and any document annexed thereto is communicated by the Registrar to the other party (Rules, article 66).

(ii) Information to the public

Unless otherwise decided by the Tribunal, copies of the pleadings are to be made available upon request to States and other entities entitled to appear before the Tribunal, as soon as possible after their filing (Rules, article 67, paragraphs 1 and 3).

Unless otherwise decided by the Tribunal, copies of the pleadings may be obtained by the public on the opening of the oral proceedings (Rules, article 67, paragraphs 2 and 3).

(c) Initial deliberations

Prior to the opening of the oral proceedings, the Tribunal meets in order to exchange views concerning the case (Rules, article 68; Resolution, article 3).

(d) Oral proceedings

(i) Hearings

In principle, the date for the opening of the oral proceedings falls within a period of six months from the closure of the written proceedings (Rules, article 69).

The oral proceedings consist of the hearing by the Tribunal of agents, counsel, advocates, witnesses and experts (Rules, article 44, paragraph 3).

The hearings are public, unless the Tribunal decides otherwise or the parties request that the public be not admitted (Statute, article 26, paragraph 2; Rules, article 74).

Prior to the hearings, each party is requested to submit a brief outline of the issues that still divide the parties and of the arguments it wishes to make in its oral statement, and a list of authorities upon which it intends to rely in its oral statement (Guidelines, paragraph 14).

(ii) Witnesses, experts and evidence

Each party must communicate to the Registrar, in sufficient time before the opening of the oral proceedings, the information referred to in article 72 of the Rules regarding evidence it intends to produce.

During the hearings, the parties may call any witnesses or experts appearing on the list communicated to the Tribunal. Any other witness or expert may only be called if the other party raises no objection or if the Tribunal so authorizes in accordance with article 78, paragraph 1, of the Rules.

(iii) Submission of new documents by the parties

After the closure of the written proceedings, no further documents may be submitted to the Tribunal by a party except with the consent of the other party or the authorization of the Tribunal in accordance with article 71 of the Rules.

(iv) Questions addressed to the parties and requests for information

Prior to or during the hearing, the Tribunal may indicate any points which it would like the parties specially to address or on which it considers that there has been sufficient argument. Similarly, the President or other judge may put questions to agents, counsel and advocates during the hearing (Rules, article 76).

At any time prior to the closure of the oral proceedings, the Tribunal may request an intergovernmental organization to furnish information relevant to a case before it. When a case before the Tribunal concerns the interpretation of the constituent instrument of an intergovernmental organization, the organization is to be notified and may submit written observations within a time-limit fixed by the Tribunal, or by the President if the Tribunal is not sitting (Rules, article 84).

(v) Interpretation and verbatim record

According to article 85 of the Rules, speeches and statements made in one of the official languages of the Tribunal are to be interpreted into the other. When a language other than an official language is used, the party concerned shall make arrangements for interpretation into one of the official languages. In such a case, arrangements for the verification of the interpretation shall be made by the Registrar at the expense of that party.

A verbatim record of every hearing is drawn up by the Registrar. Copies of the transcript of the verbatim record are circulated to the judges and to the parties, who may request corrections of errors in the transcript relating to their statements. The same applies to witnesses and experts relating to statements made by them (Rules, article 86).

(vi) Display of charts, maps and other facilities

Visual demonstration facilities for the display of any maps, charts, diagrams, illustrations of texts, etc., which a party intends to exhibit during the oral proceedings will, at the request of that party, be provided by the Registrar upon payment of fees, if any, fixed for that purpose (Guidelines, paragraph 18).

(vii) Information to the public

The Registrar issues press releases giving all necessary information as to the dates of the hearings. Admission cards are issued to members of the diplomatic or consular corps and to representatives of the press and, upon request, to any other person. Photography and filming in the courtroom during the oral proceedings are subject to authorization.

Copies of the uncorrected verbatim records of each hearing are made available to the public.

(viii) Final submissions and closure of oral proceedings

At the conclusion of the last statement made by a party, its agent reads the final submissions of that party. A copy of the written text of these submissions, signed by the agent, is communicated to the Tribunal and to the other party (Rules, article 75, paragraph 2).

After the presentation of the case is completed, the President declares the oral proceedings closed. The agents remain at the disposal of the Tribunal (Rules, article 88).

(e) Joinder of proceedings

The Tribunal may direct that the proceedings in two or more cases be joined (Rules, article 47).

(f) Default

When one of the parties does not appear before the Tribunal or fails to defend its case, the other party may request the Tribunal to continue the proceedings and make its decision. Before making its decision, the Tribunal must satisfy itself not only that it has jurisdiction over the dispute, but also that the claim is well founded in fact and law (Statute, article 28).

(g) Deliberations

After the closure of the oral proceedings, the Tribunal withdraws to deliberate (Rules, article 88, paragraph 2). The deliberations are and remain confidential (Rules, article 42, paragraph 1). The Resolution contains detailed provisions on the different steps followed during the deliberations of the Tribunal.

(h) Judgment

(i) Reading of the judgment

The judgment is read at a public sitting. The parties are notified of the date of the public sitting (Rules, article 124).

(ii) Finality and binding force

The judgment of the Tribunal is final. It is binding on the parties to the dispute on the day of its reading (Statute, article 33, paragraphs 1 and 2; Rules, article 124).

(iii) Official languages and translation

The judgment is prepared in both official languages; it contains a statement as to which text is authoritative (Rules, article 125, paragraph 1(m)).

When an official language of the United Nations other than one of the official languages of the Tribunal is chosen by the parties, article 64 of the Rules allows for any party to request the translation of the decision of the Tribunal into that official language of the United Nations. The translation is made at no cost to the parties.

(iv) Separate or dissenting opinions and declarations

The judgment indicates the number and names of the judges constituting the majority and those constituting the minority, on each operative provision (Rules, article 125, paragraph 1(l)). Any judge may attach a separate or dissenting opinion to the judgment. A judge may record concurrence or dissent without stating reasons in the form of a declaration (Rules, article 125, paragraph 2).

(v) Copies of the judgment

One copy of the judgment is signed by the President and the Registrar, then sealed and placed in the archives of the Tribunal. Copies are handed to each party. Others are sent to States Parties, the Secretary-General of the United Nations, the Secretary-General of the International Seabed Authority and, in a case submitted under an agreement other than the Convention, the parties to such agreement (Rules, article 125, paragraph 3).

Copies of the judgment are available to the public upon request.

(i) Costs

Each party bears its own costs unless otherwise decided by the Tribunal (Statute, article 34).

2. Incidental Proceedings

(a) Provisional measures

A request for the prescription of provisional measures under article 290, paragraph 1, of the Convention is made in writing by a party to a dispute before the Tribunal. It may be submitted at any time during the course of the proceedings (Rules, article 89, paragraph 1).

A request for the prescription of provisional measures under article 290, paragraph 5, of the Convention may be submitted (a) at any time if the parties have so agreed, or (b) at any time after two weeks from the notification to the other party of a request for provisional measures if the parties have not agreed that such measures may be prescribed by another court or tribunal.

Such request should indicate the legal grounds upon which the arbitral tribunal which is to be constituted would have jurisdiction and the urgency of the situation. A certified copy of the notification or of any document instituting the proceedings before the arbitral tribunal is also required to be annexed (Rules, article 89, paragraphs 2 and 4).

A request for provisional measures has priority over all other proceedings in accordance with article 90, paragraph 1, of the Rules.

The Chamber of Summary Procedure may be convened to carry out the functions of the Tribunal under the conditions provided for by article 91 of the Rules.

Any provisional measures prescribed or any modification or revocation thereof are forthwith notified to the parties and to such other States Parties as the Tribunal considers appropriate (Rules, article 94). Each party must also inform the Tribunal as soon as possible as to its compliance with any provisional measures prescribed by the Tribunal (Rules, article 95, paragraph 1).

(b) Preliminary proceedings

When an application is made in respect of a dispute referred to in article 297 of the Convention, the Tribunal determines, at the request of the respondent or *proprio motu*, in accordance with article 294 of the Convention, whether the claim constitutes an abuse of legal process or whether *prima facie* it is well founded (Rules, article 96, paragraph 1).

A request for a determination under article 294 of the Convention must be in writing and filed within the time-limit fixed by the Tribunal. The Registrar, when transmitting a certified copy of the application, notifies the respondent of the time-limit. If the Tribunal decides *proprio motu* to make a determination, its decision has to be taken within two months from the date of the application (Convention, article 294; Rules, article 96, paragraphs 2 to 4).

Preliminary proceedings suspend the proceedings on the merits. Parties may submit written observations and submissions within a time-limit not exceeding 60 days. Unless the Tribunal decides otherwise, the further proceedings are oral (Rules, article 96, paragraphs 5 and 6).

The Tribunal gives its decision in the form of a judgment (Rules, article 96, paragraph 8).

(c) Preliminary objections

Any objection to the jurisdiction of the Tribunal or to the admissibility of an application, or other objection the decision upon which is requested before any further proceedings on the merits, shall be made in writing within 90 days from the institution of proceedings (Rules, article 97, paragraph 1).

Preliminary objections suspend the proceedings on the merits. The other party may present its written observations and submissions within a time-limit not exceeding 60 days. Upon receipt of such observations and submissions, the objecting party may present its written observations and submissions in reply within a time-limit not exceeding 60 days. In principle, the further proceedings are oral (Rules, article 97, paragraphs 3 and 4).

The Tribunal gives its decision in the form of a judgment (Rules, article 97, paragraph 6).

(d) Counter-claims

A counter-claim must be directly connected with the subject matter of the claim of the other party and come within the jurisdiction of the Tribunal. The counter-claim is made in the counter-memorial of the party presenting it and appears as part of the submissions of that party (Rules, article 98).

(e) Intervention

(i) Request to intervene under article 31 of the Statute

A State Party to the Convention may request to be permitted to intervene if it considers that it has an interest of a legal nature which may be affected by the decision in the case

(Statute, article 31; Rules, article 99, paragraph 3). The request is filed not later than 30 days after the counter-memorial becomes available unless otherwise decided by the Tribunal (Rules, article 99, paragraph 1). It must fulfil the formal requirements referred to in article 99, paragraphs 2 and 3, of the Rules.

If the request is granted, the decision of the Tribunal in respect of the dispute is binding upon the intervenor in so far as it relates to matters in respect of which it intervened (Statute, article 31).

(ii) Right to intervene under article 32 of the Statute

If a case relates to the interpretation or application of the Convention or another international agreement, the parties to the agreement concerned are notified by the Registrar and have the right to intervene in the proceedings. A declaration to that effect must be filed not later than 30 days after the counter-memorial becomes available unless otherwise decided by the Tribunal (Statute, article 32; Rules, article 100, paragraph 1). The declaration must fulfil the formal requirements referred to in article 100, paragraph 2, of the Rules.

The interpretation given by the judgment is binding upon the intervenor.

(f) Discontinuance

At any time before the judgment on the merits has been delivered, the parties may notify the Tribunal in writing that they have agreed to discontinue the proceedings. The discontinuance will then be recorded in an order of the Tribunal and the Registrar will be directed to remove the case from the List of cases (Rules, article 105).

Article 106 of the Rules deals with the discontinuance, at the instance of the applicant, of proceedings instituted by means of an application.

3. Prompt Release of Vessels and Crews

(a) Application by the flag State or on its behalf

An application for the release of a vessel or its crew from detention may be submitted, in accordance with article 292 of the Convention, by any State Party (Rules, article 110, paragraph 1).

The application is made by the flag State of the vessel or on its behalf. For the purpose of an application to be made on its behalf, any State Party may at any time notify the Tribunal of the State authorities competent to authorize persons to make applications on its behalf or the name and address of any person who is authorized to make such application on its behalf (Rules, article 110, paragraphs 1 and 2).

In addition to general requirements applicable to any application, an application under article 292 of the Convention contains a statement of the facts and legal grounds upon which it is based (Rules, article 111). Where the application is made on behalf of the flag State, it must meet the specific requirements referred to in article 110, paragraph 3, of the Rules.

(b) Proceedings

The application is required to be given priority over all other proceedings in accordance with article 112, paragraph 1, of the Rules.

Upon receipt of the application, it is forthwith transmitted by the Registrar to the detaining State.

A hearing is fixed at the earliest possible date but not exceeding ten days from the date of the application. The detaining State may submit a statement in response to be filed no later than 24 hours before the hearing (Rules, article 111, paragraph 4). At the hearing, each party is normally accorded one day to present its case (Rules, article 112, paragraph 3).

If requested by the applicant, the application is dealt with by the Chamber of Summary Procedure, provided that the detaining State consents to the request within five days of receiving notice of the application (Rules, article 112, paragraph 2).

(c) Judgment and financial security

The decision of the Tribunal is in the form of a judgment and is read at a public sitting to be held not later than ten days after the closure of the hearing (Rules, article 112, paragraph 4).

If the Tribunal decides that the allegation of the flag State is well-founded, it determines the amount, nature and form of the bond or financial security to be posted for the release of the vessel or the crew (Rules, article 113, paragraph 2). The bond or other financial security is to be posted with the detaining State unless the parties agree otherwise (Rules, article 113, paragraph 3). The possibility of posting the bond or other financial security with the Tribunal is provided for in article 114 of the Rules.

4. Interpretation and Revision of Judgments

The judgments of the Tribunal are final and without appeal (Statute, article 33). However, in the event of dispute as to the meaning or scope of a judgment, any party may make a request for its interpretation (Statute, article 33; Rules, article 126, paragraph 1). A request for revision of a judgment may also be made in certain circumstances referred to in article 127, paragraph 1, of the Rules and under the conditions provided for in articles 126 to 129 of the Rules.

5. Proceedings before the Seabed Disputes Chamber

(a) General rules

Subject to the provisions of the Convention and the Rules relating specifically to them, proceedings before the Seabed Disputes Chamber and its *ad hoc* chambers are governed by the Rules applicable in contentious cases before the Tribunal (Rules, article 115).

Articles 117 to 121 of the Rules apply to proceedings in all disputes before the Chamber with the exception of disputes exclusively between States Parties and between States Parties and the International Seabed Authority (Rules, article 116).

(b) Proceedings instituted on behalf of the International Seabed Authority

Proceedings by the Council on behalf of the International Seabed Authority under article 185, paragraph 2, of the Convention are instituted by means of an application. The application is submitted to the Chamber together with a certified copy of the decision or resolution upon which it is based and the full records of all discussions within the International Seabed Authority on the matter (Rules, article 122).

(c) Question submitted by a commercial arbitral tribunal

When a commercial arbitral tribunal refers a question of interpretation of Part XI of the Convention to the Chamber, in accordance with article 188, paragraph 2, of the Convention, a precise statement of the question must be contained in the document submitting the question, together with all relevant documents and information in support (Rules, article 123, paragraph 1).

Upon receipt of the document, the parties to the proceedings before the arbitral tribunal and the States Parties are notified of the time-limit fixed by the President of the Chamber within which they may submit their written observations (Rules, article 123, paragraph 2).

There will be oral proceedings if the conditions provided for in article 123, paragraph 3, of the Rules are satisfied.

6. Proceedings before Special Chambers

(a) Applicable rules

Proceedings before a standing chamber of the Tribunal, an *ad hoc* chamber or the Chamber of Summary Procedure are governed by the Rules applicable in contentious cases before the Tribunal, subject to the provisions of the Convention and the Rules relating specifically to the special chambers (Rules, article 107).

(b) Request to submit the case to a special chamber

A case is dealt with by a standing chamber or the Chamber of Summary Procedure when a request to this effect has been made in the document instituting the proceedings and the parties are in agreement (Rules, article 108, paragraph 1).

A request for the formation of an *ad hoc* chamber must be made within two months from the date of the institution of proceedings. The chamber is constituted if the parties are in agreement. It is composed in the manner provided for in articles 30 and 31 of the Rules.

The President of the Tribunal convenes the special chamber at the earliest date compatible with the requirements of the procedure (Rules, article 108, paragraph 4).

(c) Proceedings

Written proceedings in a case before a chamber consist of a single pleading by each party, to be filed within a time-limit fixed by the chamber or its President if the chamber is not sitting. If necessary, the chamber may also authorize or decide the filing of further pleadings (Rules, article 109, paragraphs 1 and 2).

Oral proceedings take place unless the parties agree to dispense with them and the chamber so consents (Rules, article 109, paragraph 3).

III. Advisory Proceedings

1. Advisory Proceedings before the Seabed Disputes Chamber under the Convention

(a) Applicable rules

In proceedings relating to advisory opinions, the Seabed Disputes Chamber applies articles 130 to 137 of the Rules and is guided, where appropriate, by the provisions of the Convention and the Rules applicable in contentious cases.

(b) Request for an advisory opinion

The request for an advisory opinion on a legal question arising within the scope of the activities of the Assembly or the Council of the International Seabed Authority should contain a precise statement of the question. All relevant documents should be annexed to the request or transmitted as soon as possible thereafter in the number of copies required by the Registry (Rules, article 131, paragraphs 1 and 2).

(c) Notification, written statements and information to the public

Notification of the request is forthwith given by the Registrar to all States Parties and intergovernmental organizations able to furnish information on the question, which may present written statements within a time-limit fixed by the Chamber, or its President if the Chamber is not sitting (Rules, article 133, paragraphs 1 to 3). The written statements are made accessible to the public as soon as possible after their presentation (Rules, article 134).

(d) Reading of the advisory opinion

The advisory opinion is read at a public sitting of the Chamber, the date of which is notified to the Secretary-General of the International Seabed Authority, the States Parties and the intergovernmental organizations immediately concerned (Rules, articles 135 and 136).

(e) Copies of the advisory opinion

After being signed by the President and the Registrar, one copy of the opinion is sealed and archived. Other copies are sent to the Secretary-General of the International Seabed

Authority, the Secretary-General of the United Nations, States Parties and the intergovernmental organizations concerned (Rules, article 137).

2. Advisory Proceedings before the Tribunal on the Basis of Other International Agreements

When a request for an advisory opinion is submitted to the Tribunal in accordance with the provisions of an international agreement related to the purposes of the Convention, article 138 of the Rules is applicable.

CHAPTER IV

JUDICIAL WORK OF THE TRIBUNAL

I. Cases before the Tribunal

During the period under review, the Tribunal delivered a Judgment[5] in the *"Camouco" Case (Panama* v. *France)* on 7 February 2000. It also delivered a Judgment[6] in the *"Monte Confurco" Case (Seychelles* v. *France)* on 18 December 2000. Proceedings were instituted in the *Case concerning the Conservation and Sustainable Exploitation of Swordfish Stocks in the South-Eastern Pacific Ocean (Chile/European Community)*. The Tribunal made an Order[7] on 20 December 2000 concerning the constitution of a chamber to deal with this case.

1. *The "Camouco" Case*

(a) Introduction

On 17 January 2000, an Application under article 292 of the Convention was filed on behalf of Panama against France for the prompt release of the *Camouco*, a fishing vessel flying the flag of Panama, and its Master from detention by the French authorities. The Application was entered in the List of cases as Case No. 5 and named: *The "Camouco" Case*.

The events leading up to the proceedings may be presented as follows:

On 28 September 2000, the *Camouco* was arrested by a French frigate, allegedly for unlawful fishing and failure to notify its presence in the exclusive economic zone of the Crozet Islands, and subsequently escorted to Réunion. French authorities seized the vessel, fish catch, navigation and communication equipment and documents of the vessel and of the crew. The Master was charged and placed under court supervision. A French court ordered that the release of the arrested vessel would be subject to the payment of a bond in the amount of 20 million FF in cash, certified cheque or bank draft, to be paid into the Deposits and Consignments Office.

---

[5] The Judgment of 7 February 2000, the pleadings and the verbatim records are available on the United Nations website of the Tribunal: *http://www.un.org/Depts/los*

[6] The Judgment of 18 December 2000, the pleadings and the verbatim records are available on the United Nations website: *http://www.un.org/Depts/los*

[7] The Order of 20 December 2000 is available on the United Nations website: *http://www.un.org/Depts/los*

By Order dated 17 January 2000, the President fixed 27 and 28 January 2000 as the dates for the hearing.

France filed its Statement in Response on 25 January 2000.

Prior to the opening of the hearing, the Tribunal held initial deliberations on 26 January 2000.

Four public sittings to hear the oral arguments of the parties and to present evidence were held on 27 and 28 January 2000.

(b) Final submissions of the parties

In their concluding statements, the representatives of the parties read their final submissions as follows:

On behalf of Panama:

[Translation from French]

The Tribunal is requested:

1. To declare that the Tribunal has jurisdiction to entertain the application pursuant to article 292 of the United Nations Convention on the Law of the Sea.

2. To declare that the present application made by the Republic of Panama on 17 January 2000 is admissible.

3. To declare that the French Republic has violated article 73, paragraph 4, by tardy and incomplete notification of the arrest and seizure of the vessel *Camouco* to the Republic of Panama of the measures taken and of those which were to be taken.

4. To find that the French Republic has failed to observe the provisions of the Convention concerning prompt release of the Master of the vessel *Camouco*.

5. To find that the French Republic has failed to observe the provisions of the Convention concerning prompt release of the vessel *Camouco*.

6. To find that the non-observance by the French Republic of the provisions of article 73, paragraph 3 – by applying to the Master of the *Camouco* provisional measures of a penal character – constitutes unlawful detention.

7. To demand that the French Republic promptly release the vessel *Camouco* and, concomitantly, release its Master, against payment of a reasonable bond of one million three hundred thousand francs (1,300,000 FF) before deduction of the price of the cargo seized (350,000 FF), i.e. a final guarantee in a maximum amount of nine hundred and fifty thousand francs (950,000 FF).

8. To order that said amount be paid by means of a bank guarantee of a major European bank, to be entrusted to the care of the International Tribunal for the Law

of the Sea in order that it may be duly delivered to the French authorities in exchange for the release of the vessel and of its Master.

9. Pursuant to article 64, paragraph 4, of the rules of procedure, to prepare a Spanish translation of the judgment of the International Tribunal for the Law of the Sea.

On behalf of France:

[Translation from French]

The Government of the French Republic requests the Tribunal, while rejecting all submissions to the contrary presented on behalf of the Republic of Panama, to declare and adjudge:

(1) that the application requesting the Tribunal to order the prompt release of the *Camouco* and of its captain is not admissible.

(2) as a subsidiary submission, if it decides that the *Camouco* is to be released upon the deposit of a bond, that the bond shall be not less than the sum of 20,000,000 francs and that this sum shall be posted in the form of a certified cheque or bank draft.

(c) Judgment

On 7 February 2000, the Tribunal delivered its Judgment in the case.

In its Judgment, the Tribunal found that it had jurisdiction to entertain the Application.

The Tribunal observed that there was disagreement between the parties on whether the Application was admissible. The Tribunal rejected the objections to admissibility raised by the Respondent based on delay in the presentation of the Application and non-exhaustion of local remedies. It also decided that the Applicant's submissions based on alleged violations of article 73, paragraphs 3 and 4, of the Convention and of the provisions of the Convention on freedom of navigation were not admissible.

Pursuant to article 113, paragraph 1, of the Rules, the Tribunal dealt with the allegation that the detaining State had not complied with the provisions of the Convention for the prompt release of the vessel and its Master upon the posting of a reasonable bond or other financial security, and noted that for the application for release to succeed this allegation should be well-founded. The Tribunal reiterated in this connection that the posting of a bond or other security was not necessarily a condition precedent to filing an application under article 292 of the Convention. Dealing with the Applicant's contention that the bond of 20 million FF fixed by the French court was not "reasonable", the Tribunal referred to its statement in its Judgment in the *M/V "SAIGA" (No. 2) Case* that "the criterion of reasonableness encompasses the amount, the nature and form of the bond or financial security" and that the "overall balance of the amount, form and nature of the bond or financial security must be reasonable." It also elaborated on other factors which in its view were relevant in an assessment of the reasonableness of a bond or other financial security, i.e. gravity of the alleged offences, the penalties imposed or imposable under the laws of the detaining State, the value of the detained vessel and of the cargo seized, the amount of the bond imposed by the detaining State and its form. The Tribunal concluded that the bond of 20 million FF imposed by the French court was not "reasonable". The Tribunal found that the Application was admissible and that the allegation made by the Applicant was well-founded for the purposes of the proceedings. Consequently, it ordered that France should release promptly the *Camouco* and its Master upon the posting of a bond or other financial security as determined by the Tribunal. The Tribunal determined that the bond or other security should be in the amount of 8 million FF and that, unless the parties otherwise agreed, the bond should be in the form of a bank guarantee.

(d) Operative provisions of the Judgment

The operative provisions of the Judgment read as follows:

For these reasons, the Tribunal,

(1) Unanimously,

Finds that the Tribunal has jurisdiction under article 292 of the Convention to entertain the Application made on behalf of Panama on 17 January 2000.

(2) By 19 votes to 2,

Finds that the Application for release is admissible;

...

(3) By 19 votes to 2,

Orders that France shall promptly release the *Camouco* and its Master upon the posting of a bond;

...

(4) By 15 votes to 6,

Determines that the bond shall be eight million French Francs (8,000,000 FF) to be posted with France;

...

(5) By 19 votes to 2,

Determines that the bond shall be in the form of a bank guarantee or, if agreed to by the parties, in any other form;

...

(e) Declarations, separate and dissenting opinions

Judges Mensah, Laing and Ndiaye appended declarations to the Judgment; Vice-President Nelson appended a separate opinion to the Judgment; Judges Anderson, Vukas, Wolfrum and Treves appended dissenting opinions to the Judgment.

2. *The "Monte Confurco" Case*

(a) Introduction

On 27 November 2000, an Application under article 292 of the Convention was filed on behalf of Seychelles against France concerning the release of the *Monte Confurco*, a fishing vessel flying the flag of Seychelles, and its Master from detention by French authorities. The Application was entered in the List of cases as Case No. 6 and named: *The "Monte Confurco" Case*.

The events leading up to the proceedings may be presented as follows:

On 8 November 2000, the *Monte Confurco* was arrested by a French frigate, allegedly for unlawful fishing and failure to notify its presence in the exclusive economic zone of the Kerguelen Islands in the French Southern and Antarctic Territories, and subsequently escorted to Réunion. French authorities seized the vessel, its equipment and documents, the fish on board the vessel and fishing gear. The Master was charged and placed under court supervision. A French court declared that the release of the arrested vessel would be subject to the payment of a bond in the amount of 56,400,000 FF in cash, certified cheque or banker's draft, to be paid into the Deposits and Consignments Office.

By Order dated 27 November 2000, the President fixed 7 and 8 December 2000 as the dates for the hearing.

France filed its Statement in Response on 6 December 2000.

Prior to the opening of the hearing, the Tribunal held initial deliberations on 6 December 2000.

The hearing took place at the permanent premises of the Tribunal. Four public sittings to hear the oral arguments of the parties and to present evidence were held on 7 and 8 December 2000.

(b) Final submissions of the parties

In their concluding statements, the representatives of the parties read their final submissions as follows:

On behalf of Seychelles:

[Translation from French]

The Applicant requests the Tribunal:

1. To declare that the Tribunal has jurisdiction under article 292 of the United Nations Convention on the Law of the Sea to hear the application submitted today;

2. To declare the present application *admissible*;

3. To declare that the French Republic has contravened article 73 (4) by not properly giving notice of the arrest of the vessel "MONTE CONFURCO" to the Republic of Seychelles;

4. To declare that the guarantee set by the French Republic is not reasonable as to its amount, nature or form;

5. With respect to the master of the vessel "MONTE CONFURCO", Mr. José Pérez Argibay,

- To find that the French Republic has failed to observe the provisions of the Convention concerning prompt release of masters of arrested vessels;
- To require the French Republic promptly to release the master, without bond, in light of the presence of the ship, cargo, etc. as a reasonable guarantee, given the impossibility of imposing penalties of imprisonment against him and the fact that he is a European citizen;
- To find that the failure of the French Republic to comply with the provisions of article 73 (3) in applying to the master measures of a penal character constitutes a *de facto* unlawful detention;

6. With regard to the vessel, to order its release upon the posting of a guarantee in the maximum amount of 2,200,000 FF, based upon:

- 200,000 FF for failure to notify presence;
- 2,000,000 FF for a presence of 24 hours in the exclusive economic zone without giving notice and up to 4 tonnes of catch theoretically taken in the worst of cases, as the sole admissible evidence of presumption;

7. With regard to the nature of the bond, that the Tribunal consider that the value of the cargo seized, the fishing gear seized, the bait and the gasoil constitute part of the guarantee; according to our calculations, the value of the foregoing being 9,800,000 FF;

8. That the Tribunal choose between the financial instrument (*constitution financière*) issued by a European bank or a guarantee comprised of the value of an equivalent number of tonnes or other items according to our calculations;

9. With regard to the form of the financial bond, as a subsidiary measure, in the event that the Tribunal chooses to set a symbolic financial bond, the Applicant requests that the Tribunal note its desire for a bank guarantee by a leading European bank, of the same content as the guarantee already posted with the French Republic in the *"CAMOUCO" Case* in consideration of the release of the vessel.

On behalf of France:

[Translation from French]

The Government of the French Republic requests the Tribunal, rejecting the second submission made on behalf of the Republic of Seychelles, to declare and adjudge:

1. that the bond set by the competent French court for the release of the "Monte Confurco" is reasonable in the circumstances of the case, in light of all the relevant factors;

2. that the Application submitted to the Tribunal on 27 November 2000 on behalf of the Republic of Seychelles is therefore not admissible.

(c) Judgment

On 18 December 2000, the Tribunal delivered its Judgment in the case.

In its Judgment, the Tribunal found that it had jurisdiction to entertain the Application.

The Tribunal decided that the Applicant's submissions based on alleged violations of article 73, paragraphs 3 and 4, of the Convention were not admissible.

The Tribunal noted the Applicant's submissions that the detaining State had not complied with article 73, paragraph 2, of the Convention and that the bond set by the French court in the amount of 56,400,000 FF was not "reasonable". It observed that pursuant to article 113 of the Rules, it was required to decide whether or not the Applicant's allegation was well-founded in order to proceed with the determination of the amount, nature and form of the bond or financial security to be posted for the release of the vessel or the crew. The Tribunal then examined whether the bond imposed by the French court was reasonable and noted that the balance of interests emerging from articles 73 and 292 of the Convention provided the guiding criterion for the Tribunal in its assessment of the reasonableness of the bond. The Tribunal referred to factors specified in the *"Camouco" Case* which were relevant in an assessment of the reasonableness of bonds or other financial security. In the Tribunal's view, this was a non-exhaustive list of factors which complemented the criterion of reasonableness specified in the *M/V "SAIGA" Case*. The Tribunal then proceeded to apply the various factors to the present case, i.e. gravity of the alleged offences, range of penalties imposable under French law for the alleged offences, value of the *Monte Confurco* and of the fish and fishing gear seized. The Tribunal concluded that the bond of 56,400,000 FF imposed by the French court was not "reasonable". It found that the Application with respect to the allegation of non-compliance with article 73, paragraph 2, of the Convention was admissible and that the allegation made by the Applicant was well-founded. It ordered that France must release promptly the *Monte Confurco* and its Master upon the posting of a bond or other financial security as determined by the Tribunal.

The Tribunal determined that the security should be in the total amount of 18 million FF and should consist of: (1) an amount of 9 million FF as the monetary equivalent of the 158 tonnes of fish seized by the French authorities and (2) a bond in the amount of 9 million FF. The Tribunal decided that, unless the parties otherwise agreed, the bond should be in the form of a bank guarantee.

(d) Operative provisions of the Judgment

The operative provisions of the Judgment read as follows:

For these reasons, the Tribunal,

(1) Unanimously,

Finds that the Tribunal has jurisdiction under article 292 of the Convention to entertain the Application made on behalf of Seychelles on 27 November 2000.

(2) Unanimously,

Finds that the claims of Seychelles that France failed to comply with article 73, paragraphs 3 and 4, of the Convention are inadmissible.

(3) Unanimously,

Finds that the Application with respect to the allegation of non-compliance with article 73, paragraph 2, of the Convention is admissible.

(4) By 19 votes to 1,

Finds that the allegation made by the Applicant is well-founded;
...

(5) By 19 votes to 1,

Decides that France shall promptly release the *Monte Confurco* and its Master upon the posting of a bond or other security to be determined by the Tribunal;
...

(6) By 17 votes to 3,

Determines that the bond or other security shall consist of: (1) an amount of nine million French francs (9,000,000 FF) as the monetary equivalent of the 158 tonnes of fish seized by the French authorities and (2) a bond in the amount of nine million French francs (9,000,000 FF);
...

Unanimously,

Determines that the bond shall be in the form of a bank guarantee or, if agreed to by the parties, in any other form.

By 18 votes to 2,

Decides that the bank guarantee shall be invoked only if the monetary equivalent of the security held by France is not sufficient to pay the sums as may be determined by a final judgment or decision of the appropriate domestic forum in France;
...

(e) Declarations, separate and dissenting opinions

Judges Mensah, Vukas and Ndiaye appended declarations to the Judgment; Vice-President Nelson appended a separate opinion to the Judgment; Judges Anderson, Laing and Jesus appended dissenting opinions to the Judgment.

3. *Case concerning the Conservation and Sustainable Exploitation of Swordfish Stocks in the South-Eastern Pacific Ocean*

By an exchange of letters dated 18 and 19 December 2000, Chile and the European Community agreed to submit a dispute concerning the conservation and sustainable exploitation of swordfish stocks in the South-Eastern Pacific Ocean to a special chamber of the Tribunal to be formed in accordance with article 15, paragraph 2, of the Statute.

Pursuant to article 24, paragraph 2, of the Statute, the Registrar was notified of the exchange of letters between Chile and the European Community by separate letters from the Government of Chile and the European Community dated 19 December 2000.

By Order dated 20 December 2000, the Tribunal decided to accede to the request of the parties to form a special chamber to deal with the case and determined the composition of the Special Chamber with their approval.[8/] By the same Order, the Tribunal fixed the time-limits for the filing of preliminary objection or objections and of the written pleadings. The case was entered in the List of cases as Case No. 7 and named: *Case concerning the Conservation and Sustainable Exploitation of Swordfish Stocks in the South-Eastern Pacific Ocean.*

In accordance with the provisions contained in the exchange of letters, the Special Chamber is requested to decide the following issues:

On behalf of Chile:

(a) whether the European Community has complied with its obligations under the Convention, especially articles 116 to 119 thereof, to ensure conservation of swordfish, in the fishing activities undertaken by vessels flying the flag of any of its member States in the high seas adjacent to Chile's exclusive economic zone;

(b) whether the European Community has complied with its obligations under the Convention, in particular article 64 thereof, to co-operate directly with Chile as a coastal State for the conservation of swordfish in the high seas adjacent to Chile's exclusive economic zone as also to report its catches and other information relevant to this fishery to the competent international organization and to the coastal State;

(c) in relation to the foregoing, whether the European Community has challenged the sovereign right and duty of Chile, as a coastal State, to prescribe measures within its national jurisdiction for the conservation of swordfish and to ensure their implementation in its ports, in a non-discriminatory manner, as well as the measures themselves, and whether such challenge would be compatible with the Convention;

8/ For the composition of the Special Chamber, see Chapter I.

(d) whether the obligations arising under articles 300 and 297, paragraph 1 (b), of the Convention, as also the general thrust of the Convention in that regard, have been fulfilled in this case by the European Community.

On behalf of the European Community:

(e) whether the Chilean Decree 598 which purports to apply Chile's unilateral conservation measures relating to swordfish on the high seas is in breach of, *inter alia*, articles 87, 89 and 116 to 119 of the Convention;

(f) whether the "Galapagos Agreement" signed in Santiago de Chile on 14 August 2000 was negotiated into in keeping with the provisions of the Convention and whether its substantive provisions are in consonance with, *inter alia*, articles 64 and 116 to 119 of the Convention;

(g) whether Chile's actions concerning the conservation of swordfish are in conformity with article 300 of the Convention and whether Chile and the European Community remain under a duty to negotiate an agreement on cooperation under article 64 of the Convention;

(h) whether the jurisdiction of the special chamber extends to the issue referred to in paragraph 3 (c) above.

II. Application of the Statute and Rules

1. *The "Camouco" Case (Panama* v. *France), Prompt Release*

(a) Institution of proceedings
(Statute, article 24; Rules, articles 54 and 110)

Proceedings in the case were instituted by means of an Application under article 292 of the Convention filed in the Registry on 17 January 2000 on behalf of Panama against France.

(b) Fixing of date for the opening of the hearing
(Rules, article 112, paragraph 3)

The President, by Order dated 17 January 2000, fixed 27 January 2000 as the date for the opening of the oral proceedings.

(c) Notification of the names of the Agents
(Rules, article 56)

The Application was accompanied by a certificate from the officer in charge of consular affairs in the Embassy of Panama, Brussels, dated 17 January 2000, notifying the appointment of Mr. Ramón García Gallardo, *Avocat*, Brussels and Burgos, as Agent of Panama.

By letter dated 19 January 2000, the Director of Legal Affairs, Ministry of Foreign Affairs, Paris, notified the Registrar of the appointment of Mr. Jean-François Dobelle, Deputy Director of Legal Affairs of the Ministry of Foreign Affairs of France, as Agent of France.

(d) Notification to the States Parties to the Convention
(Statute, article 24, paragraph 3)

States Parties to the Convention were notified of the Application by a note verbale from the Registrar dated 18 January 2000.

(e) Statement in Response
(Rules, article 111, paragraph 4)

By note verbale from the Registrar dated 17 January 2000, the Minister for Foreign Affairs of France was informed that the Statement in Response of France could be filed in the Registry not later than 24 hours before the hearing. France transmitted its Statement in Response on 25 January 2000.

(f) Consultations with the parties
(Rules, article 45)

On 20 January 2000, the President held a teleconference with the Agents of the parties and ascertained their views regarding the order and timing of presentation by each of the parties and the evidence to be produced during the oral proceedings.

On 27 January 2000, prior to the hearing, the President held consultations with the Agents of the parties regarding the procedure for the oral proceedings.

(g) Initial deliberations
(Rules, article 68)

After the closure of the written proceedings and prior to the opening of the oral proceedings, the Tribunal held its initial deliberations in the case on 26 January 2000.

(h) Issues to be addressed by the parties
(Rules, article 76)

On 27 January 2000, a list of issues which the Tribunal wished the parties specially to address was communicated to the Agents of the parties.

On 28 January 2000, the Agent of Panama submitted a written response to the questions addressed by the Tribunal. During the hearing, on 28 January 2000, the Agent of France replied orally to those questions.

(i) Information regarding witnesses and experts
(Rules, article 72)

Information regarding witnesses and experts was submitted by the Agent of Panama to the Tribunal on 18 and 21 January 2000 and by the Agent of France on 24 January 2000.

(j) Presentation of new documents
(Rules, article 71)

During the hearing on 28 January 2000, the President drew the attention of the parties to article 71 of the Rules, and to additional documents referred to by the parties in the hearing on 27 and 28 January 2000, copies of which were communicated to the other party. Since no objection was raised by the parties, the President stated that those additional documents should be filed with the Registry together with, where necessary, a translation in one of the official languages of the Tribunal.

(k) Accessibility of documents to the public
(Rules, article 67, paragraph 2)

Copies of the pleadings and documents annexed thereto were made accessible to the public from the date of the opening of the oral proceedings.

(l) Verbatim records
(Rules, article 86)

A transcript of the verbatim record of each public sitting of the hearing was prepared and circulated to the judges sitting in the case. Copies of the transcripts were also circulated to the parties and made available to the public in printed and electronic form.

(m) Oral proceedings
(Rules, articles 75, 78, 80 and 85, paragraph 2)

Oral statements were presented by the parties at four public sittings held on 27 and 28 January 2000.

Two experts, called by the Agent of Panama, gave evidence at a public sitting held on 27 January 2000. The two experts gave evidence in Spanish. The necessary arrangements were made for the statements of those experts to be interpreted into the official languages of the Tribunal.

The experts were examined and one of them was cross-examined. A list of questions to be put to both experts, a curriculum vitae of one expert and a technical report concerning the *Camouco* were submitted by the party calling the experts.

The Agent of Panama, in the course of his statement, presented a number of exhibits which were displayed on video monitors, including nautical charts, a slide, a video film and photographs. The original of each exhibit was delivered to the Registrar and duly registered.

(n) Final submissions
(Rules, article 75, paragraph 2)

In their concluding statements, on 28 January 2000, the Agent of each party read its final submissions, copies of which were communicated to the Tribunal and to the other party.

(o) Reading of the judgment
(Rules, articles 112, paragraph 4, and 113)

The Judgment of 7 February 2000 was read at a public sitting held on 7 February 2000.

(p) Declarations, separate and dissenting opinions
(Statute, article 30; Rules, article 125, paragraph 2)

Three Judges appended declarations to the Judgment; the Vice-President appended his separate opinion to the Judgment; four Judges appended dissenting opinions to the Judgment.

(q) Translation of the judgment
(Rules, article 64, paragraph 4)

In its Judgment of 7 February 2000, the Tribunal stated that article 64, paragraph 4, of the Rules deals with the situation where the parties chose a language other than English or French for their written pleadings, which was not the case in the proceedings before it. Accordingly, the Tribunal could not accede to the request of the Applicant that the Judgment be translated into Spanish pursuant to that provision.

2. *The "Monte Confurco" Case (Seychelles v. France), Prompt Release*

(a) Institution of proceedings
(Statute, article 24; Rules, articles 54 and 110)

Proceedings in the case were instituted by means of an Application under article 292 of the Convention filed in the Registry on 27 November 2000 on behalf of Seychelles against France.

(b) Fixing of date for the opening of the hearing
(Rules, article 112, paragraph 3)

The President, by Order dated 27 November 2000, fixed 7 and 8 December 2000 as the dates for the hearing.

(c) Corrections to the Application
(Rules, article 65, paragraph 4)

On 27 November 2000, the Agent of Seychelles transmitted to the Tribunal a list of corrections to the initial submission of the Application. These corrections, being of a formal nature, were accepted by leave of the President of the Tribunal

(d) Notification of the names of the Agents
(Rules, article 56)

The Registrar was notified of the appointment of Mr. Ramón García Gallardo, *Avocat*, Brussels and Burgos, as Agent of Seychelles, and of Mr. Jean-Jacques Morel, *Avocat*, Saint-Denis, as Deputy Agent, by a letter dated 20 November 2000 from the Minister of Agriculture and Marine Resources of Seychelles.

On 30 November 2000, the Registrar was notified of the appointment of Mr. Michel Trinquier, Deputy Director for the Law of the Sea, Fisheries and the Antarctic of the Office of Legal Affairs of the Ministry of Foreign Affairs of France, as Agent of France, by a letter from the Deputy Director of Legal Affairs, Ministry of Foreign Affairs, Paris.

(e) Notification to the States Parties to the Convention
(Statute, article 24, paragraph 3)

States Parties to the Convention were notified of the Application by a note verbale from the Registrar dated 29 November 2000.

(f) Statement in Response
(Rules, article 111, paragraph 4)

By note verbale from the Registrar dated 27 November 2000, the Minister for Foreign Affairs of France was informed that the Statement in Response of France could be filed in the Registry not later than 24 hours before the hearing. France transmitted its Statement in Response on 6 December 2000.

(g) Consultations with the parties
(Rules, article 45)

On 1 December 2000, the President held a teleconference with the Agents of the parties and ascertained their views regarding the order and duration of the presentation by each party and the evidence to be produced during the oral proceedings.

On 7 December 2000, prior to the hearing, the President held consultations with the Agents of the parties regarding the procedure for the oral proceedings and the submission of documents required under the Rules and the Guidelines.

(h) Initial deliberations
(Rules, article 68)

After the closure of the written proceedings and prior to the opening of the oral proceedings, the Tribunal held its initial deliberations in the case on 6 December 2000.

(i) Issues to be addressed by the parties
(Rules, article 76)

On 7 December 2000, a list of points and issues which the Tribunal would like the parties specially to address was communicated to the Agents of the parties. On 8 December 2000, the Agents of the parties submitted written responses to those points and issues.

(j) Information regarding witnesses and experts
(Rules, article 72)

Information regarding witnesses and experts was submitted by the Agent of Seychelles to the Tribunal on 28 November 2000 and on 5 and 8 December 2000 and by the Agent of France on 1 and 7 December 2000.

(k) Presentation of new documents
(Rules, article 71)

On 8 December 2000, the Agent of Seychelles submitted additional documents referred to by that party during the hearing. Copies of the documents were communicated to the other party and the opportunity was given to it to transmit to the Tribunal its comments on one of those documents.

(l) Accessibility of documents to the public
(Rules, article 67, paragraph 2)

Copies of the pleadings and documents annexed thereto were made accessible to the public from the date of the opening of the oral proceedings.

(m) Verbatim records
(Rules, article 86)

A transcript of the verbatim record of each public sitting of the hearing was prepared and circulated to the judges sitting in the case. Copies of the transcripts were also circulated to the parties and made available to the public in printed and electronic form.

(n) Oral proceedings
(Rules, articles 75, 78, 80 and 85, paragraph 2)

Oral statements were presented by the parties at four public sittings held on 7 and 8 December 2000.

On 7 December 2000, an expert called by the Agent of France was examined and cross-examined. In the course of the testimony of the expert, a number of exhibits were displayed on video monitors, including a nautical chart and a map. The original of each exhibit was delivered to the Registrar and duly registered.

On 8 December 2000, an expert was called by the Agent of Seychelles and examined. The expert gave evidence in Spanish. The necessary arrangements were made for the statement of the expert to be interpreted into the official languages of the Tribunal.

The Agent of Seychelles, in the course of his statement, presented a number of computer-generated exhibits which were displayed on video monitors, including nautical charts and slides. He also presented a lamp, radio transmitter and battery said to be components of buoys, and referred to a number of photographs. The original of each exhibit was delivered to the Registrar and duly registered.

(o) Final submissions
(Rules, article 75, paragraph 2)

In their concluding statements, on 8 December 2000, the Agent of each party read its final submissions, copies of which were communicated to the Tribunal and to the other party.

(p) Reading of the judgment
(Rules, articles 112, paragraph 4, and 113)

The Judgment of 18 December 2000 was read at a public sitting held on 18 December 2000.

(q) Declarations, separate and dissenting opinions
(Statute, article 30; Rules, article 125, paragraph 2)

Three Judges appended declarations to the Judgment; the Vice-President appended his separate opinion to the Judgment; three Judges appended dissenting opinions to the Judgment.

3. *Case concerning the Conservation and Sustainable Exploitation of Swordfish Stocks in the South-Eastern Pacific Ocean (Chile/European Community)*

(a) Institution of proceedings
(Statute, article 24, paragraph 1; Rules, article 55)

Proceedings in the case were brought before the Tribunal by the notification of an exchange of letters between Chile and the European Community, by a letter dated 19 December 2000 from the Government of Chile and by a letter dated 19 December 2000 from the European Community.

(b) Notification of the names of the Agents
(Rules, article 56)

In their respective notifications dated 19 December 2000, the Government of Chile and the European Community stated that Ambassador Jorge Berguño had been appointed Agent of Chile and that Mr. Allan Rosas, Principal Legal Adviser, had been appointed Agent of the European Community.

(c) Constitution of a Special Chamber
(Statute, article 15, paragraph 2; Rules, articles 30 and 31)

In the exchange of letters dated 18 and 19 December 2000, respectively, the parties requested the Tribunal that the case be submitted to a special chamber composed of five members. By separate letters dated 19 December 2000, the parties informed the Tribunal of their views regarding the composition of the Special Chamber of the Tribunal.

By its Order dated 20 December 2000, the Tribunal constituted a special chamber composed of five judges to deal with the case and determined its composition. It decided that the quorum required for meetings of the Special Chamber was to be three members of the Special Chamber.

(d) Judge ad hoc
(Statute, article 17; Rules, article 19)

By letters dated 19 December 2000, the Government of Chile notified the Tribunal of its choice of Mr. Orrego Vicuña to sit as judge *ad hoc* in the Chamber, and the European

Community confirmed the choice of judge *ad hoc* made by Chile. Since no objection to such choice appeared to the Tribunal itself, Mr. Orrego Vicuña became member, as judge *ad hoc*, of the Special Chamber.

(e) Modifications or additions to the Rules
(Rules, article 48)

In its Order dated 20 December 2000, the Tribunal decided to accede to the request made by the parties that the proceedings before the Special Chamber be governed by the provisions contained in Part III, sections A, B and C, of the Rules.

(f) Preliminary objections
(Rules, article 97)

In its Order dated 20 December 2000, the Tribunal decided that any preliminary objection should be dealt with by the Special Chamber in accordance with article 97, paragraphs 1 to 6, of the Rules.

(g) Written proceedings
(Rules, article 59)

In its Order dated 20 December 2000, the Tribunal determined the number and the order of the pleadings and the time-limits within they should be filed. It reserved the subsequent procedure for further decision by the Special Chamber.

CHAPTER V

ACTIVITIES OF THE TRIBUNAL

I. Administrative Sessions of the Tribunal

In 2000, the Tribunal held two sessions devoted to administrative matters. The Ninth Session took place from 6 to 17 March 2000, and the Tenth Session took place from 18 September to 29 September 2000.

The work of the sessions was mainly devoted to the following matters:

1. Establishment of Chambers

New members of the Chamber of Summary Procedure were selected on 27 September 2000 for the period ending on 30 September 2001. During 2000, a vacancy occurred in the Seabed Disputes Chamber due to the death of Judge Lihai Zhao, who had been a member of this chamber. The composition of the Chamber for Fisheries Disputes and the Chamber for Marine Environment Disputes did not change during 2000.

The Tribunal, by Order dated 20 December 2000, constituted a special chamber to deal with the *Case concerning the Conservation and Sustainable Exploitation of Swordfish Stocks in the South-Eastern Pacific Ocean*.

2. Committees and Working Group

The members of the Committees were selected at the Eighth Session, on 4 October 1999, to serve for the period ending 30 September 2000. On 27 September 2000, the Tribunal decided to extend the terms of office of the members of the Committees until 30 September 2001.

A Working Group on Bonds and Other Financial Security was established on 15 March 2000. The terms of office of the members of the Working Group were extended on 27 September 2000 until 30 September 2001.

3. Rules of the Tribunal

During the Tenth Session, the Committee on Rules and Judicial Practice considered the Rules for the Preparation of Typed and Printed Texts, the question of costs to be borne by parties appearing before the Tribunal and time factors in the handling of applications for prompt release cases. During the same session, the Tribunal decided that communications received from parties concerning implementation of judgments and orders should be reported in the Tribunal's publications, including Yearbooks, Annual Reports and Pleadings, Minutes of Public Sittings and Documents. Relevant information in this respect may be found in Annex VIII.

During the Tenth Session, the Working Group on Bonds and Other Financial Security began consideration of the issue of bonds or other financial security in prompt release proceedings.

4. Privileges and Immunities

During the Ninth and Tenth Sessions of the Tribunal, the President reported on the status of negotiations with the German authorities on the headquarters agreement between the International Tribunal for the Law of the Sea and the Federal Republic of Germany. At the end of 2000, the negotiations on the headquarters agreement were still ongoing.

5. Premises of the Tribunal

During the Tenth Session, the Registrar reported on the conclusion of the Agreement between the International Tribunal for the Law of the Sea and the Government of the Federal Republic of Germany on the Occupancy and Use of the Premises of the International Tribunal for the Law of the Sea in the Free and Hanseatic City of Hamburg. The Agreement was signed on 18 October 2000 by the President of the Tribunal, Mr. P. Chandrasekhara Rao, the Federal Minister of Justice of the Federal Republic of Germany, Mrs. Herta Däubler-Gmelin, and the State Secretary for Foreign Affairs, Mr. Wolfgang Ischinger.

During the period under review, the Tribunal considered practical arrangements to facilitate the move to the permanent premises. The transfer of the permanent premises to the Tribunal took place on 6 November 2000. A facility manager was appointed to carry out the operation and maintenance of the premises in accordance with the Agreement. The move from the temporary premises located at Wexstrasse 4, in the centre of Hamburg, to the permanent premises took place from 20 to 24 November 2000. The Tribunal started working in its permanent premises on 27 November 2000.

6. Finances

At its Ninth Session, the Tribunal adopted budget proposals for the year 2001.

At its Tenth Session, the Tribunal gave preliminary consideration to the draft budget for 2002, based on the proposals by the Registrar. During the same session, the audit report for the 1999 financial statements of the Tribunal was presented by the Registrar.

7. Trust Fund and Donations

At the Tenth Session, the President informed the Tribunal of the decision taken by the tenth Meeting of States Parties to recommend to the General Assembly that a trust fund for assisting States in proceedings before the Tribunal be established.[9/]

8. Staff Regulations and Rules

At its Ninth Session, the Tribunal approved amendments to the Staff Regulations of the Tribunal dealing with rates of staff assessment and the salary scales for staff in the professional and higher categories.

At its Tenth Session, the Tribunal approved the Staff Rules of the Tribunal with provisional effect from 1 October 2000. In accordance with Staff Regulation 12.4, the Staff Rules were due to enter into force on 1 January 2001.

9. Instructions for the Registry

On 17 March 2000, the Tribunal adopted Instructions for the Registry.

10. Role of the President

During its Ninth and Tenth Sessions, the Tribunal adopted a decision and a supplementary decision on the role of the President regarding the administration of the Tribunal, including staff-related matters such as appointments, promotions or grant of allowances to staff members, and financial matters.

11. Internship Programme

An Internship Programme of the Tribunal was established in 1997, based on the United Nations Internship Programme. During the period under review, 16 interns took part in this programme. At its Tenth Session, the Tribunal approved changes to the Programme.

12. Buildings and Electronic Systems

At its Ninth and Tenth Sessions, the Tribunal requested the Registrar to examine certain aspects of building requirements for the new premises as regards the Library, interpretation booths and electronic equipment. These matters were the subject of consultations between the Registrar and the German authorities.

13. Public Access to the Premises

At its Tenth Session, the Tribunal, on the Registrar's proposal, established conditions concerning guided tours for the general public, groups of visitors with a relevant interest in the Tribunal's functions and open days.

[9/] See "Decision regarding the establishment of a trust fund for assisting States in proceedings before the International Tribunal for the Law of the Sea", SPLOS/57.

14. Use of the Premises

Following the decision of the Tribunal at its Seventh Session, the final and semi-final rounds of the Charles Rousseau International Law Moot Court Competition for the year 2000 were held at the temporary premises of the Tribunal on 5 and 6 May 2000.

At its Eighth Session, the Tribunal agreed to a request by the Max Planck Institute for Comparative Public Law and International Law to hold an international symposium on the occasion of the moving of the Tribunal into its new building. The symposium, entitled "The International Dispute Settlement System", took place at the permanent premises on 23 September 2000.

At its Ninth Session, the Tribunal agreed to a request by the International Ocean Institute to hold its annual conference *Pacem et Maribus 2000, The European Challenge* at the permanent premises. The conference took place from 3 to 6 December 2000.

At its Ninth Session, the Tribunal agreed to a request by the Center of Oceans Law and Policy to hold its annual conference at the permanent premises in March 2001.

15. Balance between Official Languages of the Tribunal

At its Ninth Session, the Tribunal adopted guidelines for ensuring a better balance between the two official languages of the Tribunal and decided that these guidelines would be implemented in a flexible manner.

16. Foundation for International Law of the Sea

During its Tenth Session, the Tribunal welcomed the proposed establishment of a foundation for international law of the sea on the lines of a draft statute of the foundation submitted to the Tribunal. The Tribunal decided that the President could serve as an *ex officio* chairman of the curatorium and that judges could also serve on the advisory council of the proposed foundation.

II. Relations with the United Nations and Other Organizations

1. Observer Status with the General Assembly

As an observer to the General Assembly of the United Nations, the President and the Registrar of the Tribunal participated in meetings of the fifty-fifth session of the General Assembly.

On 30 October 2000, President Chandrasekhara Rao delivered a statement on agenda item 34 (a) entitled "Oceans and the law of the sea". The statement is reproduced in Annex XI. On 30 October 2000, the General Assembly adopted resolution 55/7 on "Oceans and the law of the sea". The text of the resolution is reproduced in Annex XII.

2. Relationship Agreement with the United Nations

The Registrar reported to the Tribunal on developments regarding the implementation of the Agreement on Cooperation and Relationship between the United Nations and the International Tribunal for the Law of the Sea.

3. International Tribunal for the Law of the Sea Trust Fund

Upon the proposal of a delegation, the tenth Meeting of States Parties recommended to the General Assembly that it consider, at its fifty-fifth session, the establishment of a trust fund, to be financed through voluntary contributions, for the purpose of providing financial assistance for States in order to help them in proceedings before the International Tribunal for the Law of the Sea[10/]. During the consideration of this item by the tenth Meeting of States Parties, the President of the Tribunal made a statement in which he expressed the Tribunal's appreciation of this proposal[11/].

The recommendation was endorsed by the General Assembly which, in its resolution 55/7 on "Oceans and the law of the sea", requested the Secretary-General to establish and administer a voluntary trust fund to assist States in the settlement of disputes through the Tribunal. The texts of the resolution and of the terms of reference of the Trust Fund attached to it are reproduced in Annex XII.

4. Relationship with other Organizations and Bodies

The Registrar reported to the Tribunal on consultations regarding working contacts with international organizations whose activities were relevant to the work of the Tribunal.

III. Other Activities

On 23 August 2000, the President was requested by Chile to appoint an arbitrator pursuant to article 3 of Annex VII to the Convention. The arbitrator was to sit on the arbitral tribunal to be constituted to consider the dispute between Chile and the European Community concerning swordfish stocks in the South-Eastern Pacific Ocean. The President held consultations with the parties with regard to the appointment of an arbitrator. The Chilean request was not proceeded with following the agreement by the Government of Chile and the European Community to submit the case to a special chamber of the Tribunal.

[10/] See SPLOS/57.

[11/] See SPLOS/60, paras. 42–44.

CHAPTER VI

FINANCES OF THE TRIBUNAL

I. Financial Arrangements

1. General

(a) Method of covering expenditure

By virtue of article 19, paragraph 1, of the Statute, the expenses of the Tribunal are borne by the States Parties and by the International Seabed Authority "on such terms and in such a manner as shall be decided at meetings of the States Parties". For the financial period 2000, the ninth Meeting of States Parties decided that the budget of the Tribunal was to be financed by all States and international organizations that were parties to the Convention. This decision was made without prejudice to the application of the provisions of article 19 of the Statute in respect of future budgets regarding the contribution by the International Seabed Authority.[12/] In accordance with the decision taken by the fourth Meeting of States Parties, States that became Parties to the Convention thereafter and during the period of the budget contributed *pro rata* for the remainder of the financial period.[13/]

The ninth Meeting of States Parties decided that the contributions to be made by States Parties would be based upon the scale of assessments for the regular budget of the United Nations for the corresponding financial year, adjusted to take account of participation in the Convention. It also decided that a floor rate of 0.01 per cent and a ceiling rate of 25.00 per cent would be used in establishing the scale of assessments for States Parties for the budget of the Tribunal for 2000.[14/]

As of 31 December 2000, 58 States Parties had made their contributions to the 2000 budget (in the full amount assessed or above), totalling US$ 7,033,073. Partial contributions totalling US$ 154,094 had been made by 16 States Parties, leaving a balance of unpaid contributions in respect of those 16 States Parties of US$ 242,061. Payment of assessed contributions in the amount of US$ 421,663 towards the 2000 budget by 61 States Parties was still pending.

[12/] See SPLOS/46, para. 4.

[13/] See SPLOS/8, para. 2.

[14/] See SPLOS/46, para. 5.

Furthermore, assessed contributions amounting to US$ 730,203 in respect of the 1996/1997, 1998 and 1999 budgets were still pending as of 31 December 2000, resulting in an unpaid balance of assessed contributions to the overall budget of the Tribunal in the amount of US$ 1,393,927.

In accordance with the decision of the fourth Meeting of States Parties, the collection and management of all contributions is undertaken by the Registry. The Tribunal periodically notifies States Parties of the status of contributions.

All contributions by States Parties are paid in a convertible currency into a bank account designated by the Registrar.

In the event that an entity other than a State Party or the International Seabed Authority is party to a case submitted to the Tribunal, the Tribunal will fix the amount which that party is to contribute towards the expenses of the Tribunal (Statute, article 19, paragraph 2).

(b) Drafting of the budget

According to the applicable financial regulations, the Registrar is responsible for preparing the draft budget of the Tribunal. The draft budget is submitted to the Committee on Budget and Finance for consideration and recommendations, and then to the Tribunal for approval. The proposed budget as approved by the Tribunal is submitted to the Meeting of States Parties for consideration and adoption.

The financial period of the Tribunal consists of one calendar year. The Tribunal decided, at its Third Session, to operate on the basis of this financial period, pending adoption of a biennial period by the Meeting of States Parties.

(c) Financing of appropriations and accounts

The Registrar is responsible for the accounts and financial administration in accordance with the financial procedures of the Tribunal (Rules, article 36, paragraph 1(l)). Regulation 4.1 of the financial regulations applicable to the Tribunal provides that the appropriations adopted by the Meeting of States Parties constitute an authorization for the Registrar to incur obligations and make payments for the purposes for which the appropriations were adopted and up to the amounts adopted.

The accounts of the Tribunal are audited after the end of each financial period.

2. Salaries and Expenses of Judges

(a) Emoluments

The salaries, allowances and compensation of members of the Tribunal are determined from time to time at meetings of the States Parties, taking into account the work load of the Tribunal. They may not be decreased during the term of office (Statute, article 18, paragraph 5).

The overall remuneration of the members of the Tribunal currently consists of three elements: an annual allowance, a special allowance for each day that they are engaged on the business of the Tribunal, and a subsistence allowance for each day that they are required to be present at the seat of the Tribunal. In considering the level of remuneration of a member of the Tribunal, the second Meeting of States Parties decided that the level of remuneration of a judge of the International Court of Justice would be the comparator (SPLOS/4, 26 July 1995). The ninth Meeting of States Parties decided to approve an adjustment of the annual remuneration of the members of the Tribunal to the level of the emoluments of the International Court of Justice established in General Assembly resolution 53/214 of 18 December 1998, with effect from 1 January 2000.[15/]

The annual allowance has been set at one-third of the overall annual remuneration. The special allowance and the subsistence allowance are each subject to a maximum limit of one-third of the overall remuneration. The members of the Tribunal may also be paid a special allowance for preparatory work undertaken by them before meetings of the Tribunal. A subsistence allowance for preparatory work is also payable to judges when they undertake business in connection with the Tribunal away from their normal place of residence.

Consistent with article 18, paragraph 2, of the Statute, the President of the Tribunal, who resides at the seat of the Tribunal, receives an overall annual remuneration of US$ 160,000 and a special annual allowance of US$ 15,000. The Vice-President of the Tribunal is entitled to receive a special allowance for each day on which he or she acts as President.

Judges *ad hoc* are entitled to receive compensation for each day on which they exercise their functions (Statute, article 18, paragraph 4).

(b) Pensions

Regulations adopted at meetings of the States Parties determine the conditions under which retirement pensions may be given to members of the Tribunal and the Registrar (Statute, article 18, paragraph 7). Pension Scheme Regulations for members of the Tribunal were adopted by the ninth Meeting of States Parties[16/].

(c) Travelling expenses

The travelling expenses of the members of the Tribunal are met in accordance with regulations adopted at meetings of the States Parties (Statute, article 18, paragraph 7).

3. Salaries, Allowances and Expenses of the Registrar and Officials of the Registry

(a) Emoluments

The salary of the Registrar is determined at meetings of the States Parties, on the proposal of the Tribunal (Statute, article 18, paragraph 6). As determined at the fourth Meeting of States Parties, the Registrar has a rank equivalent to an Assistant Secretary-General of the United Nations. The Deputy Registrar has the rank of a Director (D-2).

[15/] See SPLOS/44, para. 3.

[16/] See SPLOS/47.

The staff of the Registry is remunerated according to the practice of the United Nations common system of salaries, allowances and benefits, as administered by the International Civil Service Commission. Information relating to the application of the practice is provided in Decisions on Budgetary Matters of the International Tribunal for the Law of the Sea for the Year 1998 (SPLOS/L.7, 28 May 1997).

(b) Pensions

The Tribunal participates in the United Nations Joint Staff Pension Fund. Pursuant to a decision of the General Assembly of the United Nations (A/RES/51/217), membership in the Pension Fund became effective from 1 January 1997. In 1998, a special agreement was concluded between the Tribunal and the United Nations which extends the jurisdiction of the Administrative Tribunal of the United Nations to the Tribunal with respect to applications by staff members of the Tribunal alleging non-observance of the regulations of the United Nations Joint Staff Pension Fund.

(c) Travelling expenses

The travelling expenses of staff of the Registry are paid under the conditions set out in the Staff Regulations of the Tribunal and in the Staff Rules of the United Nations, which are applied by the Tribunal *mutatis mutandis*.

II. Financial Regulations

The Tribunal applies the Financial Regulations and Rules of the United Nations (ST/SGB/Financial Rules/1/Rev.3 (1985)) *mutatis mutandis*, in accordance with the decision of the fourth Meeting of States Parties.

Pursuant to the decision of the fifth Meeting of States Parties, the Tribunal prepared draft financial regulations. At its Sixth Session, on 8 October 1999, the Tribunal approved the Financial Regulations of the Tribunal, as recommended by the Committee on Budget and Finance. The Financial Regulations of the Tribunal were submitted to the ninth Meeting of States Parties for its consideration. The ninth and tenth Meetings of States Parties considered the Financial Regulations. It was agreed that the discussions would continue at the eleventh Meeting of States Parties on the basis of a revised version of the Financial Regulations to be prepared by the Registry of the Tribunal and the Secretariat of the Meeting of States Parties.[17/]

III. Budget for 2000

The budget of the Tribunal covering the 2000 financial period was adopted by the ninth Meeting of States Parties on 28 May 1999.[18/]

[17/] SPLOS/60, para. 36.

[18/] SPLOS/46.

The eighth Meeting of States Parties had approved the establishment of a Working Capital Fund and provided on an exceptional basis for up to US$ 200,000 to be credited to the fund from savings from the 1999 appropriations. The ninth Meeting of States Parties approved an additional amount of US$ 50,000 for advances to the Working Capital Fund in 2000. It also decided that, on an exceptional basis, savings from the appropriations in the budget for 2000, up to US$ 200,000, would also be credited to the fund.[19]

With a view to providing the Tribunal with the necessary financial means to consider cases, in particular those requiring expeditious proceedings, the ninth Meeting of States Parties approved an amount of US$ 679,364 in 2000 as the contingency funds of the Tribunal. The Meeting decided that the contingency funds would be used only in the event of cases being submitted to the Tribunal.

The budget of the Tribunal for 2000 was as follows:

Objects of expenditure	US$
A. *Recurrent expenditure*	
Remuneration of judges:	
Annual allowances	1 295 107
Special allowances and subsistence allowances	311 717
Travel of judges to sessions	240 000
Judges' pension scheme	16 666
Established posts	2 413 725
Common staff costs	806 184
General temporary assistance	120 000
Overtime	45 330
Representation allowance	7 600
Official travel	90 200
Communications	151 000
Supplies and materials	85 000
External printing and binding	50 600
Temporary assistance for meetings	129 091
Maintenance of premises	350 000
Rental and maintenance of equipment	240 000

[19] *Ibid.*, para. 3.

Objects of expenditure	US$
Hospitality	7 100
Special services (external audit)	15 400
Library: procurement of books and publications	60 000
Start-up costs of library	60 000
Miscellaneous services (including bank charges)	25 000
Training	15 400
Security (contractual services)	137 135
B. *Non-recurrent expenditure*	
Hospitality	8 400
Furniture and equipment:	
Purchase of equipment	230 000
Purchase of special equipment	17 000
Contingency	679 364
Working Capital Fund	50 000
TOTAL	7 657 019

IV. Audit of Accounts

In accordance with the practice of the United Nations system, arrangements were made for the accounts of the Tribunal for 1999 to be audited by an internationally recognized auditing firm.

The tenth Meeting of States Parties took note of the audit report for the 1998 financial statements of the Tribunal as presented by the Registrar.

Pursuant to the decision taken by the Tribunal at its Ninth Session, the Registrar communicated to the tenth Meeting of States Parties the audit report for the 1999 financial statements of the Tribunal. He informed the Meeting of States Parties that the Tribunal had not yet reviewed the report. The Meeting decided to defer consideration of the report until the eleventh Meeting of States Parties.

The audit report for the 1999 financial statements of the Tribunal was presented by the Registrar to the Tribunal at its Tenth Session. The auditor, having reviewed the transactions and operations over that period, was satisfied that the financial statements presented fairly, in all material respects, the financial position of the Tribunal. The Tribunal took note of the report.

At its Tenth Session, the Tribunal authorized the re-appointment of the external auditor for 2000 and decided that the situation would be reconsidered in 2001.

CHAPTER VII

PRIVILEGES AND IMMUNITIES

I. United Nations Convention on the Law of the Sea

The Statute contains general provisions concerning the privileges and immunities of the members of the Tribunal. According to article 10 of the Statute, the members of the Tribunal, when engaged on the business of the Tribunal, enjoy diplomatic privileges and immunities. The salaries, allowances and compensation received by elected members of the Tribunal, members chosen under article 17 of the Statute and the Registrar are free of all taxation (Statute, article 18, paragraph 8).

II. Agreement on the Privileges and Immunities

The Agreement on the Privileges and Immunities of the International Tribunal for the Law of the Sea was adopted on 23 May 1997. This Agreement, of which the Secretary-General of the United Nations is the depository, was opened for signature at United Nations Headquarters for twenty-four months on 1 July 1997. The Agreement will enter into force 30 days after the date of deposit of the tenth instrument of ratification or accession. As of 30 June 1999, the closing date for signature, 21 States had signed the Agreement. By 31 December 2000, four States had ratified it.

III. Headquarters Agreement

At the end of 2000, the negotiations for a headquarters agreement between the Tribunal and the Federal Republic of Germany were still ongoing.

The relations with the host country are at present regulated on the basis of international practice, set out in the Convention on the Privileges and Immunities of the Specialized Agencies of 21 November 1947, as applied by the host country in accordance with its Ordinance on the Privileges and Immunities of the International Tribunal for the Law of the Sea of 10 October 1996.

CHAPTER VIII

BIOGRAPHIES OF THE JUDGES, THE REGISTRAR AND THE DEPUTY REGISTRAR

I. MEMBERS OF THE TRIBUNAL ON 31 DECEMBER 1999

President P. Chandrasekhara Rao

(Member of the Tribunal since 1 October 1996; re-elected as from 1 October 1999;
President of the Tribunal since 1 October 1999;
President of the Special Chamber formed to deal with the
Case concerning the Conservation and Sustainable Exploitation of Swordfish Stocks in the South-Eastern Pacific Ocean)

Born: India, 22 April 1936.
Education: B.A., B.L., M.L., LL.D., University of Madras, India.
Professional Experience: Research Officer, Indian Society of International Law (1963–1967); Law Officer (1967–1971), Assistant Legal Adviser (1971–1976), Legal and Treaties Division, Ministry of External Affairs; Counsel for the Government of India in the case concerning the *Appeal relating to the Jurisdiction of the International Civil Aviation Organization Council (India v. Pakistan)* before the International Court of Justice (1972); Legal Adviser to the Permanent Mission of India to the UN, New York (1972–1976); Deputy Legislative Counsel, Additional Legal Adviser, Joint Secretary and Legal Adviser, Additional Secretary (1976–1988), Secretary (1988–1996), Union Ministry of Law; Sole Arbitrator in Government contracts (1979–1983); Secretary-General, International Center for Alternative Dispute Resolution, New Delhi (1995–1996); Visiting Professor of Law: Osmania University, Hyderabad (1994–1995), Kakatiya University, Warangal (1994–1995), University of Madras (1995–1996).
Member: Board of Editors, *Indian Journal of International Law* (1970–present); Indian Society of International Law (Vice-President 1994–2000); Indian delegation to: Legal Sub-Committee on the Peaceful Uses of Outer Space (1969–1973, 1975); International Legal Conference on Marine Pollution Damage, Brussels (1969); UNCTAD Working Group on International Shipping Legislation, Geneva (1969); UN Special Committee on Principles of International Law concerning Friendly Relations and Cooperation among States, Geneva (1970); UN Committee on the Peaceful Uses of the Seabed and the Ocean Floor beyond the Limits of National Jurisdiction (1971, 1973); Third UN Conference on the Law of the Sea (1973–1976); UN General Assembly (1972–1975); UNCITRAL (Head of delegation 1972, 1988–1994); Legal Committee of the ICAO (1973); *Ad hoc* Committee on International Terrorism (1973); *Ad hoc* Committee on the UN Charter (1975); Commonwealth Law Ministers Meetings held at Bridgetown (1980); Harare (1986); Christchurch (1990); Port

Louis (1993); Kuala Lumpur (1996); Ministerial-level Meeting of GATT Contracting Parties, Punta del Este, Uruguay (1986); UN Conference on the Liability of Operators of Transport Terminals in International Trade, Vienna (Chairman of Drafting Committee 1990); Meeting of the International Seabed Authority, Kingston (1996), (Head of delegation); Meeting of States Parties to the UN Convention on the Law of the Sea, New York (1996), (Head of delegation).

Publications: Author of books entitled *The New Law of Maritime Zones*, 1982; *The Indian Constitution and International Law*, 1993; *The Arbitration and Conciliation Act, 1996: A Commentary*, 1997; *Alternative Dispute Resolution: What it means and how it works* (ed.), 1996; *The International Tribunal for the Law of the Sea: Law and Practice* (co-ed.), 2000.

Vice-President Dolliver Nelson
(Member of the Tribunal since 1 October 1996;
Vice-President of the Tribunal since 1 October 1999)

Born: Sauteurs, Grenada, 27 June 1932.
Education: B.A., University of the West Indies (1954); LL.M., London School of Economics (1964); Ph.D., London School of Economics (1969); Barrister-at-Law, Gray's Inn, London (1971); admitted to the Bar of Grenada (1972).
Professional Experience: Lecturer in Law, London School of Economics (1970–1977); Law of the Sea Officer (1974–1976), Senior Law of the Sea Officer (1976–1984), Deputy-Director (1984–1994), Office of Legal Affairs, Division for Ocean Affairs and the Law of the Sea; Secretary, Drafting Committee of the Third UN Conference on the Law of the Sea (1974–1982); Visiting Professor at Dalhousie University, Halifax, Canada (1980); Executive Secretary, Preparatory Commission for the International Seabed Authority and for the International Tribunal for the Law of the Sea (1983–1994); acted as Legal Adviser in the Secretary-General's informal consultations on deep seabed mining issues which concluded in 1994 with the adoption of the Agreement relating to the implementation of Part XI of the UN Convention on the Law of the Sea (1990–1994); Secretary, Conference on Straddling Fish Stocks and Highly Migratory Fish Stocks (1993–1994); Visiting Professor of International Law, London School of Economics (1995–present); lectured on aspects of the law of the sea in several institutions and actively participated in numerous seminars and workshops in various parts of the world.
Member: Committee on the Outer Continental Shelf, International Law Association (Chairman, 2000–present); Editorial Board, *Marine Policy* (1993–present); Committee on Coastal State Jurisdiction relating to Marine Pollution, International Law Association (1992–2000); research team responsible for the Commentary on the UN Convention on the Law of the Sea, Center for Oceans Law and Policy, University of Virginia (1984–1994); Committee on the Exclusive Economic Zone (EEZ), International Law Association (Rapporteur 1982–1989); Committee on the Law of the Sea, International Law Association (1974–1980); American Society of International Law (1970–present).
Publications: Contributed to various international legal periodicals and publications, including *The British Year Book of International Law*, *The American Journal of International Law*, *The International and Comparative Law Quarterly*, *The Modern Law Review* and *The Netherlands International Law Review*; and reports to conferences of the International Law Association on Exclusive Economic Zone matters.
Honours: Fiftieth Anniversary Distinguished Graduate Award, University of the West Indies, 1998.

Judge Hugo Caminos
(Member of the Tribunal since 1 October 1996;
President of the Chamber for Fisheries Disputes 1997–1999;
Member of the Special Chamber formed to deal with the
Case concerning the Conservation and Sustainable Exploitation of Swordfish Stocks in the South-Eastern Pacific Ocean)

Born: Buenos Aires, Argentina, 16 March 1921.
Education: School of Law and Social Sciences, University of Buenos Aires, Lawyer (1942); Dr. Jur. (1964); post-graduate studies in International Law, University of California, Berkeley and Los Angeles, and Columbia University, New York (1945–1946); post-graduate studies in International Relations, New School for Social Research, New York (1946).
Professional Experience: Professor of Public International Law, School of Law and Social Sciences, University of Buenos Aires (Assistant 1956–1957, Associate 1958–1962, Full Professor 1963–1987, Professor Emeritus 1988); Professor, Foreign Service Institute, Ministry of Foreign Affairs, Argentina (1963, 1967 and 1972); Director, Department of International Organizations (1971–1972), Legal Counsel (1972–1973), Ministry of Foreign Affairs, Argentina; Director of Studies, English-speaking section (Public International Law), The Hague Academy of International Law (1973); Lecturer at international law courses and courses on the law of the sea organized by UNITAR in Africa, Asia, Europe and Latin America (1973–1985); Deputy Director, Office of the Secretary-General of the United Nations for the Third United Nations Conference on the Law of the Sea, New York (1974–1981); Ambassador of Argentina to Brazil (1981–1984); Under-Secretary for Legal Affairs and Legal Counsel, Organization of American States, Washington, D.C. (1984–1994); Lecturer at The Hague Academy of International Law (1987 and 1998) and at various sessions of the External Programme of the Academy; Lecturer at the annual courses offered by the Institute of International Public Law and International Relations, Thessaloniki (1986, 1992, 1994 and 1999); Co-ordinator of the annual course in international law organized by the OAS Inter-American Juridical Committee, Rio de Janeiro (1984–1994); Visiting Professor of International Law and Law of the Sea, University of Miami School of Law (1995–present).
Member: Permanent Court of Arbitration (1962–1976); Institut de Droit international (Associate 1979, Member 1983–present); International Curatorium of the Institute of International Public Law and International Relations, Thessaloniki (1987–present); International Law Association (Argentine Branch); Argentine Council for International Relations; Argentine National Academy of Law and Social Sciences.
Publications: Author of numerous articles, monographs and papers on public international law, law of the sea, human rights and international organizations.

Judge Vicente Marotta Rangel

(Member of the Tribunal since 1 October 1996; re-elected as from 1 October 1999)

Born: São Paulo, Brazil, 14 March 1924.
Education: Bachelor, School of Law, University of São Paulo (1946); Brevet in Juridical Terminology, Institut de Droit Comparé, University of Paris (1949); Doctor of University, University of Paris (1950); Ph.D., School of Law, University of São Paulo (1954); Participant, The Hague Academy of International Law, Centre for studies and research (1960); Visiting Scholar, Columbia University (1972–1973); Visiting Scholar, Columbia University, Parker School of Foreign and Comparative Law (1973).
Professional Experience: Assistant Professor (1954–1963), Associate Professor (1963–1967), Full Professor (1967–1994), Head of International Law Department (1970–1982), Director of Law School (1982–1986), University of São Paulo; Lecturer, Institute of Public International Law, Thessaloniki (1976); Lecturer, UN/UNITAR, Regional Training Course in International Law, Buenos Aires (1983); Lecturer, The Hague Academy of International Law (1985); Legal Adviser to the Ministry of Foreign Affairs (1990–1993); Professor, University of Brasilia (1990–1993); Member of the Examination Board, Advanced Studies Courses, School of Diplomacy, Instituto Rio Branco (1978–1990); Member of Brazilian delegation to: The Geneva Diplomatic Conference on Humanitarian Law (1974–1977), Third United Nations Conference on the Law of the Sea (1973–1982), The Diplomatic Conference for the Adoption of the Draft Unidroit Convention on the International Return of Stolen or Illegally Exported Cultural Objects, Rome (head of delegation, 1995); Director, Legal Department, Brazilian Space Agency (1994–1997).
Member: Institut de Droit International; American Society of International Law; International Law Association; Instituto Hispano-Luso-Americano de Derecho Internacional; Arbitral Tribunal, Mercosur; Permanent Court of Arbitration, The Hague (Brazilian group); Association Henri Capitant (Brazilian group); Société française pour le droit international; Asociación Argentina de Derecho Internacional (correspondent).
Distinctions: Silver medal awarded by the "Association Henri Capitant des Amis de la Culture Juridique Française"; Member *ad honorem* of the UNIDROIT Governing Council (1999); Doctor *honoris causa*, University of Coimbra (1999).
Publications: Author of numerous books, articles, monographs and papers in the field of public and private international law, international organizations and the law of the sea, including: *Public International Law: the Last Five Decades*, *Panorama of Brazilian Law*, University of Miami, 1992; *Le droit de la mer dans la jurisprudence de la Cour Internationale de Justice*, Thesaurus Acroasium, volume VII, 1977; *Le plateau continental dans la Convention de 1982 sur le droit de la mer*, Collected Courses, The Hague, 1985–V.

Judge Alexander Yankov
(Member of the Tribunal since 1 October 1996;
President of the Chamber for Marine Environment Disputes since 4 October 1999;
Member of the Special Chamber formed to deal with the
Case concerning the Conservation and Sustainable Exploitation of Swordfish Stocks in the South-Eastern Pacific Ocean)

Born: Bourgas, Bulgaria, 24 June 1924.
Education: Graduated in Law, Faculty of Law, Sofia University (1951); Ph.D. in International Law, Sofia University (1963).
Academic Experience: Professor of International Law (1968–present), Head of the International Law Department (1980–1989), Sofia University; Member (1981–present), Head of the International Law Section (1988–1989), Vice-President in charge of social, political, legal studies and humanities (1988–1991), Bulgarian Academy of Sciences; gave post-graduate and special courses on international law and law of the sea at Sofia University, many foreign universities and The Hague Academy of International Law.
Executive Experience: Vice-Chairman, National Oceanographic Committee of Bulgaria (1969–present); Ambassador of Bulgaria to the United Kingdom of Great Britain and Northern Ireland (1972–1976); Deputy Minister for Foreign Affairs, Ambassador, Permanent Representative of Bulgaria to the UN in New York (1976–1980); Minister of Science and Higher Education (1989–1990).
Judicial Experience: Member of the Court of Commercial Arbitration at the Bulgarian Chamber of Commerce and Industry (1971–1987).
Member: Permanent Court of Arbitration at The Hague (1971–1998); International Ocean Institute, Malta (Vice-President); Executive Council of the International Law Association (1973–present); International Law Commission (1977–1996, Chairman 1984); Institut de Droit international (1979–present); Advisory Committee on the Protection of the Sea, London (Vice-Chairman 1980–1996); Bulgarian Society for International Law (President 1980–present); National Assembly (the Parliament) of Bulgaria, its Committee on the Elaboration of the Constitution, and its Foreign Policy Committee (1986–1991); Union of Bulgarian Scientists (President 1987–1989); National Association for International Relations (President 1994–present); Independent World Commission on the Oceans, Lisbon (1995–1998); Bulgarian delegation to: UN General Assembly and the Security Council (1964–1984, Deputy Head); Legal Sub-Committee, UN Committee on the Peaceful Uses of the Sea-Bed and the Ocean Floor beyond the Limits of National Jurisdiction (Vice-Chairman 1968–1973); International Maritime Organization, Eighth Assembly, London (President 1973–1974); International Conference for the Prevention of Pollution from Ships, London (Chairman of the Fourth Committee 1973); Third UN Conference on the Law of the Sea (Chairman of the Third Committee 1973–1982); International Council of Environmental Law, Bonn (1976); IOC (Vice-Chairman 1987–1991).
Publications: Author of numerous books, articles, monographs and publications in the field of international law, law of the sea, international organizations, international adjudication and environmental law.

Judge Soji Yamamoto
(Member of the Tribunal since 1 October 1996)

Born: Nagano, Japan, 25 February 1928.
Education: LL.B., Faculty of Law, University of Tokyo (1953); Doctor of Law, University of Tokyo (1969).
Professional Experience: Associate Professor of International Law, Faculty of Law and Literature, Kumamoto University, Japan (1955–1961); Professor of International Law and Organization, College of Liberal Arts, International Christian University, Tokyo (1961–1967); Professor of International Law, Faculty of Law, Seikei University, Tokyo (1967–1976); Professor of International Law (1976–1988), Professor Emeritus (1988–present), Faculty of Law, Tohoku University, Sendai; Professor of International Law, Sophia University, Tokyo (1988–1998).
Member: Postal Administration Council, Ministry of Post and Telecommunications (1973–1982); Ocean Development Council, Cabinet (1976–1984); Japanese Association of International Law, Executive Council (1976–1991), President (1988–1991), Honorary Councillor (1992–present); Meeting of 17 Experts to Study the Practice of States relating to the UN Convention on the Law of the Sea, New York (1992); American Society of International Law; Japanese delegation to: UN Legal Subcommittee on Peaceful Uses of Outer Space (Special Adviser 1967–1982); INTELSAT, Intergovernmental Conference for Definitive Arrangements (Adviser 1969); Antarctic Treaty Consultative Meeting (Special Adviser 1976–1979, and 1986); Third UN Conference on the Law of the Sea (Alternate Representative 1978); Legal Expert Panel of INTELSAT (1982–1993); Permanent Court of Arbitration (2000–present).
Publications: Author of numerous books, articles and papers in the field of public international law, the law of international organizations, international environmental law, international telecommunications and international criminal law, including *On Definitive Agreements Relating to INTELSAT* (in Japanese), 1973; *International Law of Space Telecommunications: A Type of International Enterprise* (in Japanese), 1976; *Space Development and Law* (in Japanese), 1976; *International Fishery Disputes and Law* (in Japanese), 1976; *Freedom and Regulation in Direct Broadcast Satellites* (in Japanese), 1979; *Function of Liability for Risk in International Law* (in Japanese), 1982; *International Criminal Law* (in Japanese), 1991; *Law of the Sea* (in Japanese), 1992; *International Law* (in Japanese), 1985, 2nd new ed. 1994; Editor-in-Chief of *The Japanese Annual of International Law* (1978–present).

Judge Anatoly Lazarevich Kolodkin

(Member of the Tribunal since 1 October 1996; re-elected as from 1 October 1999)

Born: St. Petersburg, Russian Federation, 27 February 1928.
Education: Faculty of Law, State University, St. Petersburg (1945–1950); Doctor of Legal Sciences (1971); Professor (1985).
Professional Experience: Researcher and Head of Department, Central Marine Scientific Research Institute, St. Petersburg (1956–1968); Head of International Law of the Sea Department (1968–1978), Deputy Director (1981–present), State Scientific Research and Project Development Institute of Maritime Transport, Moscow; Director, International Communications Department of the All-Union *Morsvyazsputnik* Association (1978–1981); Professor, Moscow State Law Academy (1994–present); Chairman, National Committee of the Russian Federation on UN Decade of International Law (1996–present); Co-Chairman, Expert Council on International Law of the State Duma of the Federal Assembly of the Russian Federation (1997–present); President, Maritime Law Association (1981–present); President, Russian International Law Association (1994–present); Main Scientific Fellow, Institute of the State and Law of the Russian Academy of Sciences (1998–present).
Member: Expert Council on Legal Sciences of the Russian Federation Higher Degree Committee (1985–present); Permanent Court of Arbitration (1990–present); Academic Council on International Law, Russian Academy of Sciences Institute of the State and Law (1993–present); two Academic Councils of Moscow University (1985–present); Academic Council of Moscow, State Institute of Foreign Relations; Comité Maritime International, Vice-President (1981–1994), Honorary Vice-President (1994–present); Law of the Sea Institute (Council member 1989–1995); Planning Council, International Ocean Institute *Pacem in Maribus* (1971–1990); Delegate to Conference on establishing INMARSAT and sessions of the Assembly and Council (1972–1982); Head of USSR delegations to Diplomatic Conferences on Privileges and Immunities of INMARSAT and on the Headquarters Agreement between INMARSAT and UK Government (1981); Expert, Intergovernmental Oceanographic Commission of UNESCO; elaborated (co-author) and presented to IMO Draft Convention on the Legal Regime of Vessels in Foreign Ports (1974); elaborated and presented to IOC, UNESCO Draft Convention on the Legal Regime of Ocean Data Acquisition Systems (1993 and 1995); USSR delegate and spokesman of East-European States to the Preparatory Groups and the Conference on elaborating and adopting the UN Convention on Conditions for Registration of Ships (1982–1986).
Publications: Author of more than 240 books and articles published in Russia, USA, UK, FRG, Belgium, Italy, India, Poland, etc. on international law, law of the sea, maritime and shipping law and international organizations, including *World Ocean: International Legal Regime* (in Russian), 1973, (in English), 1974; *History of International Law of the Sea*, 1974; *The UN Convention on the Law of the Sea and the Legislative Practice of States* (co-author), 1984; *The International Legal Regime of Territorial Waters and Contiguous Zones* (in Russian), 1992; *Stability in the Law of the Sea–Beyond Confrontation: International Law for the Post-Cold War Era* (co-author, in Russian and English), 1995 and 1996; *International Tribunal for the Law of the Sea – a New Judicial International Institution* (in Russian and in English), 1998.

Judge Choon-Ho Park
(Member of the Tribunal since 1 October 1996)

Born: Namwon, Korea, 15 April 1930.
Education: B.A. in Political Science, Seoul National University, Korea (1959); Graduate Diploma in Applied Linguistics, University of Edinburgh, Great Britain (1965); Ph.D. in International Law, Faculty of Law, University of Edinburgh (1971).
Professional Experience: Research Associate, Harvard Law School (1972–1978); Fellow, Woodrow Wilson International Center for Scholars, Washington, D.C. (1973); Research Associate, East-West Center, Hawaii (1978–1982); Professor of International Law, Faculty of Law, Korea University (1982–1995); Director, Asiatic Research Center, Korea University (1992–1995); Professor of International Law, Faculty of Law, Seinan Gakuin University, Japan (1995–present); Distinguished Professor of International Law, Graduate School of International Studies, Korea University (1997–present); participation in the Third United Nations Conference on the Law of the Sea and the Preparatory Commission for the International Seabed Authority and for the International Tribunal for the Law of the Sea representing the Republic of Korea and the International Law Association (1974–1995).
Member: Institut de Droit international (Associate member 1997–present); Editorial Board of: *Marine Policy* (1977–present), *Ocean Development and International Law* (1977–2000), *Ocean and Shore-Line Management* (1988–present), *The Asian Review* (1993–present).
Publications: Articles and monographs on law of the sea, energy and Chinese law.
Honours: Distinguished Scholarship Award (Social Sciences), Academy of Sciences, The Republic of Korea (1989); Doctor of Law (*honoris causa*), University of Edinburgh (1998).

Judge Paul Bamela Engo
(Member of the Tribunal since 1 October 1996; re-elected as from 1 October 1999)

Born: Cameroon, 5 October 1931.
Education: Lawyer, Jurist; called to the English Bar (Middle Temple Inn, London, 1959).
Professional Experience: Her Majesty's Crown Counsel, Legal Departments of Lagos, Nigeria, and Southern Cameroons (1959–1961); Magistrate, Southern Cameroons (1961–1965); Senior Member, Cameroon's Federal Judicial Commission (1961–1969); Minister Plenipotentiary, *Hors Hiérarchie* (since 1969); Deputy Agent for Cameroon in the *Northern Cameroons* (*Cameroon* v. *United Kingdom*) case before the International Court of Justice (1963); Minister Counsellor, Cameroon Embassies in Bonn, Germany (1964) and Washington, D.C. (1965–1968); Deputy, Permanent Mission of Cameroon to the UN (1968–1973); Lecturer on Law of the Sea, Cameroon Institute for International Relations, University of Yaoundé (1973–1979); Technical Adviser, Cabinet of the Minister of Foreign Affairs (1973–1982); Cameroon Ambassador, Permanent Representative to the UN (1984–1991 and 1996, until election as a Judge, ITLOS); Lecturer on English Common Law, National School of Administration and Magistracy (ENAM); Senior Counsel for Cameroon in the *Land and Maritime Boundary between Cameroon and Nigeria* (*Cameroon* v. *Nigeria*) case before the International Court of Justice (1995–1996, until election as a Judge, ITLOS).
Member: Cameroonian and Nigerian Bars (since 1959); Cameroonian delegation to: Second African Heads of State Conference in Cairo (Legal Adviser 1964); Sessions of the UN General Assembly (1965–1990, 1996); UN Special Committee on Principles of International Law concerning Friendly Relations and Co-operation among States (Drafting Committee Chairman 1966, Chairman 1967); Sixth Committee of the UN General Assembly (Vice-Chairman 1969, Chairman 1970); UN *Ad Hoc* Committee to Study the Peaceful Uses of the Seabed and the Ocean Floor beyond the Limits of National Jurisdiction (Chairman of the First Subcommittee 1971); UN Committee on the Peaceful Uses of the Seabed and the Ocean Floor beyond the Limits of National Jurisdiction (Chairman of the First Committee 1972–1973); Third UN Conference on the Law of the Sea (Special Representative of the Cameroonian Head of State as from 1973, Chairman of the First Committee 1973–1982); Presidential Commission on the Law of the Sea (Chairman 1980–1984); Council for Namibia (Chairman of Standing Committee III, 1984); Chairman, African Group that negotiated the Declaration on the Critical Economic Situation in Africa at the General Assembly (Chairman 1984–1985); Head of delegation (1984–1990); UN Human Rights Commission (Vice-Chairman 1985); UN Disarmament Commission (Vice-Chairman 1985–1988, Chairman of Working Group III, 1985–1988); Organization of African Unity Ministerial Conference, Lomé (Rapporteur General and Head of Cameroonian delegation 1985); Preparatory Committee for the International Conference on Disarmament and Development (1985–1986); Third Pledging Conference for the World Disarmament Campaign (Vice-President 1986); Head of delegation of the Council for Namibia on the first publicity campaign in Asia (Singapore, 1986); Vice-President of the UN General Assembly (1987–1988).UNICEF Executive Board (Vice-Chairman of Bureau 1989); International Environmental Law Association (Governor for the African Region 1989–1996);
Publications: Author of numerous articles on international law, including *Africa's Contribution to Development of International Law: Africa and International Organizations*.

Judge Thomas A. Mensah
(Member of the Tribunal since 1 October 1996; President of the Tribunal 1996–1999)

Born: Kumasi, Ghana, 12 May 1932.
Education: B.A., University of Ghana (1956); LL.B., University of London (1959); LL.M., Yale University Law School (1962); J.S.D., Yale University Law School (1964).
Professional Experience: Lecturer in Law (1963–1968), Dean of the Faculty (1966–1968), University of Ghana; Associate Legal Officer, International Atomic Energy Agency, Vienna (1965–1966); Assistant Secretary-General and Legal Counsel, International Maritime Organization, London (1968–1990); Special Advisor on Environmental Law and Institutions, UN Environment Programme (UNEP), Nairobi (1991–1992); Visiting Professor, World Maritime University, Malmö, Sweden (1981–1990); Cleveringa Professor of Law, Leiden University, Leiden, The Netherlands (1993–1994); Professor and Director, Law of the Sea Institute, University of Hawaii, USA (1993–1995); High Commissioner of Ghana to the Republic of South Africa (1995–1996).
Member: Institut de Droit international (since 1989); American Society of International Law; British Maritime Law Association; Titular Member, Comité Maritime International (CMI); Standing Committee, International Maritime Arbitration Organization, Paris; IUCN Commission on Environmental Law; Chairman Panel F4 (Environmental Claims), United Nations Compensation Commission (UNCC).
Publications: Articles, monographs and papers in the field of public international law, law of the sea, maritime law and international environmental law.

Judge Joseph Akl

(Member of the Tribunal since 1 October 1996; re-elected as from 1 October 1999; President of the Seabed Disputes Chamber 1997–1999)

Born: Damour, Lebanon, 5 August 1936.

Education: Licence (Master's degree) in public law, Faculty of Law, Saint Joseph University, Beirut (1961); Advanced Studies Diploma for Ph.D. in public law, Faculty of Law, University of Paris (1962).

Professional Experience: Teacher, Ministry of National Education (1956–1963); Assistant Professor of Public Law, Faculty of Law, Saint Joseph University, Beirut (1963–1972 and 1978–1982); Head of Section, Department of Administrative and Consular Affairs, Ministry of Foreign Affairs (1963–1966); Assistant Director, Department of International Organizations, Conferences and Treaties (1966–1972); First Counsellor, Lebanese Embassy, Washington, D.C. (1972–1978); Legal Adviser and Director of Research and Documentation Center, Ministry of Foreign Affairs (1978–1983 and 1994–1996); Ambassador to the German Democratic Republic (1983–1990); Ambassador to Colombia (1991–1994).

Member: Lebanese delegation to: several sessions of the UN General Assembly; second session of the UN Conference on Trade and Development, New Delhi (1968); Ministerial Meeting of the Group of 77, Lima (1971); UN Conference on Environment, Stockholm (1972); various sessions of the Council of the League of Arab States; twelfth Summit of Kings and Heads of Arab States, Fez (1982); Conference of Ministers of Foreign Affairs, Organisation of the Islamic Conference, Niamey (1982); Non-aligned Summit, Cartagena (1995); Member of the International Law Commission of the League of Arab States (1979–1985, President 1983); Head of the Lebanese delegation to: Diplomatic Conference on the Suppression of Unlawful Acts against the Safety of Civil Aviation, Montreal (1973); twentieth session of the Legal Committee, ICAO (1973); Diplomatic Conference on Succession of States in respect of Treaties, Vienna (1978); Third UN Conference on the Law of the Sea (1979–1982).

Judge David Heywood Anderson
(Member of the Tribunal since 1 October 1996)

Born: England, 14 September 1937.
Education: LL.B., Leeds University (1958); LL.M., London School of Economics (1960); Called to the Bar, Gray's Inn (1963).
Professional Experience: Assistant Legal Adviser, Foreign and Commonwealth Office (FCO) (1960–1969); Legal Adviser, British Embassy, Bonn (1969–1972); Legal Counsellor, FCO (1972–1979 and 1982–1987); Legal Adviser, Permanent Mission of the United Kingdom to the UN, New York (1979–1982); Deputy Legal Adviser (1987–1989), Second Legal Adviser (1989–1996), FCO; Visiting Professor, University of Durham (1995–present); Visiting Professor, University College, London (1996–present); Agent for the UK in the *Fisheries Jurisdiction* case (*Merits; UK* v. *Iceland*) before the International Court of Justice (1974), and in numerous cases before the European Court and Commission of Human Rights (1976–1979).
Member: UK teams for the *Factortame* and *Baselines* cases before the European Court of Justice; UK delegations to: Antarctic Treaty Consultative Meetings (1963–1978); Council of Europe Meeting on the Suppression of Marine Broadcasting (1965); UN General Assembly (1967–1995); Vienna Conference on the Law of Treaties (1969); Quadripartite Conference on Berlin (1971); International Maritime Organization MARPOL Conference (1973); UN Committee on the Peaceful Uses of the Sea-Bed and the Ocean Floor beyond the Limits of National Jurisdiction (1973); Third UN Conference on the Law of the Sea (1973–1976, 1979–1982); Conference on Conservation of Antarctic Marine Living Resources (1977–1978); UN Security Council (1979–1982); Anglo French Joint Commission for the Channel Tunnel (1987–1989); Maritime boundary negotiations with Ireland, France, Belgium, Denmark (Faroes), Bahamas, Dominican Republic, Maldives, United States, Jamaica and Cuba; Channel Islands fisheries talks with France (1989–1996); EC Senior Officials Meetings on Law of the Sea (1989–1996); South Atlantic Fisheries Commission (Argentina and UK) (1990–1996); South West Atlantic Hydrocarbons Commission (Argentina and UK) (1995–1996); UN Secretary-General's consultations concerning Part XI of the UN Convention on the Law of the Sea (1990–1994); Preparatory Commission for the International Seabed Authority and for the International Tribunal for the Law of the Sea (1990–1994); UN Conference on Straddling Fish Stocks and Highly Migratory Fish Stocks (Chairman of the UK delegation 1993–1995); Task Force of North Sea States on the introduction of EEZs and Pollution Jurisdiction (1993–1995); International Seabed Authority (1994–1996); Member of: Editorial Committee, *British Year Book of International Law* (1996–present); Study Group on *Joint Development of Offshore Oil and Gas*, British Institute of International and Comparative Law (1989); Committee on Public International Law, British Institute of International and Comparative Law (1992–present); Group of Experts, convened by the UN Office for Ocean Affairs and the Law of the Sea (1992) on the *Impact of the Convention on the Law of the Sea* (UN publication 1994); International Law Association, British Branch; American Society of International Law; Law of the Sea Institute; Greenwich Forum (1996–present).
Publications: Author of numerous articles and papers on international law, including law of the sea; Contributor to *International Maritime Boundaries* (1993 and 1997).
Appointed: CMG (Companion of the Order of St. Michael and St. George) (1982).

Judge Budislav Vukas

(Member of the Tribunal since 1 October 1996)

Born: Rijeka/Suπ ak, Croatia, 1 January 1938.
Education: LL.B. (1961), LL.M. (1965), Doctor of Law (International Law) (1974), Faculty of Law, University of Zagreb; attended courses at The Hague Academy of International Law (1961 and 1968–1970); participated in the Centre of the Academy for Studies and Research (International Law and International Relations) (1967).
Professional Experience: Professor of Public International Law, Faculty of Law, University of Zagreb (Assistant 1963–1970, Lecturer 1970–1974, Assistant Professor 1974–1977, Professor 1977–present); lectured at the Universities of Belgrade, Bologna, Boston, Brest, Maribor, Milan, Osijek, Paris, Parma, Rijeka, Rome, Split, Thessaloniki, Tilburg and Valletta; directs a course on the law of the sea at the Dubrovnik Inter-University Centre (1984–present); delivered a course on "States, Peoples and Minorities" at The Hague Academy of International Law (1992); Consultant for UNEP, Nairobi (1981 and 1991) and its Co-ordinating Unit for the Mediterranean Action Plan, Athens (1985 and 1990); participated in: Third UN Conference on the Law of the Sea (1975–1982); Preparatory Commission for the International Seabed Authority and for the International Tribunal for the Law of the Sea (1984–1990 and 1994); International Seabed Authority (1994–1996); Meetings of States Parties to the UN Convention on the Law of the Sea (1994–1996); the Sixth Committee of the UN General Assembly (1990, 1991, 1995); Working Group on the UN Decade of International Law of the Sixth Committee of the UN General Assembly (Chairman 1990); CSCE Conference on the Human Dimension, Copenhagen Meeting (1990); CSCE Meeting of Experts on National Minorities, Geneva (1991); World Conference on Human Rights, Vienna (1993); 26th International Conference of the Red Cross and Red Crescent, Geneva (1995).
Member: Committee of Experts on the Application of Conventions and Recommendations of the International Labour Organization (1985–present); Commission of Inquiry formed under Article 26 of the Constitution of the International Labour Organization to examine the observance by Romania of the Discrimination (Employment and Occupation) Convention, 1958 (No. 111) (1989–1991); Scientific Council of the European Institute for Marine Studies, Brest, France (1997–present); Scientific Council of the Institute for Economic Law of the Sea, Monaco (2000–present); Permanent Court of Arbitration (1989–1991 and 1999–present); Court of Conciliation and Arbitration within the OSCE (1995–present); Institut de Droit international (Associate member 1991–1997, Member 1997–present); Croatian Society of International Law (1961–present); Société française pour le droit international (1978–present); International Council of Environmental Law, Bonn (1978–present); Judge *ad hoc* in the case before the International Court of Justice concerning *Application of the Convention on the Prevention and Punishment of the Crime of Genocide (Croatia* v. *Yugoslavia)*.
Publications: Author of numerous books, monographs, articles and papers in various fields of public international law, in particular law of the sea, international environmental law, international protection of human rights and national minorities, including *The Relativity of Treaties* (in Croatian), 1975; *Ethnic Minorities and International Relations* (in Croatian), 1978; *The New Law of the Sea* (ed., in Croatian), 1982; *Essays on the New Law of the Sea, Vol. I–III*, (ed.), 1985–1996; *The Legal Regime of Enclosed or Semi-Enclosed Seas: The Particular Case of the Mediterranean* (ed.), 1988; *International Law, Vol. I* (with J. Andrassy and B. Bakotić, in Croatian), 1995.

Judge Rüdiger Wolfrum

(Member of the Tribunal since 1 October 1996; re-elected as from 1 October 1999;
Vice-President of the Tribunal 1996–1999;
President of the Chamber for Marine Environment Disputes 1997–1999;
Member of the Special Chamber formed to deal with the
Case concerning the Conservation and Sustainable Exploitation of Swordfish Stocks in the South-Eastern Pacific Ocean)

Born: Berlin, Germany, 13 December 1941.
Education: First State Examination (1969); Second State Examination (1973); Dr. jur., University of Bonn (1973); *Habilitation, venia legendi* for National Public and International Public Law (1980).
Professional Experience: Assistant Professor, Institute of International Law, University of Bonn (1973–1982); Research fellow, Center for Oceans Law and Policy, University of Virginia (1977–1978); Professor of National Public and International Public Law, University of Mainz (1982); Professor, Chair of National Public and International Public Law and Director, Institute of International Law, University of Kiel (1982–1993); Vice-Rector, University of Kiel (1990–1993); Judge at the Courts of Appeal for Administrative Matters, Lüneburg and Schleswig (1986–1993); Director, Max Planck Institute for Comparative Public Law and International Law, Heidelberg (1993–present); Professor, Faculty of Law, University of Heidelberg (1993–present); Vice-President, German Research Foundation (1996–present).
Member: International Law Association (Board German section, 1994–present); Executive Board, Law of the Sea Institute, University of Hawaii and University of Miami (1994–present); German delegation to: Third UN Conference on the Law of the Sea (1980–1982), Preparatory Commission for the International Seabed Authority and for the International Tribunal for the Law of the Sea (1982), 4th Special Consultative Meeting concerning Antarctic mineral resource activities (1983–1988); Chairman of the Legal Working Group of the Antarctic Treaty Consultative Meetings preparing an Annex to the Protocol on Environmental Protection to the Antarctic Treaty on responsibility for environmental damage (1993–1998); UN Committee on the Elimination of Racial Discrimination (1990, re-elected 1994 and 1998).
Publications: Author and editor of numerous books and articles on various issues of public international law, law of the sea, international environmental law, human rights, United Nations and the Antarctic, including *Internationalization of Common Spaces Outside National Jurisdiction: The Development of an International Administration for Antarctica, Outer Space, High Seas and Deep Seabed* (in German), 1984; *United Nations: law, policies, and practice*, 1995; *Enforcing Environmental Standards: Economic Mechanisms as Viable Means*, 1996; *The Right to a Fair Trial* (together with D. Weissbrodt), 1997; *Means of Ensuring Compliance with and Enforcement of International Law*, Recueil des Cours 272, 1998, 10 *et seq*.

Judge Edward Arthur Laing
(Member of the Tribunal since 1 October 1996)

Born: Belize City, Belize, 27 February 1942.
Education: B.A. Cambridge University (1964); LL.M. Cambridge University (1966); LL.M. Columbia University (1968).
Professional Experience: Assistant Magistrate, Belize (1966); Crown Counsel, Belize (1967); Associate, Baker and MacKenzie, New York and Chicago (1968–1969); private law practice, Belize (1969–1970); Lecturer in Law (1970–1975); Senior Lecturer (1975), University of the West Indies (U.W.I.), Barbados and Jamaica; Assistant Professor of Law, Notre Dame Law School, Indiana (1974–1976); Associate Professor of Law, University of Maryland (1976–1981); Professor of Law and Director, Graduate Program, Howard University, School of Law, Washington, D.C. (1980–1985); Ambassador of Belize to the U.S.A. (1985–1990); High Commissioner to Canada (1985–1990); Special Counsel to the Ministry of Foreign Affairs (1985–1990); Permanent Representative to the Organization of American States (1985–1990); Professor of Law, New York Law School (1990–1993); Ambassador and Permanent Representative of Belize to the UN (1993–1996); Belize delegations on law of the sea and UN economic, humanitarian, legal and social agendas and to UNDP Executive Board, World Bank, OAS, Caribbean Community, Commonwealth Heads of Government (1985–1990, 1993–1996); Constitution and independence adviser to Belize Chamber of Commerce and Industry (1981); consultant to international agencies, including UN Development Programme (1996–present).
Member: Bars of Barbados, Belize, England, Illinois, Washington, D.C.; American Society of International Law; International Law Association; Belize-Guatemala Permanent Joint Commission – member of the three sub-commissions (economic, political/maritime (co-chair) and security) (1987–1990); group negotiating treaty for Association of Caribbean States (1995–1996).
Publications: Numerous articles, UN interventions and papers on law of the sea, governance, inter-parliamentary institutions, Security Council reform, international development, international law, international adjudication, international trade law, public law and legal education.

Judge Tullio Treves
(Member of the Tribunal since 1 October 1996;
President of the Seabed Disputes Chamber since 4 October 1999)

Born: Tucumán, Argentina, 20 September 1942.
Education: Doctor of Law, University of Milan (1964).
Professional Experience: Professor of International Law, University of Sassari (1969–1973); University of Turin (1974–1980); University of Milan (1980–present); Legal Adviser to the Permanent Mission of Italy to the UN in New York (1984–1992); Counsel for France in the case against Canada decided by an Arbitral Tribunal concerning the Delimitation of Maritime Areas in the Region of Saint-Pierre-et-Miquelon (1990–1991); Counsel for Finland in the *Passage through the Great Belt* (*Finland* v. *Denmark*) case before the International Court of Justice (1991–1992); taught in the International Law Courses of Victoria, Spain (1984) and the Unitar Courses in International Law at The Hague (1987, 1988, 1996 and 1999); gave courses at the Geneva Institute for Advanced International Studies (1988), Universities of Paris I and II (1983, 1994 and 1995), The Hague Academy of International Law (1990), the Rhodes Academy of International Maritime Law and Policy (1997, 1998, and 2000); the Bancaja Courses of international law at Castellon, Spain (1997); the University of Aix-Marseille (2000); the International Law Courses of Thessaloniki, Greece (2000); lectured in universities in Italy, Canada, Finland, France, Mexico, Portugal, Spain, Sweden, Switzerland, the United Kingdom, the United States, Belgium, South Africa, Republic of Korea, Singapore; External examiner for Doctoral degrees at: Dalhousie University, Halifax; European University Institute, Florence; University of Valencia, Spain.
Member: Institut de Droit international (Associate member since 1999); Law of the Sea Institute; American, French and Italian Societies of International Law; European Council for Environmental Law; Steering Committee of the Project on International Courts and Tribunals (London – New York); Scientific Committee of the *Institut de droit économique de la mer* (Monaco); Editorial Boards of *Ocean Development and International Law, Espaces et ressources maritimes* and *Il diritto marittimo*; Legal Sub-Project of the Finalized Project on Oceanography of the Italian Council for Scientific Research (Board 1977–1982); Italian delegation to: Committee on the Peaceful Uses of the Seabed and the Ocean Floor beyond the Limits of National Jurisdiction (1973); Third UN Conference on the Law of the Sea (1974–1982, Coordinator of the French Language Group of the Drafting Committee); Intergovernmental Oceanographic Commission of UNESCO (1981 and 1983); Preparatory Commission for the International Seabed Authority and for the International Tribunal for the Law of the Sea (1983–1994); Sixth Committee of the UN General Assembly (1983–1991); Working Group of the Sixth Committee of the UN General Assembly for the Drafting of a UN Body of Principles for the Protection of Detained or Imprisoned Persons (Chairman 1984–1988); Special Committee of the UN General Assembly for the Drafting of a Convention Against the Recruitment, Use, Financing and Training of Mercenaries (1984–1989, Vice-Chairman); Second Vienna Conference on the Law of Treaties (1986); Special Committee for the Strengthening of the Principle of Non-Use of Force (Chairman 1987); Security Council (1987–1988); Consultations of the UN Secretary-General concerning Part XI of the UN Convention on the Law of the Sea (1990–1994); First and Second Sessions of the International Seabed Authority (1994, 1995, 1996).
Publications: Author of numerous books and articles in various fields of public and private international law, law of the sea and environmental law, including *The Exploitation of the International Seabed* (in Italian), 1982; *International Law* (with M. Giuliano and T. Scovazzi,

in Italian), 1991; *The Law of the Sea, the European Union and its Member States*, 1997; *The United Nations Compensation Commission; A Handbook* (with M. Frigessi di Ratalma), 1999; *Le controversie internazionali, nuove tendenze, nuovi tribunali* (International Disputes, New Trends, New Tribunals) 1999; editor of the *Rivista di diritto internazionale privato e processuale* and the *Italian Yearbook of International Law*.

Judge Mohamed Mouldi Marsit
(Member of the Tribunal since 1 October 1996)

Born: Kebili, Tunisia, 14 January 1944.
Education: Bachelor of Law; Post Graduate Studies in Law; Diploma, National Administration Institute, Tunis.
Professional Experience: Administrator (1969–1996), Deputy Director (1976–1996), Department of Law and Legislation, Office of the Prime Minister; Director (1980–1985), Director General (1985–1996), Legal Adviser to the Government; Head of division, Office of the Prime Minister (1989–1993); Adviser to the Administrative Mediator (Ombudsman) (1993–1994), Director General for Consular Affairs, Ministry of Foreign Affairs (1994–1996); Administrator, *Compagnie Tunisienne de Navigation*; represented the Office of the Prime Minister at the Tunis Administrative Tribunal for Litigation (1975–1980); Tunisian Legal Adviser, *Continental Shelf* (*Tunisia/Libyan Arab Jamahiriya*) case before the International Court of Justice (1981–1982 and 1985); Lecturer on International Relations, Faculty of Law, Tunis (1991–present).
Member: Tunisian delegation to: UN Committee on the Peaceful Uses of the Sea-Bed and the Ocean Floor beyond the Limits of National Jurisdiction (1973); Third UN Conference on the Law of the Sea (1974–1982); Contact Group of 77 in charge of the settlement of disputes, Preamble and final clauses (Coordinator 1976–1982); Working Group on the settlement of disputes of the group of Arab experts on the law of the sea (President 1976, 1977 and 1979); Barcelona Conference organized by Mediterranean States against pollution (member of the drafting committee, 1976); African group of the meetings of legal experts on the law of the sea, Addis Ababa and Nairobi (Rapporteur 1978–1979); Sixth Committee of the UN General Assembly (1980); Preparatory Commission for the International Seabed Authority and for the International Tribunal for the Law of the Sea (coordinator of the Group of 77, 1984–1994); International Seabed Authority (Chairman of Financial Committee 1996).
Publications: Author of books and articles on the law of the sea, including *Tunisia and the Law of the Sea* (in Arabic), 1992; *Le Tribunal du droit de la mer*, 1999; "Le règlement du Tribunal international du droit de la mer", *Annuaire du droit de la mer*, 1997.

Judge Gudmundur Eiriksson
(Member of the Tribunal since 1 October 1996;
President of the Chamber for Fisheries Disputes since 4 October 1999)

Born: Winnipeg, Canada, 26 October 1947.
Education: A.B., B.S. in Civil Engineering, Rutgers College (1970); LL.B., King's College, University of London (1973); LL.M., Columbia University (1974); Visiting Scholar, University of Virginia Law School (1984 and 1985).
Professional Experience: Law of the Sea Officer, Office of the Secretary-General of the United Nations for the Law of the Sea, New York (1974–1976); Special Consultant, Third UN Conference on the Law of the Sea, New York (1977); Assistant Legal Adviser (1977–1980), Legal Adviser (1980–1996), Ambassador (1988–1996), Ministry for Foreign Affairs of Iceland; Lecturer, University of Iceland (1987–1996); Visiting Professor of Law, University of New Mexico School of Law (1994–1995).
Member: International Law Commission (1987–1996, Rapporteur 1990, First Vice-Chairman 1993); Society of Professional Engineers, Iceland; Association of Icelandic Lawyers; International Law Association (International Committee on the Exclusive Economic Zone and International Committee on Coastal State Jurisdiction relating to Marine Pollution); Icelandic delegations to Third UN Conference on the Law of the Sea (1978–1982), Preparatory Commission for the International Seabed Authority and for the International Tribunal for the Law of the Sea and Council of the North Atlantic Salmon Conservation Organization (President 1984–1988); Panel of Conciliators and Arbitrators, Center for Arbitrations, Mediation and Conciliation, Dakar; Panel of Conciliators and Panel of Arbitrators, International Centre for the Settlement of Investment Disputes, Washington.
Publications: *The International Tribunal for the Law of the Sea*, 2000; numerous articles on the law of the sea, legal education, international criminal law, international organizations, disarmament and human rights.

Judge Tafsir Malick Ndiaye
(Member of the Tribunal since 1 October 1996)

Born: Kaolack, Senegal, 7 February 1953.
Education: Annual internship certificate, UN (1979); Diploma, Institute of Advanced International Studies, University of Paris (1980); Postgraduate Diploma (taken before completion of the doctorate) in political studies with a specialization in international relations, University of Paris (1980); Postgraduate Diploma (taken before completion of the doctorate) in public law with a specialization in public international law, University of Paris (1981); Diploma from The Hague Academy Centre for Studies and Research in International Law and International Relations, The Hague Academy of International Law (1981); Doctor of Laws, University of Paris (1984).
Professional Experience: Assistant Lecturer, University of Paris X (1981); Assistant, Collège de France, Professor René Jean Dupuy Chair of International Law (1981); Lecturer, University of Dakar (1984); Director of the Research Centre, Faculty of Law, University of Dakar (1985); Legal Adviser and Co-Representative of the Government of Senegal in the matter of the delimitation of the maritime boundary between Senegal and Guinea-Bissau (1985); Arbitration Tribunal, Geneva (1986–1989); International Court of Justice, The Hague (1989–1991); Adviser to the Government of Senegal on Senegambia (1986); UN consultant (undertook several missions for the UN, 1989); Legal Adviser to the Senegalese Government in the negotiations concerning Senegal's commercial debt, London Club (1989); Rapporteur, Commission on the Reform of the Senegalese Electoral Code (1991); Expert, Global Coalition for Africa, Washington (1992); Jurisconsult (1992); Panel of Conciliators and Arbitrators, Center for Arbitration, Mediation and Conciliation, Dakar; visiting professor at various universities (Arusha, Lilongwe, Lomé, Paris, Tunis, …).
Member: Several learned societies.
Distinctions: *Chevalier de l'ordre national du Lion*, Senegal (1995); *Commandeur de l'ordre du mérite*, Senegal (1998).
Publications: Author of books, and numerous articles and papers in the field of international law, constitutional law, international organizations and law of integration, including *Matières premières et droit international*, 1992.

Judge José Luis Jesus
(Member of the Tribunal since 1 October 1999)

Born: Ribeira Grande – Santo Antão, Cape Verde, 20 September 1950.
Education: Law Degree, School of Law, Classical University of Lisbon (1978); International Law Certificate, Saint John's University, New York (1985); M.A., Government and Politics, Saint John's University, New York (1985).
Professional Experience: Counselor (Legal Adviser) (1981–1987), Ambassador and Deputy Permanent Representative (1987–1991), Ambassador and Permanent Representative (1991–1994), Permanent Mission of Cape Verde to the United Nations, New York; Special Envoy of the Secretary-General of the United Nations for the Great Lakes Region, Central Africa (1994); Ambassador of Cape Verde to Portugal, Spain and Israel (1994–1996); Secretary of State for Foreign Affairs and Cooperation (1996–1998); Minister of Foreign Affairs and Communities (1998–1999).
Member: Head of Cape Verde delegation to the Third UN Conference on the Law of the Sea (1979–1982); Sixth Committee of the UN General Assembly (1979–1994); Preparatory Commission for the International Seabed Authority and for the International Tribunal for the Law of the Sea (Head of delegation 1983–1994, Chairman 1987–1995); Chairman, Group of 77 for the Law of the Sea (1986); Chairman, Group of African States at the UN (1986); Head of the Cape Verde delegation to UN Conference on the Law of Treaties between States and International Organizations or between International Organizations, Vienna (1986); President, UN Security Council (July 1992 and November 1993); Chairman of the National Commission on the Delimitation of Maritime Boundaries, Cape Verde; Speaker at several seminars on the Law of the Sea; Cape Verde Bar Association.
Publications: Author of publications in the fields of the law of the sea and humanitarian law.

II. FORMER JUDGE

Judge Zhao Lihai †

(Member of the Tribunal from 1 October 1996 to 10 October 2000)

Born: Shan Xi, China, 3 July 1916.
Education: B.A., Yenching University (1939); M.A., University of Chicago (1941); Ph.D. in International Law, Harvard University (1944).
Professional Experience: Professor of Law, National Wuhan University, China (1945–1947); Professor of Law, National Central University, Nanjing, China (1947–1949); Professor of Law, Nanjing University, China (1949–1957); Professor of International Law, Peking University (1957–2000); Visiting Professor, New York University School of Law (1983); Vice-President, Chinese Association of International Marine Affairs (1981–1989); Vice-President, Chinese Society of the Law of the Sea (1989–1999); President, Chinese Society of the Law of the Sea (2000); Senior Legal Adviser, China Ocean Mineral Research and Development Association (1991–1996).
Member: Board of Directors, Chinese Society of Oceanography (1989–1994; Adviser 1994–2000); China Law Society (1982–1986; Adviser 1986–1991); Board of Directors, Chinese Society of Politics and Law (1956–1966); Board of Directors, Chinese Society of International Law (1980–1994; Adviser 1994–2000); Member, Curatorium Internationale, Institute of International Public Law and International Relations, Greece (1983–2000); Member, The 7th National Committee, The Chinese People's Political Consultative Conference (1988–1993); Member, The Legal System Committee, CPPCC (1988–1993); Deputy Director, The Legal System Committee, China Democratic League (1989–2000); Member, China Council for the Promotion of Peaceful National Reunification (1988–1996).
Publications: Author of numerous treatises, including *Public International Law* (in Chinese), 1947; *Revision of the United Nations Charter* (in Chinese), 1982; *New Developments in the Law of the Sea* (in Chinese), 1984; *Basic Theories of International Law* (in Chinese), 1990; *Current Problems of International Law* (in Chinese), 1993; *Current Problems of the Law of the Sea* (in Chinese), 1996.

III. JUDGE *AD HOC*

Judge *ad hoc* Francisco Orrego Vicuña

(Judge *ad hoc* in the *Case concerning the Conservation and Sustainable Exploitation of Swordfish Stocks in the South-Eastern Pacific Ocean*)

Born: Santiago, Chile, 12 June 1942.
Education: Doctoral Degree in Law, University of Chile Law School (1965); Ph.D., (International Law), London School of Economics and Political Science, University of London (1986).
Professional Experience: Senior Legal Adviser, Department of Legal Affairs of the Organization of American States (1965–1969; 1972–1974); Professor of International Law at the Law School and Institute of International Studies, University of Chile (1969–present); Director, School of Law and Institute of International Studies, University of Chile (1974–1983; 2001–present); Member of the Commission on the Papal Mediation in the boundary dispute between Chile and Argentina (1978–1985); President of the Chilean branch of the International Law Association (1979–present); Vice-President and President of the Chilean Delegation to the Third United Nations Conference on the Law of the Sea (1973–1983); Visiting Professsor, Stanford University (1981) and at the Université de Droit, d'Economie et de Sciences Sociales de Paris (1988); Ambassador to Great Britain (1983–1985); Inter-American Juridical Committee; Chilean Academy of Social Sciences (1983–present); Course on the Exclusive Economic Zone at the Hague Academy of International Law (1986); World Bank Administrative Tribunal (Judge 1991–present, President 2001–present); President of the F2 Claims Panel, United Nations Compensation Commission (1998–2001); Lecturer at numerous universities in Latin America, Europe, the United States and Asia.
Member: American Society of International Comparative Law (1974–present); Fellow Royal Geographical Society (FRGS 1985–present); Société Française pour le Droit International (1988–present); Royal Institution of Great Britain (MRI 1985–present); Institut de Droit International (1991–present).
Publications: Author of books and articles, including *Antarctic Mineral Exploitation* (1988); *The Exclusive Economic Zone, Regime and Legal Nature under International Law* (1986); *Antarctic Resources Policy* (Editor, 1983); *The Changing International Law of High Seas Fisheries* (1999).

IV. THE REGISTRAR AND THE DEPUTY REGISTRAR

Gritakumar E. Chitty
(Registrar of the Tribunal since 23 October 1996)

Born: Colombo, Sri Lanka, 14 June 1939.
Education: Bachelor of Laws (LL.B.) University of Sri Lanka, Faculty of Law (1965); Professional Examination for Attorneys, Ceylon Law College (1967); Called to the Bar in May 1968.
Professional Experience: Advocate of the Supreme Court, Sri Lanka; Practising Attorney in trial and appeal courts (1968–1975); Legal Officer and Special Assistant to Under-Secretaries-General and Special Representatives of the Secretary-General of the United Nations for the Law of the Sea, responsible for the subject of settlement of disputes relating to the Law of the Sea (1975–1994); Committee Secretary of Informal Plenary of the Third United Nations Conference on the Law of the Sea; Secretary to the Groups of Legal Experts and Negotiating Groups on the Settlement of Disputes concerning Sea Bed Mining; and in the Exclusive Economic Zone; and the Group of 77 on subjects of the Plenary (1975–1982); Secretary of Special Commission IV of the Preparatory Commission for the International Seabed Authority and for the International Tribunal for the Law of the Sea, mandated to prepare all legal, procedural, administrative and budgetary texts, reports and proposals for the Meeting of States Parties to the Convention (1983–1994); Principal Legal Officer (since 1990); Specially designated by the Legal Counsel of the United Nations to coordinate the First session and the Ceremonial Inauguration of the International Criminal Tribunal for the former Yugoslavia (The Hague, November 1993–January 1994); Special Assistant for the Law of the Sea to the Legal Counsel of the UN (1994); Secretary of the Meeting of States Parties to the Convention on the Law of the Sea, First to Fourth Sessions (1994–1996); Specially appointed by the Secretary-General of the United Nations as Officer responsible for the establishment of the International Tribunal for the Law of the Sea under General Assembly resolution 49/28 (1995–1996); Director of the Tribunal (August–October 1996); First Registrar of the International Tribunal for the Law of the Sea (1996–present).
Member: Panel of Counsel of the United Nations (1975–1996), Appointment and Promotion Board of the United Nations (1994–1995); Joint Disciplinary Committee (1985–1986); Representative to Advisory Committee on Teaching, Study and Dissemination of International Law (1982–1996); Ex-officio Secretary to Advisory Panel for the Amerasinghe Fellowship on the Law of the Sea (1983–1996); Delegate to ESCAP Group of Experts on Guidelines to Maritime Legislation, Thailand (1991/1994); Delegate to First Ministerial Conference on Indian Ocean Marine Affairs Cooperation (IOMAC), Colombo, Sri Lanka (1992); Head of UN Delegation to Second IOMAC Ministerial Conference, Arusha, Tanzania (1993).
Publications: Principal Contributor to: *United Nations Convention on the Law of the Sea 1982, a Commentary*, Volume V, University of Virginia, Center for Oceans Law and Policy, Martinus Nijhoff, 1989; Principal author of UN Secretariat documentation for: The Third UN Conference on the Law of the Sea on the Settlement of Disputes, Preamble, General Provisions and the Final Act and Resolution on the Preparatory Commission (1975–1982); Special Commission 4 of the Preparatory Commission for the Tribunal (1982–1994); Meeting of States Parties to the Convention on the Law of the Sea; General Assembly Reports under the item Law of the Sea; Reports on Needs of States for Assistance in realizing their benefits under the Law of the Sea Convention (1991–1992).

Philippe Gautier
(Deputy Registrar of the Tribunal since 19 January 1997)

Born: Bujumbura, Burundi, 1 February 1960.
Education: Licence en droit (1982), Licence en philosophie (1983), Diplôme d'études spécialisées en droit européen (1985), Docteur en droit (1992), Catholic University of Louvain (Louvain-la-Neuve).
Professional Experience: Administrator (Treaty Direction, 1984–1988; Law of the Sea/Antarctica Office, 1988–1991), Deputy Director, Head of the Law of the Sea/Antarctica Office (1991–1995), Director, Head of the Treaties Division (1995–1997), Ministry of Foreign Affairs of Belgium; Assistant (1985–1993), Lecturer (1993–1996), Visiting Professor (1996–present), Faculty of Law, Catholic University of Louvain (Louvain-la-Neuve).
Member: Belgian delegation to: Maritime boundary negotiations with France, United Kingdom and The Netherlands (1991–1996), Preparatory Commission for the International Seabed Authority and for the International Tribunal for the Law of the Sea (1989–1990, Head 1991–1994), Consultations of the UN Secretary-General concerning Part XI of the UN Convention on the Law of the Sea (1991–1994), UN Conference on Straddling Fish Stocks and Highly Migratory Fish Stocks (1993), Antarctic Consultative meetings (1990, Head 1991–1996); Belgian Society of International Law; French Society for International Law.
Publications: Author of publications on international law, including: *Essai sur la définition des traités entre Etats*, 1993; "De 1982 à 1994: les étapes d'une modification 'singulière' de la partie XI de la Convention des Nations Unies sur le droit de la mer de 1982", *RBDI*, 1995; "Le plateau continental de la Belgique et sa délimitation – quelques réflexions sur la notion d'accord implicite", *RBDI*, 1995; "Institutional developments in the Antarctic Treaty System", *International Law for Antarctica*, 1996; "La procédure devant le Tribunal International du droit de la mer", *Espaces et ressources maritimes*, 1998; "The Reparation for Injuries Case Revisited: The Personality of the European Union", *Max-Planck Yearbook of United Nations Law*, 2000.

CHAPTER IX

SELECT BIBLIOGRAPHY ON SETTLEMENT OF DISPUTES CONCERNING THE LAW OF THE SEA[20]

I. GENERAL

Eiriksson, Gudmundur. THE INTERNATIONAL TRIBUNAL FOR THE LAW OF THE SEA (The Hague, Martinus Nijhoff Publishers, 2000).

Gautier, Philippe. La procédure devant le Tribunal international du droit de la mer, 12 COLLECTION ESPACES ET RESSOURCES MARITIMES (1998), pp. 24–43.

Jagota, S.P. Developments in the law of the sea between 1970 and 1998: a historical perspective, 2 (1) *JOURNAL OF THE HISTORY OF INTERNATIONAL LAW/REVUE D'HISTOIRE DU DROIT INTERNATIONAL* (2000), pp. 91–119.

McDorman, Ted L. Global ocean governance and international adjudicative dispute resolution, 43 *OCEAN & COASTAL MANAGEMENT* (2000), pp. 255–275.

Rao, P. Chandrasekhara. Settlement of the law of the sea disputes and the insurance industry, *LLOYD'S MARITIME AND COMMERCIAL LAW QUARTERLY* (August 2000), pp. 328–337.

Rosenne, Shabtai. International Tribunal for the Law of the Sea: 1999 survey, 15 (4) *INTERNATIONAL JOURNAL OF MARINE AND COASTAL LAW* (2000), pp. 443–474.

Treves, Tullio. Advisory opinions of the International Court of Justice on questions raised by other international tribunals, 4 *MAX PLANCK YEARBOOK OF UNITED NATIONS LAW* (2000), pp. 215–231.

Treves, Tullio. Le Tribunal international du droit de la mer et la multiplication des jurisdictions internationales *in* JUSTICE ET JURIDICTIONS INTERNATIONALES (Actes de la IVe Rencontre internationale de la Faculté des sciences juridiques, politiques et sociales de Tunis, 13, 14 et 15 avril 2000, Paris, Éditions A. Pedone, 2000), 101–123.

Vaughan, Lowe. Overlapping jurisdiction in international tribunals, 20 *AUSTRALIAN YEARBOOK OF INTERNATIONAL LAW, 1999* (2000), pp. 191–204.

[20] The list also includes articles on the settlement of disputes concerning the law of the sea that were not included in the *Yearbook 1999*.

Vukas, Budislav. Règlement du Tribunal international du droit de la mer, 12 COLLECTION ESPACES ET RESSOURCES MARITIMES (1998), pp. 15–23.

Wolfrum, Rüdiger. Der Internationale Seegerichtshof – eine erste Bilanz, 48 (4) *VEREINTE NATIONEN* (2000), pp. 127–132.

II. CASES BEFORE THE TRIBUNAL

Aoki, Takashi. Camouco-go Iken senpaku-syakuho hanke-tsu [The ITLOS judgment in the "Camouco" case], 73 (6) *JOURNAL OF LAW, POLITICS AND SOCIOLOGY* (2000), pp. 83–102.

Bialek, Dean. Australia & New Zealand v Japan: Southern Bluefin Tuna Case, 1 *MELBOURNE JOURNAL OF INTERNATIONAL LAW* (2000), pp. 153–161.

Baldock, Julia. [Commentary] Determining the fate of Southern Bluefin Tuna – International Tribunal for the Law of the Sea (1999) New Zealand v Japan; Australia v Japan, 17 (3) *ENVIRONMENTAL AND PLANNING LAW JOURNAL* (2000), pp. 157–164.

Brevern, Hartmut von and Leopold von Carlowitz. Die erste Hauptsacheentscheidung des Internationalen Seegerichtshof, 45 (11) *RECHT DER INTERNATIONALEN WIRTSCHAFT* (1999), pp. 856–866.

Chigara, Ben. The International Tribunal for the Law of the Sea and customary international law, 22 (4) *LOYOLA OF LOS ANGELES INTERNATIONAL & COMPARATIVE LAW REVIEW* (2000), pp. 433–452.

Churchill, Robin. The Southern Bluefin Tuna cases (*New Zealand* v. *Japan; Australia* v. *Japan*): Order for Provisional Measures of 27 August 1999, 49 (4) *INTERNATIONAL AND COMPARATIVE LAW QUARTERLY* (2000), pp. 979–990.

Dissars, Björn-Axel. [International News: The Camouco] International Tribunal for the Law of the Sea: ship arrest. New case before the International Tribunal for the Law of the Sea, 7 (1) *INTERNATIONAL MARITIME LAW* (2000), p. 23.

Dissars, Björn-Axel. [International News] International Tribunal for the Law of the Sea: prompt release. Belize v France (The MV "Grand Prince") 20 April 2001, 7 (8) *INTERNATIONAL MARITIME LAW* (2000), pp. 279–281.

Eiriksson, Gudmundur. Prompt release of vessels and crews in accordance with Article 292 of the United Nations Convention on the Law of the Sea, 1 *CUADERNOS DE DERECHO PESQUERO* (2000), pp. 19–34.

Evans, Malcolm D. [Case and Comment] Bonded reason *The Camouco*, (3) *LLOYD'S MARITIME AND COMMERCIAL LAW QUARTERLY* (2000), pp. 315–322.

Evans, Malcolm D. The Southern Bluefin Tuna dispute: provisional thinking on provisional measures?, 10 *YEARBOOK OF INTERNATIONAL ENVIRONMENTAL LAW, 1999* (2000), pp. 7–14.

Fabra, Adriana. The LOSC and the implementation of the precautionary principle, 10 *Yearbook of International Environmental Law, 1999* (2000), pp. 15–24.

Fayette, Louise de la. International Tribunal for the Law of the Sea. The M/V "Saiga" (No. 2) Case (St. Vincent and the Grenadines v. Guinea), Judgment, 49 (1) *International and Comparative Law Quarterly* (2000), pp. 467–476.

Fayette, Louise de la. ITLOS and the saga of the Saiga: peaceful settlement of a law of the sea dispute, 15 (3) *The International Journal of Marine and Coastal Law* (2000), pp. 355–392.

Freestone, David. Caution or precaution: "a rose by any other name ..."?, 10 *Yearbook of International Environmental Law, 1999* (2000), pp. 25–32.

García Gallardo, Ramón. [Case Note] Fifth case of the International Tribunal for the Law of the Sea (ITLOS), Part 2 *The International Journal of Shipping Law* (2000), pp. 130–132.

Hayashi, Moritaka. The Southern Bluefin Tuna Cases: prescription of provisional measures by the International Tribunal for the Law of the Sea, 13 (2) *Tulane Environmental Law Journal* (2000), pp. 361–385.

Johnston, Douglas M. Fishery diplomacy and science and the judicial function, 10 *Yearbook of International Environmental Law, 1999* (2000), pp. 33–39.

Kwiatkowska, Barbara. The Saint Vincent and the Grenadines v. Guinea M/V Saiga cases before the International Tribunal for the Law of the Sea, *in* Navigational Rights and Freedoms and the New Law of the Sea (Donald Rothwell and W.S.G. Bateman, eds., The Hague, Martinus Nijhoff, 2000), pp. 275–292.

Kwiatkowska, Barbara. [Case Note] Southern Bluefin Tuna (New Zealand v. Japan; Australia v. Japan), Order on Provisional Measures (ITLOS Cases Nos. 3 and 4), 94 (1) *American Journal of International Law* (2000), pp. 150–155.

Kwiatkowska, Barbara. The Southern Bluefin Tuna (New Zealand v Japan; Australia v. Japan) Cases, 15 (1) *The International Journal of Marine and Coastal Law* (2000), pp. 1–37.

Leggett, Kristina. The *Southern Bluefin Tuna Cases*: ITLOS Order on Provisional Measures, 9 (1) *Review of European Community and International Environmental Law* (2000), pp. 75–79.

Lux, Jonathan and Philip Carney. The Camouco case: Panama v. France, 28 (10) *International Business Lawyer* (2000), pp. 461–462, 464.

Mahinga, Jean-Grégoire. Les affaires du M/V Saiga devant le Tribunal du Droit de la Mer, 104 (3) *Revue Générale de Droit International Public* (2000), pp. 695–730.

Marr, Simon. The Southern Bluefin Tuna cases: the precautionary approach and conservation and management of fish resources, 11 (4) *European Journal of International Law* (2000), pp. 815–832.

O'Keefe, Roger. ITLOS flags its intent (International Tribunal for the Law of the Sea), 59 (3) *Cambridge Law Journal* (2000), pp. 428–431.

Orrego Vicuña, Francisco. L'affaire SAIGA et l'interprétation judiciaire des droits et devoirs des États dans la Z.E.E., 13 *Collection Espaces et Ressources Maritimes* (1999–2000), pp. 43–60.

Orrego Vicuña, Francisco. From the 1893 Bering Sea Fur-Seals Case to the 1999 Southern Bluefin Tuna cases: a century of efforts at conservation of the living resources of the high seas, 10 *Yearbook of International Environmental Law, 1999* (2000), pp. 40–47.

Oxman, Bernard H. and Vincent Bantz. [Case Note] The "Camouco" (Panama v. France) (Judgment). ITLOS Case No. 5, 94 (4) *American Journal of International Law* (2000), pp. 713–721.

Oxman, Bernard H. and Vincent Bantz. [Case Note] The M/V "Saiga" (No.2) (Saint Vincent and the Grenadines v. Guinea), Judgment (ITLOS Case No. 2), 94 (1) *American Journal of International Law* (2000), pp. 140–150.

Rabe, Dieter and Björn-Axel Dissars. International news: Panama v France (The mv "Camouco" International Tribunal for the Law of the Sea, Hamburg) 7 February 2000, 7 (2) *International Maritime Law* (2000), pp. 49–52.

Schiffman, H.S. The Southern Bluefin Tuna Case: ITLOS hears its first fishery dispute, 2 *Journal of International Wildlife Law and Policy* (1999), pp. 318–333.

Scott, Shirley V. Australia's first tuna negotiations with Japan, 24 (4) *Marine Policy* (2000), pp. 309–318.

Van Dyke, Jon M. Louis B. Sohn and the settlement of ocean disputes (a festschrift honoring Professor Louis B. Sohn), 33 (1) *The George Washington International Law Review* (2000), pp. 31–47.

ANNEXES

ANNEX I

(A) STATUS OF THE UNITED NATIONS CONVENTION ON THE LAW OF THE SEA OF 10 DECEMBER 1982

Status as at 31 December 2000.

State, entity	Signature, succession (s)	Ratification, accession (a), formal confirmation (fc), succession (s)
Afghanistan	18 March 1983	
Algeria	10 December 1982	11 June 1996
Angola	10 December 1982	5 December 1990
Antigua and Barbuda	7 February 1983	2 February 1989
Argentina	5 October 1984	1 December 1995
Australia	10 December 1982	5 October 1994
Austria	10 December 1982	14 July 1995
Bahamas	10 December 1982	29 July 1983
Bahrain	10 December 1982	30 May 1985
Bangladesh	10 December 1982	
Barbados	10 December 1982	12 October 1993
Belarus	10 December 1982	
Belgium	5 December 1984	13 November 1998
Belize	10 December 1982	13 August 1983
Benin	30 August 1983	16 October 1997
Bhutan	10 December 1982	
Bolivia	27 November 1984	28 April 1995
Bosnia and Herzegovina		12 January 1994 (s)
Botswana	5 December 1984	2 May 1990
Brazil	10 December 1982	22 December 1988
Brunei Darussalam	5 December 1984	5 November 1996
Bulgaria	10 December 1982	15 May 1996
Burkina Faso	10 December 1982	
Burundi	10 December 1982	
Cambodia	1 July 1983	
Cameroon	10 December 1982	19 November 1985
Canada	10 December 1982	
Cape Verde	10 December 1982	10 August 1987
Central African Republic	4 December 1984	
Chad	10 December 1982	
Chile	10 December 1982	25 August 1997
China	10 December 1982	7 June 1996
Colombia	10 December 1982	
Comoros	6 December 1984	21 June 1994
Congo	10 December 1982	
Cook Islands	10 December 1982	15 February 1995
Costa Rica	10 December 1982	21 September 1992
Côte d'Ivoire	10 December 1982	26 March 1984
Croatia		5 April 1995 (s)
Cuba	10 December 1982	15 August 1984
Cyprus	10 December 1982	12 December 1988
Czech Republic	22 February 1993 (s)	21 June 1996
Democratic People's Republic of Korea	10 December 1982	

Democratic Republic of the Congo	22 August 1983	17 February 1989
Denmark	10 December 1982	
Djibouti	10 December 1982	8 October 1991
Dominica	28 March 1983	24 October 1991
Dominican Republic	10 December 1982	
Egypt	10 December 1982	26 August 1983
El Salvador	5 December 1984	
Equatorial Guinea	30 January 1984	21 July 1997
Ethiopia	10 December 1982	
European Community	7 December 1984	1 April 1998 (fc)
Fiji	10 December 1982	10 December 1982
Finland	10 December 1982	21 June 1996
France	10 December 1982	11 April 1996
Gabon	10 December 1982	11 March 1998
Gambia	10 December 1982	22 May 1984
Georgia		21 March 1996 (a)
Germany		14 October 1994 (a)
Ghana	10 December 1982	7 June 1983
Greece	10 December 1982	21 July 1995
Grenada	10 December 1982	25 April 1991
Guatemala	8 July 1983	11 February 1997
Guinea	4 October 1984	6 September 1985
Guinea-Bissau	10 December 1982	25 August 1986
Guyana	10 December 1982	16 November 1993
Haiti	10 December 1982	31 July 1996
Honduras	10 December 1982	5 October 1993
Hungary	10 December 1982	
Iceland	10 December 1982	21 June 1985
India	10 December 1982	29 June 1995
Indonesia	10 December 1982	3 February 1986
Iran (Islamic Republic of)	10 December 1982	
Iraq	10 December 1982	30 July 1985
Ireland	10 December 1982	21 June 1996
Italy	7 December 1984	13 January 1995
Jamaica	10 December 1982	21 March 1983
Japan	7 February 1983	20 June 1996
Jordan		27 November 1995 (a)
Kenya	10 December 1982	2 March 1989
Kuwait	10 December 1982	2 May 1986
Lao People's Democratic Republic	10 December 1982	5 June 1998
Lebanon	7 December 1984	5 January 1995
Lesotho	10 December 1982	
Liberia	10 December 1982	
Libyan Arab Jamahiriya	3 December 1984	
Liechtenstein	30 November 1984	
Luxembourg	5 December 1984	5 October 2000
Madagascar	25 February 1983	
Malawi	7 December 1984	
Malaysia	10 December 1982	14 October 1996
Maldives	10 December 1982	7 September 2000
Mali	19 October 1983	16 July 1985
Malta	10 December 1982	20 May 1993
Marshall Islands		9 August 1991 (a)
Mauritania	10 December 1982	17 July 1996
Mauritius	10 December 1982	4 November 1994

Mexico	10 December 1982	18 March 1983
Micronesia (Federated States of)		29 April 1991 (a)
Monaco	10 December 1982	20 March 1996
Mongolia	10 December 1982	13 August 1996
Morocco	10 December 1982	
Mozambique	10 December 1982	13 March 1997
Myanmar	10 December 1982	21 May 1996
Namibia	10 December 1982	18 April 1983
Nauru	10 December 1982	23 January 1996
Nepal	10 December 1982	2 November 1998
Netherlands	10 December 1982	28 June 1996
New Zealand	10 December 1982	19 July 1996
Nicaragua	9 December 1984	3 May 2000
Niger	10 December 1982	
Nigeria	10 December 1982	14 August 1986
Niue	5 December 1984	
Norway	10 December 1982	24 June 1996
Oman	1 July 1983	17 August 1989
Pakistan	10 December 1982	26 February 1997
Palau		30 September 1996 (a)
Panama	10 December 1982	1 July 1996
Papua New Guinea	10 December 1982	14 January 1997
Paraguay	10 December 1982	26 September 1986
Philippines	10 December 1982	8 May 1984
Poland	10 December 1982	13 November 1998
Portugal	10 December 1982	3 November 1997
Qatar	27 November 1984	
Republic of Korea	14 March 1983	29 January 1996
Romania	10 December 1982	17 December 1996
Russian Federation	10 December 1982	12 March 1997
Rwanda	10 December 1982	
Saint Kitts and Nevis	7 December 1984	7 January 1993
Saint Lucia	10 December 1982	27 March 1985
Saint Vincent and the Grenadines	10 December 1982	1 October 1993
Samoa	28 September 1984	14 August 1995
Sao Tome and Principe	13 July 1983	3 November 1987
Saudi Arabia	7 December 1984	24 April 1996
Senegal	10 December 1982	25 October 1984
Seychelles	10 December 1982	16 September 1991
Sierra Leone	10 December 1982	12 December 1994
Singapore	10 December 1982	17 November 1994
Slovakia	28 May 1993 (s)	8 May 1996
Slovenia		16 June 1995 (s)
Solomon Islands	10 December 1982	23 June 1997
Somalia	10 December 1982	24 July 1989
South Africa	5 December 1984	23 December 1997
Spain	4 December 1984	15 January 1997
Sri Lanka	10 December 1982	19 July 1994
Sudan	10 December 1982	23 January 1985
Suriname	10 December 1982	9 July 1998
Swaziland	18 January 1984	
Sweden	10 December 1982	25 June 1996
Switzerland	17 October 1984	
Thailand	10 December 1982	

The former Yugoslav Republic of Macedonia		19 August 1994 (s)
Togo	10 December 1982	16 April 1985
Tonga		2 August 1995 (a)
Trinidad and Tobago	10 December 1982	25 April 1986
Tunisia	10 December 1982	24 April 1985
Tuvalu	10 December 1982	
Uganda	10 December 1982	9 November 1990
Ukraine	10 December 1982	26 July 1999
United Arab Emirates	10 December 1982	
United Kingdom of Great Britain and Northern Ireland		25 July 1997 (a)
United Republic of Tanzania	10 December 1982	30 September 1985
Uruguay	10 December 1982	10 December 1992
Vanuatu	10 December 1982	10 August 1999
Viet Nam	10 December 1982	25 July 1994
Yemen	10 December 1982	21 July 1987
Yugoslavia	10 December 1982	5 May 1986
Zambia	10 December 1982	7 March 1983
Zimbabwe	10 December 1982	24 February 1993
TOTALS	**158**	**135**

(B) STATUS OF THE AGREEMENT RELATING TO THE IMPLEMENTATION OF PART XI OF THE UNITED NATIONS CONVENTION ON THE LAW OF THE SEA OF 10 DECEMBER 1982, ADOPTED ON 28 JULY 1994

Status as at 31 December 2000.

State, entity	Signature	Provisional application by virtue of a notification (n), signature, adoption of the Agreement or accession thereto	Notification under article 7(1)(b) that the Agreement will not apply provisionally	Ratification, accession (a), formal confirmation (fc) definitive signature (s), simplified procedure (p) or consent to be bound after deposit of an instrument of ratification, accession or succession in respect of the Convention (P)
Afghanistan		16 November 1994		
Albania		16 November 1994		
Algeria	29 July 1994	16 November 1994		11 June 1996 (P)
Andorra		16 November 1994		
Argentina	29 July 1994	16 November 1994		1 December 1995
Armenia		16 November 1994		
Australia	29 July 1994	16 November 1994		5 October 1994

Austria	29 July 1994	16 November 1994		14 July 1995
Bahamas	29 July 1994	16 November 1994		28 July 1995 (p)
Bahrain		16 November 1994		
Bangladesh		16 November 1994		
Barbados	15 November 1994	16 November 1994		28 July 1995 (p)
Belarus		16 November 1994		
Belgium	29 July 1994	16 November 1994		13 November 1998
Belize		16 November 1994		21 October 1994 (s)
Benin		16 November 1994		16 October 1997 (P)
Bhutan		16 November 1994		
Bolivia		16 November 1994		28 April 1995 (P)
Botswana		16 November 1994		
Brazil	29 July 1994		29 July 1994	
Brunei Darussalam		16 November 1994		5 November 1996 (P)
Bulgaria		15 May 1996	15 November 1994	15 May 1996 (a)
Burkina Faso	30 November 1994	30 November 1994		
Burundi		16 November 1994		
Cambodia		16 November 1994		
Cameroon	24 May 1995	24 May 1995	15 November 1994	
Canada	29 July 1994	16 November 1994		
Cape Verde	29 July 1994	16 November 1994		
Chile		16 November 1994		25 August 1997 (a)
China	29 July 1994	16 November 1994		7 June 1996 (P)
Congo		16 November 1994		
Cook Islands				15 February 1995 (a)
Côte d'Ivoire	25 November 1994	16 November 1994		28 July 1995 (p)
Croatia				5 April 1995 (P)
Cuba		16 November 1994		
Cyprus	1 November 1994	27 July 1995	15 November 1994	27 July 1995
Czech Republic	16 November 1994	16 November 1994		21 June 1996
Denmark	29 July 1994		29 July 1994	
Egypt	22 March 199	16 November 1994		
Equatorial Guinea				21 July 1997 (P)
Eritrea		16 November 1994		
Estonia		16 November 1994		
Ethiopia		16 November 1994		
European Community	29 July 1994	16 November 1994		1 April 1998 (fc)
Fiji	29 July 1994	16 November 1994		28 July 1995
Finland	29 July 1994	16 November 1994		21 June 1996
France	29 July 1994	16 November 1994		11 April 1996
Gabon	4 April 1995	16 November 1994		11 March 1998 (P)
Georgia				21 March 1996 (P)
Germany	29 July 1994	16 November 1994		14 October 1994
Ghana		16 November 1994		
Greece	29 July 1994	16 November 1994		21 July 1995
Grenada	14 November 1994	16 November 1994		28 July 1995 (p)
Guatemala				11 February 1997 (P)
Guinea	26 August 1994	16 November 1994		28 July 1995 (p)
Guyana		16 November 1994		
Haiti				31 July 1996 (P)
Honduras		16 November 1994		

Hungary		16 November 1994		
Iceland	29 July 1994	16 November 1994		28 July 1995 (p)
India	29 July 1994	16 November 1994		29 June 1995
Indonesia	29 July 1994	16 November 1994		2 June 2000
Iran (Islamic Republic of)			1 November 1994	
Iraq	16 November 1994			
Ireland	29 July 1994		29 July 1994	21 June 1996
Italy	29 July 1994	16 November 1994	29 July 1994	13 January 1995
Jamaica	29 July 1994	16 November 1994		28 July 1995 (p)
Japan	29 July 1994	16 November 1994		20 June 1996
Jordan			14 November 1994	27 November 1995 (P)
Kenya		16 November 1994		29 July 1994 (s)
Kuwait		16 November 1994		
Lao People's Democratic Republic	27 October 1994	16 November 1994		5 June 1998 (P)
Lebanon				5 January 1995 (P)
Libyan Arab Jamahiriya		16 November 1994		
Liechtenstein		16 November 1994		
Luxembourg	29 July 1994	16 November 1994		5 October 2000
Madagascar		16 November 1994		
Malaysia	2 August 1994	16 November 1994		14 October 1996 (P)
Maldives	10 October 1994	16 November 1994		7 September 2000 (P)
Malta	29 July 1994	16 November 1994		26 June 1996
Marshall Islands		16 November 1994		
Mauritania	2 August 1994	16 November 1994		17 July 1996 (P)
Mauritius		16 November 1994		4 November 1994 (P)
Mexico			2 November 1994	
Micronesia (Federated States of)	10 August 1994	16 November 1994		6 September 1995
Monaco	30 November 1994	16 November 1994		20 March 1996 (P)
Mongolia	17 August 1994	16 November 1994		13 August 1996 (P)
Morocco	19 October 1994		19 October 1994	
Mozambique		16 November 1994		13 March 1997 (a)
Myanmar		16 November 1994		21 May 1996 (a)
Namibia	29 July 1994	16 November 1994		28 July 1995 (p)
Nauru				23 January 1996 (P)
Nepal		16 November 1994		2 November 1998 (P)
Netherlands	29 July 1994	16 November 1994		28 June 1996
New Zealand	29 July 1994	16 November 1994		19 July 1996
Nicaragua				3 May 2000 (P)
Nigeria	25 October 1994	16 November 1994		28 July 1995 (p)
Norway		16 November 1994		24 June 1996 (a)
Oman		16 November 1994		26 February 1997 (a)
Pakistan	10 August 1994	16 November 1994		26 February 1997 (P)
Palau				30 September 1996 (P)
Panama				1 July 1996 (P)
Papua New Guinea		16 November 1994		14 January 1997 (P)
Paraguay	29 July 1994	16 November 1994		10 July 1995
Philippines	15 November 1994	16 November 1994		23 July 1997

Poland	29 July 1994	23 February 1995		13 November 1998 (P)
Portugal	29 July 1994		29 July 1994	3 November 1997
Qatar		16 November 1994		
Republic of Korea	7 November 1994	16 November 1994		29 January 1996
Republic of Moldova		16 November 1994		
Romania			4 October 1994	17 December 1996 (a)
Russian Federation		11 January 1995		12 March 1997 (a)
Samoa	7 July 1995	16 November 1994		14 August 1995 (P)
Saudi Arabia			9 November 1994	24 April 1996 (P)
Senegal	9 August 1994	16 November 1994		25 July 1995
Seychelles	29 July 1994	16 November 1994		15 December 1994
Sierra Leone		16 November 1994		12 December 1994 (P)
Singapore		16 November 1994		17 November 1994 (P)
Slovakia	14 November 1994	16 November 1994		8 May 1996
Slovenia	19 January 1995	16 June 1995	15 November 1994	16 June 1995
Solomon Islands		8 February 1995		23 June 1997 (P)
South Africa	3 October 1994	16 November 1994		23 December 1997
Spain	29 July 1994			15 January 1997
Sri Lanka	29 July 1994	16 November 1994		28 July 1995 (p)
Sudan	29 July 1994	16 November 1994		
Suriname		16 November 1994		9 July 1998 (P)
Swaziland	12 October 1994	16 November 1994		
Sweden	29 July 1994		29 July 1994	25 June 1996
Switzerland	26 October 1994	16 November 1994		
The former Yugoslav Republic of Macedonia		16 November 1994		19 August 1994 (P)
Togo	3 August 1994	16 November 1994		28 July 1995 (p)
Tonga				2 August 1995 (P)
Trinidad and Tobago	10 October 1994	16 November 1994		28 July 1995 (p)
Tunisia	15 May 1995	16 November 1994		
Uganda	9 August 1994	16 November 1994		28 July 1995 (p)
Ukraine	28 February 1995	16 November 1994		26 July 1999
United Arab Emirates		16 November 1994		
United Kingdom of Great Britain and Northern Ireland	29 July 1994	16 November 1994		25 July 1997
United Republic of Tanzania	7 October 1994	16 November 1994		25 June 1998
United States of America	29 July 1994	16 November 1994		
Uruguay	29 July 1994		29 July 1994	
Vanuatu	29 July 1994	16 November 1994		10 August 1999(p)
Viet Nam		16 November 1994		
Yugoslavia	12 May 1995			28 July 1995 (p)
Zambia	13 October 1994	16 November 1994		28 July 1995 (p)
Zimbabwe	28 October 1994	16 November 1994		28 July 1995 (p)

ANNEX II

(A) DECLARATIONS OF STATES PARTIES RELATING TO SETTLEMENT OF DISPUTES IN ACCORDANCE WITH ARTICLE 287 (CHOICE OF PROCEDURE)

Algeria

[Original: French]

The People's Democratic Republic of Algeria does not consider itself bound by the provisions of article 287, paragraph 1 (b), of the United Nations Convention on the Law of the Sea dealing with the submission of disputes to the International Court of Justice.

The People's Democratic Republic of Algeria declares that, in order to submit a dispute to the International Court of Justice, prior agreement between all the parties concerned is necessary in each case.

Argentina

[Original: Spanish]

In accordance with the provisions of article 287, the Argentine Government declares that it accepts, in order of preference, the following means for the settlement of disputes concerning the interpretation or application of the Convention:

(a) the International Tribunal for the Law of the Sea;
(b) an arbitral tribunal constituted in accordance with Annex VIII for questions relating to fisheries, protection and preservation of the marine environment, marine scientific research and navigation, in accordance with Annex VIII, article 1.

Austria

"In the absence of any other peaceful means to which it would give preference the Government of the Republic of Austria hereby chooses one of the following means for the settlement of disputes concerning the interpretation or application of the [United Nations Convention on the Law of the Sea and the Agreement relating to the Implementation of Part XI of the United Nations Convention on the Law of the Sea] in accordance with article 287 of the Convention on the Law of the Sea, in the following order:

1. the International Tribunal for the Law of the Sea established in accordance with Annex VI;
2. a special arbitral tribunal constituted in accordance with Annex VIII;
3. the International Court of Justice.

Also in absence of any other peaceful means, the Government of the Republic of Austria hereby recognizes as of today the validity of special arbitration for any dispute concerning the interpretation or application of the Convention on the Law of the Sea relating to fisheries, protection and preservation of the marine environment, marine scientific research and navigation, including pollution from vessels and by dumping."

Belgium

Declaration made upon signature
[Original: French]
In the absence of any other peaceful means to which it obviously gives priority, the Government of the Kingdom of Belgium deems it expedient to choose alternatively, and in order of preference, as article 287 of the Convention leaves it free to do, the following means of settling disputes concerning the interpretation or application of the Convention:

1. an arbitral tribunal constituted in accordance with Annex VIII;
2. the International Tribunal for the Law of the Sea established in accordance with Annex VI;
3. the International Court of Justice.

Still in the absence of any other peaceful means, the Government of the Kingdom of Belgium wishes here and now to recognize the validity of the special arbitration procedure for any dispute concerning the interpretation or application of the provisions of the Convention in respect of fisheries, protection and preservation of the marine environment, marine scientific research or navigation, including pollution from vessels and by dumping.

Declaration made upon ratification
[Original: French]
In accordance with article 287 of the Convention, the Kingdom of Belgium hereby declares that it chooses, as a means for the settlement of disputes concerning the interpretation or application of the Convention, in view of its preference for pre-established jurisdictions, either the International Tribunal for the Law of the Sea established in accordance with Annex VI (art. 287(1)(a)) or the International Court of Justice (art. 287(1)(b)), in the absence of any other means of peaceful settlement of disputes that it might prefer.

Cape Verde

"The Republic of Cape Verde declares that, in the absence of or failing any other peaceful means, it chooses, in order of preference and in accordance with article 287 of the United Nations Convention on the Law of the Sea, the following procedures for the settlement of disputes regarding the interpretation or application of the said Convention:

(a) The International Tribunal for the Law of the Sea;
(b) The International Court of Justice."

Chile

[Original: Spanish]
With regard to Part XV of the Convention, the Republic of Chile declares that:
(a) In accordance with article 287 of the Convention, it accepts, in order of preference, the following means for the settlement of disputes concerning the interpretation or application of the Convention:
(i) the International Tribunal for the Law of the Sea established in accordance with Annex VI;

(ii) a special arbitral tribunal, established in accordance with Annex VIII, for the categories of disputes specified therein relating to fisheries, protection and preservation of the marine environment, marine scientific research and navigation, including pollution from vessels and by dumping.

(b) in accordance with articles 280 to 282 of the Convention, the choice of means for the settlement of disputes indicated in the preceding paragraph shall in no way affect the obligations deriving from the general, regional or bilateral agreements to which the Republic of Chile is a party concerning the peaceful settlement of disputes.

Croatia

"In implementation of article 287 of the United Nations Convention on the Law of the Sea, the Government of the Republic of Croatia has the honour to declare that, for the settlement of disputes concerning the application or interpretation of the Convention and of the Agreement adopted on 28 July 1994 relating to the Implementation of Part XI, it chooses, in order of preference, the following means:

1. The International Tribunal for the Law of the Sea established in accordance with Annex VI;
2. The International Court of Justice."

Cuba

[Original: Spanish]

With regard to article 287 on the choice of procedure for the settlement of disputes concerning the interpretation or application of the Convention, the Government of the Republic of Cuba declares that it does not accept the jurisdiction of the International Court of Justice and, consequently, will not accept either the jurisdiction of the Court with respect to the provisions of either article 297 or 298.

Egypt

[Original: Arabic]

The Arab Republic of Egypt,

In ratifying the United Nations Convention on the Law of the Sea, hereinafter referred to as "the Convention", which it signed at Montego Bay, Jamaica, on 10 December 1982,

Acting in conformity with article 287 of the Convention,

Hereby issues the following declaration:

The Arab Republic of Egypt declares that it accepts the arbitral procedure the modalities of which are defined in Annex VII to the Convention as the procedure for the settlement of any dispute which might arise between Egypt and any other State concerning the interpretation or application of the Convention.

The Arab Republic of Egypt further declares that it excludes from the scope of application of this procedure those disputes considered to be exceptions under article 297 of the Convention.

Finland

"In accordance with article 287 of the Convention, Finland chooses the International Court of Justice and the International Tribunal for the Law of the Sea as means for the settlement of disputes concerning the interpretation or application of the Convention as well as of the Agreement Relating to the implementation of its Part XI."

Germany

[Original: German]

In the absence of any other peaceful means, which would be given preference by the Government of the Federal Republic of Germany, that Government considers it useful to choose one of the following means for the settlement of disputes concerning the interpretation or application of the [United Nations Convention on the Law of the Sea and the Agreement relating to the Implementation of Part XI of the United Nations Convention on the Law of the Sea], as it is free to do under article 287 of the Convention on the Law of the Sea, in the following order:

1. the International Tribunal for the Law of the Sea established in accordance with Annex VI;
2. an arbitral tribunal constituted in accordance with Annex VII;
3. the International Court of Justice.

Also in the absence of any other peaceful means, the Government of the Federal Republic of Germany hereby recognizes as of today the validity of special arbitration for any dispute concerning the interpretation or application of the Convention on the Law of the Sea relating to fisheries, protection and preservation of the marine environment, marine scientific research and navigation, including pollution from vessels and by dumping.

Greece

"Pursuant to article 287 of the United Nations Convention on the Law of the Sea, the Government of the Hellenic Republic hereby chooses the International Tribunal for the Law of the Sea established in accordance with Annex VI to the Convention as the means for the settlement of disputes concerning the interpretation or application of the Convention."

Guinea-Bissau

[Original: Portuguese]

The Government of the Republic of Guinea-Bissau declares that, as regards article 287 on the choice of a procedure for the settlement of disputes concerning the interpretation or application of the United Nations Convention on the Law of the Sea, it does not accept the jurisdiction of the International Court of Justice and consequently will not accept that jurisdiction with respect to articles 297 and 298.

Italy

"In implementation of article 287 of the United Nations Convention on the Law of the Sea, the Government of Italy has the honour to declare that, for the settlement of disputes concerning the application or interpretation of the Convention and of the Agreement adopted on 28 July 1994 relating to the Implementation of Part XI, it chooses the International Tribunal for the Law of the Sea and the International Court of Justice, without specifying that one has precedence over the other.

In making this declaration under article 287 of the Convention on the Law of the Sea, the Government of Italy is reaffirming its confidence in the existing international judicial organs. In accordance with article 287, paragraph 4, Italy considers that it has chosen 'the same procedure' as any other State Party that has chosen the International Tribunal for the Law of the Sea or the International Court of Justice."

Netherlands

"The Kingdom of the Netherlands hereby declares that, having regard to article 287 of the Convention, it accepts the jurisdiction of the International Court of Justice in the settlement of disputes concerning the interpretation and application of the Convention with States Parties to the Convention which have likewise accepted the said jurisdiction."

Nicaragua

[Original: Spanish]
In accordance with article 287, paragraph 1, of the Convention, Nicaragua hereby declares that it accepts only recourse to the International Court of Justice as a means for the settlement of disputes concerning the interpretation or application of the Convention.

Norway

"The Government of the Kingdom of Norway declares pursuant to article 287 of the Convention that it chooses the International Court of Justice for the settlement of disputes concerning the interpretation or application of the Convention."

Oman

[Original: Arabic]
Pursuant to article 287 of the Convention, the Sultanate of Oman declares its acceptance of the jurisdiction of the International Tribunal for the Law of the Sea, as set forth in Annex VI to the Convention, and the jurisdiction of the International Court of Justice, with a view to the settlement of any dispute that may arise between it and another State concerning the interpretation or application of the Convention.

Portugal

[Original: Portuguese]
For the purposes of article 287 of the Convention, Portugal declares that, in the absence of non-judicial means for the settlement of disputes arising out of the application of this Convention, it will choose one of the following means for the settlement of disputes:

(a) the International Tribunal for the Law of the Sea, established in pursuance of Annex VI;
(b) the International Court of Justice;
(c) an arbitral tribunal, constituted in accordance with Annex VII;
(d) a special arbitral tribunal, constituted in accordance with Annex VIII.

In the absence of any other peaceful means for the settlement of disputes, Portugal will, in accordance with Annex VIII to the Convention, choose the recourse to a special arbitral tribunal in so far as the application of the provisions of the Convention, or the interpretation thereof, to the matters relating to fisheries, protection and preservation of marine living resources and the marine environment, marine scientific research, navigation and marine pollution are concerned.

Russian Federation

Declaration made upon signature by the Union of Soviet Socialist Republics
[Original: Russian]

The Union of Soviet Socialist Republics declares that, under article 287 of the United Nations Convention on the Law of the Sea, it chooses an arbitral tribunal constituted in accordance with Annex VII as the basic means for the settlement of disputes concerning the interpretation or application of the Convention. It opts for a special arbitral tribunal constituted in accordance with Annex VIII for the consideration of matters relating to fisheries, the protection and preservation of the marine environment, marine scientific research, and navigation, including pollution from vessels and dumping. It recognizes the competence of the International Tribunal for the Law of the Sea, as provided for in article 292, in matters relating to the prompt release of detained vessels and crews.

Spain

[Original: Spanish]

In accordance with the provisions of paragraph 1 of article 287, Spain chooses the International Court of Justice as the means for the settlement of disputes concerning the interpretation or application of the Convention.

Sweden

"The Government of the Kingdom of Sweden hereby chooses, in accordance with article 287 of the Convention, the International Court of Justice for the settlement of disputes concerning the interpretation or application of the Convention and the Agreement Implementing Part XI of the Convention."

Ukraine

Declaration made upon signature by the Ukrainian Soviet Socialist Republic
[Original: Russian]

The Ukrainian Soviet Socialist Republic declares that, in accordance with article 287 of the United Nations Convention on the Law of the Sea, it chooses as the principal means for the settlement of disputes concerning the interpretation or application of this Convention an arbitral tribunal constituted in accordance with Annex VII. For the consideration of questions relating to fisheries, protection and preservation of the marine environment, marine scientific research and navigation, including pollution from vessels and by dumping, the Ukrainian SSR chooses a special arbitral tribunal constituted in accordance with Annex VIII. The Ukrainian SSR recognizes the competence, as stipulated in article 292, of the International Tribunal for the Law of the Sea in respect of questions relating to the prompt release of detained vessels or their crews.

Declaration made upon ratification

[Original: Ukrainian]

Ukraine declares that, in accordance with article 287 of the United Nations Convention on the Law of the Sea of 1982, it chooses as the principal means for the settlement of disputes concerning the interpretation or application of this Convention an arbitral tribunal constituted in accordance with Annex VII. For the consideration of disputes concerning the interpretation or application of the Convention in respect of questions relating to fisheries, protection and preservation of the marine environment, marine scientific research and navigation, including pollution from vessels and by dumping, Ukraine chooses a special arbitral tribunal constituted in accordance with Annex VIII.

Ukraine recognizes the competence, as stipulated in article 292 of the Convention, of the International Tribunal for the Law of the Sea in respect of questions relating to the prompt release of detained vessels or their crews.

United Kingdom of Great Britain and Northern Ireland

"In accordance with article 287, paragraph 1, of the United Nations Convention on the Law of the Sea, the United Kingdom of Great Britain and Northern Ireland chooses the International Court of Justice for the settlement of disputes concerning the interpretation or application of the Convention.

The International Tribunal for the Law of the Sea is a new institution, which the United Kingdom hopes will make an important contribution to the peaceful settlement of disputes concerning the law of the sea. In addition to those cases where the Convention itself provides for the compulsory jurisdiction of the Tribunal, the United Kingdom remains ready to consider the submission of disputes to the Tribunal as may be agreed upon on a case-by-case basis."

United Republic of Tanzania

"In accordance with article 287 of the United Nations Convention on the Law of the Sea, the United Republic of Tanzania declares that it chooses the International Tribunal for the Law of the Sea for the settlement of disputes concerning the interpretation or application of the Convention."

Uruguay

[Original: Spanish]

Pursuant to the provisions of article 287, Uruguay declares that it chooses the International Tribunal for the Law of the Sea for the settlement of such disputes relating to the interpretation or application of the Convention as are not subject to other procedures, without prejudice to its recognition of the jurisdiction of the International Court of Justice and of such agreements with other States as may provide for other means for peaceful settlement.

(B) DECLARATIONS OF STATES PARTIES RELATING TO SETTLEMENT OF DISPUTES IN ACCORDANCE WITH ARTICLE 298 (OPTIONAL EXCEPTIONS TO THE APPLICABILITY OF PART XV, SECTION 2, OF THE CONVENTION)

Argentina

[Original: Spanish]

The Argentine Government also declares that it does not accept the procedures provided for in Part XV, section 2, with respect to the disputes specified in article 298, paragraph 1 (a), (b) and (c).

Cape Verde

"The Republic of Cape Verde, in accordance with article 298 of the United Nations Convention on the Law of the Sea, declares that it does not accept the procedures provided for in Part XV, Section 2, of the said Convention for the settlement of disputes concerning military activities, including military activities by government-operated vessels and aircraft engaged in non-commercial service, as well as disputes concerning law enforcement activities in regard to the exercise of sovereign rights or jurisdiction excluded from the jurisdiction of a court or tribunal under article 297, paragraphs 2 and 3, of the aforementioned Convention."

Chile

[Original: Spanish]

In accordance with article 298 of the Convention, Chile declares that it does not accept any of the procedures provided for in Part XV, section 2, with respect to the disputes referred to in article 298, paragraphs 1 (a), (b) and (c), of the Convention.

Cuba

[Original: Spanish]

With regard to article 287 on the choice of procedure for the settlement of disputes concerning the interpretation or application of the Convention, the Government of the Republic of Cuba declares that it does not accept the jurisdiction of the International Court of Justice and, consequently, will not accept either the jurisdiction of the Court with respect to the provisions of either article 297 or 298.

France

[Original: French]

With reference to the provisions of article 298, paragraph 1, France does not accept any of the procedures provided for in Part XV, section 2, with respect to the following disputes:

- Disputes concerning the interpretation or application of articles 15, 74 and 83 relating to sea boundary delimitations, or those involving historic bays or titles;
- Disputes concerning military activities, including military activities by governmental vessels and aircraft engaged in non-commercial service, and disputes concerning law enforcement activities in regard to the exercise of sovereign rights or jurisdiction excluded from the jurisdiction of a court or tribunal under article 297, paragraph 2 or 3;

- Disputes in respect of which the Security Council of the United Nations is exercising the functions assigned to it by the Charter of the United Nations, unless the Security Council decides to remove the matter from its agenda or calls upon the parties to settle it by the means provided for in the Convention.

Guinea-Bissau

[Original: Portuguese]
The Government of the Republic of Guinea-Bissau declares that, as regards article 287 on the choice of a procedure for the settlement of disputes concerning the interpretation or application of the United Nations Convention on the Law of the Sea, it does not accept the jurisdiction of the International Court of Justice and consequently will not accept that jurisdiction with respect to articles 297 and 298.

Iceland

"Upon depositing the instrument of ratification of the United Nations Convention on the Law of the Sea, the Permanent Representative of Iceland, on behalf of the Government of Iceland, declares that under article 298 of the Convention the right is reserved that any interpretation of article 83 shall be submitted to conciliation under annex V, section 2 of the Convention."

Italy

"Italy has the honour to declare, under paragraph 1 (a) of article 298 of the Convention, that it does not accept any of the procedures provided for in section 2 of Part XV with respect to disputes concerning the interpretation of articles 15, 74 and 83 relating to sea boundary delimitations as well as those involving historic bays or titles."

Nicaragua

[Original: Spanish]
Nicaragua hereby declares that it accepts only recourse to the International Court of Justice as a means for the settlement of the categories of disputes set forth in subparagraphs (a), (b) and (c) of paragraph 1 of article 298 of the Convention.

Norway

"The Government of the Kingdom of Norway declares pursuant to Article 298 of the Convention that it does not accept an arbitral tribunal constituted in accordance with Annex VII for any of the categories of disputes mentioned in Article 298."

Portugal

[Original: Portuguese]
Portugal declares that, without prejudice to the provisions contained in Part XV, section 1, of the Convention, it does not accept the compulsory procedures referred to in section 2 of the said Part, with respect to one or more of the categories specified in article 298, subparagraphs 1 (a), (b) and (c), of the Convention.

Russian Federation

Declaration made upon signature by the Union of Soviet Socialist Republics
[Original: Russian]
The Union of Soviet Socialist Republics declares that, in accordance with article 298 of the Convention, it does not accept the compulsory procedures entailing binding decisions for the consideration of disputes relating to sea boundary delimitations, disputes concerning military activities, or disputes in respect of which the Security Council of the United Nations is exercising the functions assigned to it by the Charter of the United Nations.

Declaration made upon ratification
[Original: Russian]
The Russian Federation declares that, in accordance with article 298 of the United Nations Convention on the Law of the Sea, it does not accept the procedures, provided for in section 2 of Part XV of the Convention, entailing binding decisions with respect to disputes concerning the interpretation or application of articles 15, 74 and 83 of the Convention, relating to sea boundary delimitations, or those involving historic bays or titles; disputes concerning military activities, including military activities by government vessels and aircraft, and disputes concerning law-enforcement activities in regard to the exercise of sovereign rights or jurisdiction; and disputes in respect of which the Security Council of the United Nations is exercising the functions assigned to it by the Charter of the United Nations.

Tunisia

[Original: Arabic]
The Republic of Tunisia, in accordance with the provisions of article 298 of the United Nations Convention on the Law of the Sea, declares that it does not accept the procedures provided for in Part XV, section 2, of the said Convention with respect to the following categories of disputes:

(a) (i) Disputes concerning the interpretation or application of articles 15, 74 and 83 relating to sea boundary delimitations, or those involving historic bays or titles, provided that a State having made such a declaration shall, when such a dispute arises subsequent to the entry into force of this Convention and where no agreement within a reasonable period of time is reached in negotiations between the parties, at the request of any party to the dispute, accept submission of the matter to conciliation under Annex V, section 2; and provided further that any dispute that necessarily involves the concurrent consideration of any unsettled dispute concerning sovereignty or other rights over continental or insular land territory shall be excluded from such submission;

(ii) After the conciliation commission has presented its report, which shall state the reasons on which it is based, the parties shall negotiate an agreement on the basis of that report; if these negotiations do not result in an agreement, the parties shall, by mutual consent, submit the question to one of the procedures provided for in section 2, unless the parties otherwise agree;

(iii) This subparagraph does not apply to any sea boundary dispute finally settled by an agreement between the parties, or to any such dispute which is to be settled in accordance with a bilateral or multilateral agreement binding upon those parties;

(b) Disputes concerning military activities, including military activities by governmental vessels and aircraft engaged in non-commercial service, and disputes concerning law enforcement activities in regard to the exercise of sovereign rights or jurisdiction excluded from the jurisdiction of a court or tribunal under article 297, paragraph 2 or 3;

(c) Disputes in respect of which the Security Council of the United Nations is exercising the functions assigned to it by the Charter of the United Nations, unless the Security Council decides to remove the matter from its agenda or calls upon the parties to settle it by the means provided for in this Convention.

Ukraine

Declaration made upon signature by the Ukrainian Soviet Socialist Republic

[Original: Russian]

The Ukrainian Soviet Socialist Republic declares, in accordance with article 298 of the Convention, that it does not accept compulsory procedures, involving binding decisions, for the consideration of disputes relating to sea boundary delimitations, disputes concerning military activities and disputes in respect of which the Security Council of the United Nations is exercising the functions assigned to it by the Charter of the United Nations.

Declaration made upon ratification

[Original: Ukrainian]

Ukraine declares, in accordance with article 298 of the Convention, that it does not accept, unless otherwise provided by specific international treaties of Ukraine with relevant States, the compulsory procedures entailing binding decisions for the consideration of disputes relating to sea boundary delimitations, disputes involving historic bays or titles, and disputes concerning military activities.

Uruguay

[Original: Spanish]

Pursuant to the provisions of article 298, Uruguay declares that it will not accept the procedures provided for in Part XV, section 2, of the Convention, in respect of disputes concerning law enforcement activities in regard to the exercise of sovereign rights or jurisdiction excluded from the jurisdiction of a court or tribunal under article 297, paragraphs 2 and 3.

ANNEX III

RELEVANT PROVISIONS OF INTERNATIONAL AGREEMENTS CONFERRING JURISDICTION ON THE TRIBUNAL

Below is a list of international agreements containing provisions relating to the jurisdiction of the International Tribunal for the Law of the Sea. The list is not necessarily exhaustive.

(A) 1996 PROTOCOL TO THE CONVENTION ON THE PREVENTION OF MARINE POLLUTION BY DUMPING OF WASTES AND OTHER MATTER, 1972

Adopted on 7 November 1996 by the Special Meeting of Contracting Parties to the London Convention 1972.

NOT YET IN FORCE
TEXT: IMO document LC/SM 1/6 of 14 November 1996; 36 ILM (1997) 7-20

Article 16
Settlement of disputes

1. Any disputes regarding the interpretation or application of this Protocol shall be resolved in the first instance through negotiation, mediation or conciliation, or other peaceful means chosen by parties to the dispute.

2. If no resolution is possible within twelve months after one Contracting Party has notified another that a dispute exists between them, the dispute shall be settled, at the request of a party to the dispute, by means of the Arbitral Procedure set forth in Annex 3, unless the parties to the dispute agree to use one of the procedures listed in paragraph 1 of Article 287 of the 1982 United Nations Convention on the Law of the Sea. The parties to the dispute may so agree, whether or not they are also States Parties to the 1982 United Nations Convention on the Law of the Sea.

3. In the event an agreement to use one of the procedures listed in paragraph 1 of article 287 of the 1982 United Nations Convention on the Law of the Sea is reached, the provisions set forth in Part XV of that Convention that are related to the chosen procedure would also apply, *mutatis mutandis*.

4. The twelve month period referred to in paragraph 2 may be extended for another twelve months by mutual consent of the parties concerned.

5. Notwithstanding paragraph 2, any State may, at the time it expresses its consent to be bound by this Protocol, notify the Secretary-General that, when it is a party to a dispute about the interpretation or application of article 3.1 or 3.2, its consent will be required before the dispute may be settled by means of the Arbitral Procedure set forth in Annex 3.

(B) AGREEMENT FOR THE IMPLEMENTATION OF THE PROVISIONS OF THE UNITED NATIONS CONVENTION ON THE LAW OF THE SEA OF 10 DECEMBER 1982 RELATING TO THE CONSERVATION AND MANAGEMENT OF STRADDLING FISH STOCKS AND HIGHLY MIGRATORY FISH STOCKS

Adopted on 4 August 1995 by the United Nations Conference on Straddling Fish Stocks and Highly Migratory Fish Stocks at New York. Opened for signature on 4 December 1995.

NOT YET IN FORCE
TEXT: Doc. A/CONF.164/37; 34 ILM (1995) 1547-80

Article 30
Procedures for the settlement of disputes

1. The provisions relating to the settlement of disputes set out in Part XV of the Convention apply *mutatis mutandis* to any dispute between States Parties to this Agreement concerning the interpretation or application of this Agreement, whether or not they are also Parties to the Convention.

2. The provisions relating to the settlement of disputes set out in Part XV of the Convention apply *mutatis mutandis* to any dispute between States Parties to this Agreement concerning the interpretation or application of a subregional, regional or global fisheries agreement relating to straddling fish stocks or highly migratory fish stocks to which they are parties, including any dispute concerning the conservation and management of such stocks, whether or not they are also Parties to the Convention.

3. Any procedure accepted by a State Party to this Agreement and the Convention pursuant to article 287 of the Convention shall apply to the settlement of disputes under this Part, unless that State Party, when signing, ratifying or acceding to this Agreement, or at any time thereafter, has accepted another procedure pursuant to article 287 for the settlement of disputes under this Part.

4. A State Party to this Agreement which is not a Party to the Convention, when signing, ratifying or acceding to this Agreement, or at any time thereafter, shall be free to choose, by means of a written declaration, one or more of the means set out in article 287, paragraph 1, of the Convention for the settlement of disputes under this Part. Article 287 shall apply to such a declaration, as well as to any dispute to which such State is a party which is not covered by a declaration in force. For the purposes of conciliation and arbitration in accordance with Annexes V, VII and VIII to the Convention, such State shall be entitled to nominate conciliators, arbitrators and experts to be included in the lists referred to in Annex V, article 2, Annex VII, article 2, and Annex VIII, article 2, for the settlement of disputes under this Part.

5. Any court or tribunal to which a dispute has been submitted under this Part shall apply the relevant provisions of the Convention, of this Agreement and of any relevant subregional, regional or global fisheries agreement, as well as generally accepted standards for the conservation and management of living marine resources and other rules of international

law not incompatible with the Convention, with a view to ensuring the conservation of the straddling fish stocks and highly migratory fish stocks concerned.

Article 31
Provisional measures

1. Pending the settlement of a dispute in accordance with this Part, the parties to the dispute shall make every effort to enter into provisional arrangements of a practical nature.

2. Without prejudice to article 290 of the Convention, the court or tribunal to which the dispute has been submitted under this Part may prescribe any provisional measures which it considers appropriate under the circumstances to preserve the respective rights of the parties to the dispute or to prevent damage to the stocks in question, as well as in the circumstances referred to in article 7, paragraph 5, and article 16, paragraph 2.

3. A State Party to this Agreement which is not a Party to the Convention may declare that, notwithstanding article 290, paragraph 5, of the Convention, the International Tribunal for the Law of the Sea shall not be entitled to prescribe, modify or revoke provisional measures without the agreement of such State.

Article 32
Limitations on applicability of procedures for the settlement of disputes

Article 297, paragraph 3, of the Convention applies also to this Agreement.

(C) AGREEMENT TO PROMOTE COMPLIANCE WITH INTERNATIONAL CONSERVATION AND MANAGEMENT MEASURES BY FISHING VESSELS ON THE HIGH SEAS

Adopted on 24 November 1993 at the FAO Conference, Rome.

NOT YET IN FORCE
TEXT: 33 ILM (1994) 969–80

Article IX
Settlement of Disputes

1. Any Party may seek consultations with any other Party or Parties on any dispute with regard to the interpretation or application of the provisions of this Agreement with a view to reaching a mutually satisfactory solution as soon as possible.

2. In the event that the dispute is not resolved through these consultations within a reasonable period of time, the Parties in question shall consult among themselves as soon as possible with a view to having the dispute settled by negotiation, inquiry, mediation, conciliation, arbitration, judicial settlement or other peaceful means of their own choice.

3. Any dispute of this character not so resolved shall, with the consent of all Parties to the dispute, be referred for settlement to the International Court of Justice, to the International Tribunal for the Law of the Sea upon entry into force of the 1982 United Nations Convention on the Law of the Sea or to arbitration. In the case of failure to reach agreement on referral to the International Court of Justice, to the International Tribunal for the Law of the Sea or to arbitration, the Parties shall continue to consult and cooperate with a view to reaching a settlement of the dispute in accordance with the rules of international law relating to the conservation of living marine resources.

(D) AGREEMENT FOR THE CONSERVATION OF FISHERY RESOURCES IN THE HIGH SEAS OF THE SOUTH-EAST PACIFIC

Signed at Santiago on 14 August 2000 by Chile, Colombia, Ecuador and Peru.

NOT YET IN FORCE
TEXT: Agreement for the Conservation of Fishery Resources in the High Seas of the South-East Pacific (Galapagos Agreement), Permanent Commission for the South Pacific (CPPS) (Original text in Spanish, published in *Declaración de Santiago 2000,* Comisión Permanente del Pacífico Sur, Quito, Ecuador, 2000)

Article 14
Dispute Settlement

1. Disagreements among the States Parties as to the interpretation or application of the provisions established in this Agreement, or in its complementary instruments, shall be resolved in the first instance through the dispute-settlement procedures set forth in Article 33 of the United Nations Charter, or in other international instruments in force for the States Parties.

2. If an agreement cannot be reached, disputes must be submitted either to a conciliation commission or a technical arbitration body, unless both parties have agreed upon a different procedure.

3. If the voluntary dispute-resolution measures are exhausted, or if agreement is not reached on recourse to other instances, such as the International Court of Justice or the International Law of the Sea Tribunal, either of the parties may solicit a binding arbitration procedure.

4. In no case, subject to the applicable provisions in conformity with international law, shall disputes concerning the exercise of the coastal States' sovereign rights within their respective national jurisdiction zones be submitted to the procedures set forth in paragraph 3.

ANNEX IV

INSTRUCTIONS FOR THE REGISTRY

(As adopted by the Tribunal on 17 March 2000)

The Tribunal,

Acting pursuant to the Rules of the Tribunal (hereinafter "the Rules"), in particular article 38, paragraph 3.

Approves the following Instructions for the Registry.

PART I. GENERAL
Article 1

1. The President directs the work of the Tribunal and supervises the administration of the Tribunal.

2. The Registrar is the head of the Registry. The Registrar is responsible for all departments of the Registry and is authorized to control the staff and direct the work of the Registry.

PART II. DUTIES OF THE REGISTRAR
Article 2

The Registrar is responsible for the preparation of cases for consideration by the Tribunal and assists the Committee established by the Tribunal to prepare drafts of judgments, orders and advisory opinions.

Article 3

The Registrar prepares and keeps up to date the List of cases before the Tribunal, in accordance with article 36, paragraph 1(b), of the Rules.

Article 4

1. The Registrar prepares the draft agenda for all meetings of the Tribunal, adding the necessary explanatory notes.

2. The Registrar will, at the appropriate time, place items on the draft agenda, including:

(a) the budget estimates;

(b) the selection of members of the Seabed Disputes Chamber and the selection of members and alternates of the Chamber of Summary Procedure;

(c) the formation of other chambers provided for in article 15 of the Statute; and

(d) the election of the President and Vice-President of the Tribunal.

3. As soon as the draft agenda has been approved by the President of the Tribunal, the Registrar sends copies to the Members of the Tribunal.

Article 5

1. The Registrar is responsible for the official correspondence of the Tribunal in conformity with article 36, paragraph 1(a), of the Rules.

2. Letters not reserved for the signature of the President of the Tribunal are signed by the Registrar, or by the Deputy Registrar or the Assistant Registrar or Heads of Departments or other officials, in so far as the Registrar may delegate this duty to them. Notes in the third person are drafted in the name of the Registrar.

Article 6

The Registrar will send to judges the notifications required under the Rules.

Article 7

Whenever the Tribunal has to deal with a case which has previously been before it, the Registrar will notify every judge who has already sat in the case.

Article 8

In cases submitted to the Tribunal the Registrar will issue the communications and notifications provided for in the Convention (articles 290, paragraph 4; and 294, paragraph 2), in the Statute (articles 24, paragraphs 2 and 3; 30, paragraph 4; and 32, paragraphs 1 and 2) and in the Rules (articles 19, paragraph 3; 36, paragraph 1(f) and (g); 54, paragraphs 4 and 5; 55, paragraph 1; 65, paragraph 4; 66, paragraph 1; 71, paragraph 3; 72; 75, paragraph 2; 82, paragraph 2; 84, paragraph 3; 86, paragraph 4; 94; 96, paragraph 2; 101; 104, paragraphs 1 and 2; 106, paragraph 1; 109; 111, paragraphs 4 and 5; 112, paragraph 4; 114, paragraph 1; 119, paragraphs 2 and 4; 123, paragraph 2; 124, paragraph 1; 125, paragraph 3; 128, paragraph 2; 133; 136; and 137).

Article 9

1. The Registrar will inform all concerned of the dates and hours of meetings.

2. The Registrar will cause the dates and times of public meetings to be published. When a public meeting is to be held for the reading of a judgment or order, the Registrar will send a special notice to all agents whose appointment and address at the seat of the Tribunal or in the capital of the country where the seat is located have been duly brought to the knowledge of the Registrar.

Article 10

The Registrar will make arrangements for the recruitment of temporary staff.

Article 11

1. The Registrar will take the necessary steps to ensure compliance with article 65 of the Rules.

2. The Registrar will notify parties of the Guidelines concerning the Preparation and Presentation of Cases before the Tribunal, and any other applicable guidelines.

Article 12

1. When a request for an advisory opinion is received under article 159, paragraph 10, or article 191 of the Convention, the Registrar may ask for additional information from the Secretary-General of the International Seabed Authority. The Registrar will also ask for information from the intergovernmental organizations referred to in article 133, paragraph 2, of the Rules.

2. When a request for an advisory opinion referred to in article 138 of the Rules is received, the Registrar may ask for additional information from the body making the request.

Article 13

If, under article 15, paragraph 2, of the Rules, experts are to be selected, the Registrar will collect and submit to the President of the Tribunal the information relevant to the choice of the experts.

Article 14

If the Tribunal or a Chamber is to meet at a place other than the place at which the seat of the Tribunal is established, the Registrar will make the necessary arrangements.

Article 15

The Registrar will consult the President of the Tribunal in respect of members of the staff whose presence is required during the Tribunal's judicial deliberations.

Article 16

1. In accordance with article 85 of the Rules, the Registrar will make arrangements for interpretation of speeches and statements made and evidence given at a hearing.

2. The Registrar will make arrangements for the verification of the interpretation as required by article 85, paragraph 2, of the Rules.

3. The Registrar will ensure that the interpreters provided by a party under article 85, paragraph 2, of the Rules make the solemn declaration prescribed by paragraph 4 of that article.

Article 17

The Registrar will obtain statements of expenses from persons referred to in article 83 of the Rules and will cause the amounts due to be paid to them.

Article 18

1. The Registrar is responsible for the preparation of the records referred to in article 36, paragraph 1(h), of the Rules.

2. The Registrar is also responsible for the preparation of the minutes referred to in article 86 of the Rules.

3. The Registrar will provide to judges a record of decisions adopted by the Tribunal at its meetings.

Article 19

The Registrar will place the necessary staff at the disposal of any person instructed to carry out an inquiry or to give an expert opinion under article 82 of the Rules.

Article 20

1. The Registrar is responsible for the communication of judgments or advisory opinions rendered by the Tribunal, as provided for in articles 125, paragraph 3, and article 137 of the Rules.

2. Unless otherwise decided by the Tribunal, orders will be communicated in the same manner as judgments and advisory opinions of the Tribunal.

Article 21

The Registrar will, in accordance with article 36, paragraph 1(o), of the Rules, ensure that information concerning the Tribunal and its activities is accessible to Governments, the highest national courts of justice, professional and learned societies, legal faculties and schools of law and public information media.

Article 22

1. The Registrar will arrange, in accordance with article 36, paragraph 1(k), of the Rules, for the reproduction, printing and publication of:

(a) judgments, advisory opinions and orders;

(b) pleadings, statements and minutes of public sittings in cases and such other documents relating to cases as the Tribunal may direct to be published;

(c) the Yearbooks of the Tribunal;

(d) any other documents that the Tribunal may direct to be published.

2. The Registrar will conclude the necessary contracts with printers and other appropriate persons, and will provide for distribution or electronic dissemination of the Tribunal's publications.

3. The Registrar will establish, maintain and keep up to date the website of the Tribunal, posting such material on it as the Tribunal may direct.

Article 23

1. The Registrar will ensure that copies of declarations and notices deposited in accordance with articles 287 and 298 of the Convention or article 7 of Annex IX thereto are duly kept in the archives of the Tribunal.

2. Upon the receipt of copies of declarations and notices referred to in paragraph 1, the Registrar will immediately communicate them to the Members of the Tribunal.

Article 24

The Registrar will inform the States Parties to the United Nations Convention on the Law of the Sea (hereinafter "the States Parties"), the International Seabed Authority and the Secretary-General of the United Nations of any changes which may occur in the Tribunal's composition and of any application of article 9 of the Statute.

Article 25

The Registrar will notify the States Parties by written communications of amendments to the Statute proposed by the Tribunal in accordance with article 41, paragraph 3, of the Statute.

Article 26

The Registrar will communicate to the Secretary-General of the United Nations:

(a) the date of the election fixed by the President of the Tribunal, in accordance with article 6 of the Statute, for filling a vacancy in the membership of the Tribunal;

(b) any items for inclusion in the provisional agenda of the Meeting of States Parties in accordance with Rule 6 of the Rules of Procedure for Meetings of States Parties.

(c) any report of the Tribunal on its work.

Article 27

The Registrar will, in accordance with Rule 38 of the Rules of Procedure for Meetings of States Parties, submit reports and make statements to Meetings of States Parties concerning any question relating to the administrative or financial implications for the Tribunal of any proposed action of the Meetings of States Parties.

Article 28

The Registrar will make a record of declarations referred to in articles 34 and 35 of the Rules, signed by the President of the Tribunal, the Registrar and the person concerned, and deposit it in the archives of the Tribunal.

Article 29

The Registrar will ensure the observance of article 10 of the Statute and the Agreement on the Privileges and Immunities of the International Tribunal for the Law of the Sea of 1 July 1997, and of any general or special conventions or agreements concerning the privileges and immunities of the Tribunal.

PART III. THE DEPUTY REGISTRAR AND ASSISTANT REGISTRAR

Article 30

1. The Deputy Registrar and the Assistant Registrar share the duties devolving upon the Registrar both in connection with the exercise of the judicial and advisory powers of the Tribunal and in connection with the direction of the Registry.

2. In dividing the work between the Registrar and the Deputy Registrar, the Registrar will ensure that both of them are constantly in touch with the work of the Tribunal and of the Registry.

3. In the absence of the Registrar, the functions and authority of Registrar will be exercised by the Deputy Registrar and, in the absence of the Deputy Registrar, by the Assistant Registrar. In the absence of the Registrar, the Deputy Registrar and the Assistant Registrar, the appropriate official appointed in accordance with article 37, paragraph 2, of the Rules will discharge the duties of Registrar.

PART IV. FINANCIAL ADMINISTRATION

Article 31

The financial administration of the Tribunal, including the management of all funds, will be carried out by the Registrar in accordance with the Financial Regulations of the Tribunal.

Article 32

The Registrar is responsible for the collection and management of contributions of States Parties, the Authority and other entities under article 19 of the Statute.

Article 33

1. The Registrar is responsible for the preparation of the Tribunal's draft budget and will submit it at the appropriate time to the Committee on Budget and Finance. Supplementary budget proposals, whenever necessary, will be prepared by the Registrar and will, as far as possible, be submitted in the same manner.

2. The Registrar will forward the proposed budget and any supplementary budget proposals, as approved by the Tribunal, to the Secretary-General of the United Nations for submission to the Meeting of States Parties.

Article 34

The Registrar will provide such support as may be required by the President when the President represents the Tribunal at Meetings of States Parties.

Article 35

The Registrar will notify the States Parties, at least once a year, of the status of contributions. In particular, the Registrar will report to each Meeting of States Parties the status of contributions to the current and previous budgets.

Article 36

The Registrar is responsible for the expenditure of the funds of the Tribunal and for charging expenditure to the proper items of the budget or relevant accounts, unless the Tribunal decides otherwise.

Article 37

The Registrar alone is entitled to incur obligations or liabilities in the name of the Tribunal. The Registrar may, however, delegate to any member of the staff the power to incur obligations or liabilities within the limits of the normal activities of the branch of the Registry to which the staff member belongs. The Registrar may seek prior approval for such delegation from the Tribunal, or from the President if the Tribunal is not sitting.

Article 38

The Registrar will periodically inform the Tribunal or the President if the Tribunal is not sitting of the cash flow situation and any financial or administrative constraints likely to arise as a consequence.

Article 39

The Registrar will advise the President of the financial and administrative implications of requests from Judges for travel or other administrative services.

Article 40

1. The Registrar will propose for the approval of the Tribunal appropriate draft instructions relating to the following areas of the work of the Registry:

(a) Administration and Management;

(b) Finance and Accounts;

(c) Legal Department;

(d) Library service;

(e) Information systems and documentation, publication, archives and indexing services;

(f) Conference and linguistic services;

(g) Dispatch and receipt of documents and correspondence;

(h) Buildings Management and Property maintenance; and

(i) Security and Transport services.

2. The Registrar may propose for the approval of the Tribunal additional draft instructions in respect of such other aspects of the work of the Registry as the Registrar may consider necessary or the Tribunal may request.

PART V. AMENDMENTS

Article 41

The present Instructions may be modified by the Tribunal upon the proposals of the Registrar or *proprio motu*, after seeking the views of the Registrar.

ANNEX V

INFORMATION ON THE INTERNSHIP PROGRAMME

ITLOS/INT.3
22 September 2000

PLEASE NOTE: The Internship Programme is in no way connected with recruitment for employment at the Tribunal and there should be no expectancy of such. Interns wishing to be considered for employment with the Tribunal, even if otherwise fully qualified, are not eligible to apply for employment during their internship.

PURPOSE

1. The purposes of the Internship Programme are to give the participants the opportunity to gain an understanding of the work and functions of the Tribunal and to enable the Tribunal and its Members to benefit from the assistance of persons with relevant knowledge and skills in areas within the scope of activities of the Tribunal.

Participants in the programme will be expected to be able to contribute to the work of the Tribunal in the fields of, inter alia, the law of the sea, public international law, international organizations and international relations, political science, public information, publications and library science, and translation.

STRUCTURE OF THE PROGRAMME

2. The Internship Programme of the Tribunal is normally a full-time programme. Other arrangements are possible. Under supervision the intern carries out assignments for Members of the Tribunal and the Registry.

3. The internship usually covers a period of two to six months. In exceptional cases, individual internships may be extended.

ELIGIBILITY CRITERIA

4. The following criteria are used to determine eligibility for the Internship Programme:

(a) applicants should have completed at least three years of university studies;

(b) applicants should normally be engaged in a degree-granting or postgraduate programme at the time of application and also during the internship;

(c) applicants should normally not be more than 35 years of age;

(d) applicants should have a good command of the English and/or the French language; and

(e) applicants should have an interest in international law, specifically in international law of the sea, or international affairs.

In the selection of candidates due consideration will be given to geographical diversity and gender representation.

APPLICATION PROCEDURE

5. Persons who are interested in participating in the internship programme at the Tribunal in Hamburg should submit the duly completed application form, ITLOS/INT.2. In the case of persons nominated by a Government, university, other institution, law firm or organization, Part II of the form should be filled out by the responsible official of the nominating body. A resume, with grade transcript or list of courses taken and, if available, a brief sample of research work in English or French, should accompany the application form.

Applications should be sent to the Tribunal no earlier than eight months and no later than two months before the start of the internship. Incomplete applications will not be considered.

6. Application forms can be obtained from the Registry of the International Tribunal for the Law of the Sea, Am Internationalen Seegerichtshof 1, 22609 Hamburg, Germany. Tel.: (49) (40) 35607-227, Fax: (49) (40) 35607-245, E-mail: press@itlos.org

CONDITIONS OF INTERNSHIP

7. Interns are not paid. Costs of travel and accommodation, as well as living expenses, are the responsibility of interns or their sponsoring institutions.

8. Interns are responsible for obtaining the necessary visas and arranging their travel to and accommodation in Hamburg.

9. The Tribunal accepts no responsibility for costs arising from accidents and/or illness incurred during an internship. Therefore, candidates for internship must show proof of valid regular as well as major medical insurance coverage.

10. Interns must keep confidential any and all unpublished information obtained during the course of the internship and may not publish any reports or papers based on such information even after the completion of the internship, except with the explicit authorization of the Tribunal.

11. An information sheet on temporary accommodation can be obtained from the Internship Coordinator.

CERTIFICATE

12. Upon successful completion of the internship interns receive a certificate. The certificate will inter alia state the period of internship, give examples of the allocated tasks and evaluate their performance.

ANNEX VI

(A) AGREEMENT BETWEEN THE INTERNATIONAL TRIBUNAL FOR THE LAW OF THE SEA AND THE GOVERNMENT OF THE FEDERAL REPUBLIC OF GERMANY ON THE OCCUPANCY AND USE OF THE PREMISES OF THE INTERNATIONAL TRIBUNAL FOR THE LAW OF THE SEA IN THE FREE AND HANSEATIC CITY OF HAMBURG (ADDITIONAL AGREEMENT IN ACCORDANCE WITH ARTICLE [3] OF THE HEADQUARTERS AGREEMENT)

The International Tribunal for the Law of the Sea
and
the Government of the Federal Republic of Germany

Desiring to conclude an agreement regarding the occupancy and use of the premises of the International Tribunal for the Law of the Sea and in order to regulate the terms under which the premises shall be made available by the Government of the Federal Republic of Germany to the Tribunal as its seat in the Free and Hanseatic City of Hamburg, pursuant to article 1, paragraph 2, of Annex VI to the United Nations Convention on the Law of the Sea of 10 December 1982,

Having regard to the legal personality of the Tribunal and the provisions of the Agreement on the Privileges and Immunities of the International Tribunal for the Law of the Sea, adopted by the Meeting of States Parties to the United Nations Convention on the Law of the Sea on 23 May 1997,

Whereas the Government of the Federal Republic of Germany has agreed to provide, at its own expense, appropriate accommodation for the International Tribunal for the Law of the Sea and to make it available with all necessary facilities as the premises,

Whereas the International Tribunal for the Law of the Sea has accepted the offer of the Government of the Federal Republic of Germany and has agreed to occupy and use the premises,

Whereas the Headquarters Agreement between the International Tribunal for the Law of the Sea and the Federal Republic of Germany (hereinafter referred to as "the Headquarters Agreement") *inter alia* provides for the privileges, immunities and facilities of the Tribunal in the Federal Republic of Germany,

Have agreed as follows:

Article 1
Use of terms

For the purposes of this Agreement:

a) "Tribunal" means the International Tribunal for the Law of the Sea;

b) "host country" means the Federal Republic of Germany;

c) "Government" means the Government of the Federal Republic of Germany;

d) "competent authorities" means such federal *(Bund), Land* (state) or local authorities in the Federal Republic of Germany including the "*Oberfinanzdirektion*" as may be appropriate in the context and in accordance with the laws, regulations and customs of the Federal Republic of Germany, including the laws, regulations and customs of the *Land* (state) and local authorities involved;

e) "*Oberfinanzdirektion*" means the regional finance directorate responsible for the area of the Free and Hanseatic City of Hamburg;

f) "Parties" means the parties to this Agreement;

g) “Headquarters Agreement” means the Agreement concluded between the Tribunal and the Government regarding the Headquarters of the Tribunal;

h) “Headquarters district” comprises the area with the buildings upon it of the premises of the Tribunal as described in Annex 1;

i) “premises” means the property of the Federal Republic of Germany comprising the buildings, installations, equipment, fittings and all other facilities, as well as the surrounding grounds on the site located on the street “Am Internationalen Seegerichtshof”, in the Free and Hanseatic City of Hamburg, as described in Annex 1;

j) “installations” means all immovable fixtures, such as machinery, utility and communication lines, drainage systems and all other systems and facilities which are permanently attached to the premises;

k) “fittings” means any item which, though removable, is considered to be a permanent part of the premises, such as specially fitted or built-in furniture, lamps and video screens;

l) “equipment” means any movable item which is provided as accessory to the premises and which is neither permanently fixed nor specially fitted for the premises, such as telephones, fax machines, furniture, kitchen equipment and table-ware.

Article 2
Purposes and scope of the Agreement

This Agreement establishes the terms and conditions under which the premises together with the installations, equipment, fittings and all other facilities therein which are required for the effective functioning of the Tribunal are made available by the Government to the Tribunal and are occupied and used by the Tribunal.

Article 3
Transfer and use of the premises

(1) The Government hereby agrees to transfer the premises permanently to the Tribunal, free of rent, with the right to occupy and use the premises as the Headquarters of the Tribunal for the purpose of and in accordance with the Headquarters Agreement and this Agreement. Without prejudice to the foregoing, the premises shall remain the property of the Federal Republic of Germany.

(2) The Tribunal shall have the right to enjoy the premises peaceably and quietly, without undue interruptions and disturbances, for the conduct of its activities including any ancillary activities it may decide to carry out.

(3) The Government shall make every effort to ensure that the use of the vicinity of the premises shall not adversely affect the usefulness of the premises to the Tribunal.

(4) The Tribunal may, with due notice to the Government, allow third parties use of the premises or parts of the premises, free of rent, but, if required, against compensation for expenses incurred, for the purpose of meetings, conferences, consultations, deliberations or

any other activities related to the functions or interests of the Tribunal. In respect of the obligations of the Tribunal under this Agreement any such activities shall be deemed to be activities of the Tribunal.

(5) The Government undertakes to ensure that the buildings are properly constructed and equipped for occupancy and use for the purposes of the Tribunal and that the buildings, installations and fittings are erected in compliance with the building regulations and standards that are legally binding in the host country.

(6) The Government shall make the premises available to the Tribunal safe, fit and ready for use and occupancy on 6 November 2000. On this date, the Government shall transfer the possession of the premises to the Tribunal. The responsibilities of each of the Parties for the operation, maintenance and repair of the premises under article 4, shall take effect from the date of the transfer of the possession of the premises.

(7) An inventory of the equipment, fittings and any other movable facilities provided with the building to the Tribunal shall be drawn up by the Government at least 30 days prior to the date specified in paragraph 6 and will be confirmed by the Tribunal within 30 days following the move into the premises by the Tribunal.

Article 4
Operation, maintenance, repair and alteration of the premises

(1) The Tribunal shall maintain the premises in good repair and tenantable condition. In this respect, it shall be responsible, at its own expense, for the orderly operation and adequate maintenance of the premises including installations and fittings. Adequate maintenance shall include regular inspection and servicing of installations and fittings as well as upkeep of the buildings and care of the grounds. The Tribunal shall also be responsible for replacement or repair of buildings or parts of buildings, installations and fittings as a result of faulty operation or inadequate maintenance. In respect of all other repairs of the premises including installations and fittings, particularly those arising from wear and tear, the Tribunal will be responsible for minor repairs. A detailed description of the responsibilities of the Tribunal in respect of operation and maintenance as well as repairs is set out in Annex 2.

(2) The Tribunal undertakes to secure the services of one or more providers of facility management to carry out the operation and maintenance of the premises in accordance with this article. When so requested, the *Oberfinanzdirektion* shall assist the Tribunal in the selection of the providers of facility management services. The Tribunal will notify the Government as to which of the services specified in Annex 2 will be carried out by external operators. All other services will be carried out by the Tribunal.

(3) The host country shall be responsible, at its own expense, for major repairs as specified in Annex 2. This includes in particular measures necessary to preserve the substance of the buildings, installations and fittings thereon ("in Dach und Fach") and to eliminate possible construction defects in the buildings. In addition, it shall be responsible for any necessary restoration or reconstruction of the premises in accordance with article 7. The Tribunal shall report any necessary measures that are the responsibility of the host country to the Government, which shall take prompt and effective action in response.

(4) The Tribunal may, with notice to the competent authorities, at its own expense, make alterations, attach fittings, add installations and erect additions on the premises for its own purposes. In any case involving structural alterations of the buildings or additions to be erected on the premises, the Tribunal shall obtain the prior consent of the Government and take into account the building regulations applicable in the Free and Hanseatic City of Hamburg to the extent feasible and subject to their applicability in the Headquarters district in accordance with article [4, paragraph 2,] of the Headquarters Agreement.

(5) In order to ensure the timely filing of warranty claims which may arise against a construction company or architect involved in the construction and renovation of the buildings, installations and fittings, the Tribunal shall inform the Government as soon as possible of any defects which may possibly give rise to warranty claims.

(6) To the extent to which the host country furnishes the Tribunal with equipment for its use, the Tribunal shall be responsible, at its own expense, for any servicing measure, repair or replacement of such equipment which the Tribunal may consider to be necessary or appropriate according to its own requirements. In respect of such equipment the Government shall secure the transfer of any warranty rights to the Tribunal or shall authorize the Tribunal to secure servicing or repairs of the equipment warranted by the producers or suppliers of such equipment. The Government will make available to the Tribunal all information necessary to file such warranty claims.

(7) Within one year from the date specified in article 3, paragraph 6, the Tribunal will notify the competent authorities of any conditions of the premises that do not conform to the requirements in article 3, paragraph 5. The Government shall take prompt and effective action to ensure that these requirements are met and that any necessary repairs or replacements are undertaken within a reasonable time.

Article 5
Public services for the premises

At the request of the Registrar of the Tribunal, the Oberfinanzdirektion shall use its good offices to cause the providers of public services to:

a) install and maintain, on fair conditions, the public services needed by the Tribunal, such as, but not limited to, postal, telephone, telegraph, facsimile and data communication services, electricity, water, gas, sewerage, collection of waste, fire protection and public (local) transportation;

b) extend to the Tribunal, in respect of utilities and services referred to in subparagraph (a), rates not less favourable than the rates accorded to essential agencies and organs of the Government on the territory of the Free and Hanseatic City of Hamburg.

Article 6
Access to the premises

Without prejudice to article [5] of the Headquarters Agreement, upon request, with due notice given and subject to the prior approval of the Registrar of the Tribunal, duly authorized representatives of the competent authorities may enter the premises in order to inspect the premises for the purposes of maintenance, under conditions which shall not unreasonably disturb the carrying out of the functions of the Tribunal.

Article 7
Damage to or destruction of the premises

(1) Subject to article 4, the Tribunal shall not be responsible for restoration or reconstruction of the premises including buildings, installations and fittings in case of damage or destruction by the elements, fire or other causes.

(2) Should the premises, including buildings, installations and fittings, be damaged by the elements, fire or other causes the Government shall, in case of partial damage to the premises, restore the damaged part of the premises within a reasonable time. In the event that the premises are totally destroyed or otherwise rendered unfit for the use of the Tribunal, the Government shall make other suitable premises available to the Tribunal.

Article 8
Vacation of the premises

In the event that the Tribunal vacates the premises, it shall surrender the premises to the host country in as good a condition as when taken, except for reasonable wear and tear and damage by the elements, fire or other causes. The Tribunal shall not be required to restore the premises to the shape and state existent prior to any changes or additions that may have been executed in accordance with article 4, paragraph 4. The Tribunal shall not be required to replace or repair any equipment which is not a permanent fixture of the buildings and which will be provided by the host country with the premises.

Article 9
Consultations

(1) Representatives of the Tribunal and representatives of the Government shall meet at the request of either party to resolve by mutual agreement any problems that may have been found to exist with respect to the application of this Agreement in order to find an appropriate solution with a view to securing the effective functioning of the Tribunal.

(2) Three years after the entry into force of this Agreement or upon request of either party, representatives of the Tribunal and representatives of the Government shall meet to review the application of article 4 and Annex 2.

Article 10
Settlement of disputes

Any dispute between the Tribunal and the Government concerning the interpretation or application of this Agreement shall be settled in accordance with article [34] of the Headquarters Agreement.

Article 11
General provisions

(1) This Agreement may be amended by agreement between the Tribunal and the Government, at any time, at the request of either Party.

(2) After being signed by the Parties, this Agreement shall enter into force on the same day as the Headquarters Agreement. It shall be applied provisionally as from the date of signature.

(3) The attached Annexes 1 and 2 are an integral part of this Agreement.

Done at Berlin, on 18 October 2000, in duplicate in the English, French and German languages, all texts being equally authentic.

(Signed)
P. Chandrasekhara Rao
(President of the International Tribunal for the Law of the Sea)

For the
International Tribunal for the Law of the Sea

(Signed)
Herta Däubler-Gmelin
(Minister of Justice of the Federal Republic of Germany)

(Signed)
Wolfgang Ischinger
(State Secretary for Foreign Affairs)

For the
Government of the Federal Republic of Germany

Annex 1
to the
Agreement
between
the International Tribunal for the Law of the Sea
and
the Government of the Federal Republic of Germany
on
the Occupancy and Use of the Premises of the
International Tribunal for the Law of the Sea
in the Free and Hanseatic City of Hamburg

Description of the premises
in accordance with subparagraph (i) of article 1

The premises made available to the Tribunal for occupancy and use through the Headquarters Agreement and this Agreement shall be described, as provided in subparagraph (i) of article 1, as follows:

Section 1
Owner

The owner of the premises is the Federal Republic of Germany, as entered in the Land Register for Nienstedten.

Section 2
Location

The premises are located on the street "Am Internationalen Seegerichtshof", in the district of Altona, district area of Nienstedten, in the federal state of Hamburg.

The premises comprise the plots of land designated in the Land Register for Nienstedten, volume 25, pages 1056 and 2334:

–	serial number 3	plot 1321	total area 28,369 m^2
–	serial number 1	plot 2448	total area 2,721 m^2.

Section 3
Buildings

All the buildings located on the plots referred to in section 2 form part of the premises. The buildings form a complex comprising the main building together with the security building and a nineteenth-century villa.

Section 4
Additional installations and facilities

The premises also include:

- parking spaces for vehicles near the vehicle entrance;
- boundary of the property, including the entrance gate, forming the border of the premises on the Elbchaussee, on the Elbschloßstraße, on the street "Am Internationalen Seegerichtshof" and on the adjacent site in the west;
- road- and pathways within the premises;
- electronic surveillance of the grounds;
- drainage installation for draining rainwater into the Elbe (the drains run under the Elbchaussee, plots 1406 and 1117; the drainage installation is located on plot 1117).

Annex 2
to the
Agreement
between
the International Tribunal for the Law of the Sea
and
the Government of the Federal Republic of Germany
on
the Occupancy and Use of the Premises of the
International Tribunal for the Law of the Sea
in the Free and Hanseatic City of Hamburg

Distribution of responsibilities in accordance with article 4

Section 1
General provisions

The purpose of this Annex is to lay down in detail the distribution of the respective responsibilities of the Parties in respect of repairs, operation and maintenance as well as upkeep of the premises as provided for in article 4. This Annex is not exhaustive: insofar as responsibilities are not expressly provided for in this Annex, article 4 shall apply.

Section 2
Responsibilities of the host country

The host country shall be responsible, at its own expense, for major repairs as provided in article 4, paragraph 3. This includes in particular measures necessary to preserve the substance of the buildings, installations and fittings thereon ("in Dach und Fach") and to eliminate possible construction defects in the buildings as well as any necessary restoration or reconstruction of the premises in accordance with article 7.

Any single repair measure exceeding the amount of 2,500 Euro shall be considered to be a major repair. Subject to section 3 (a), the costs of major repairs shall be borne by the host country. The host country, in accordance with the procedure in section 3 (a), shall carry out the necessary repairs or authorize the Tribunal to do so on its behalf and at its expense.

Section 3
Responsibilities of the Tribunal

Pursuant to article 4, paragraphs 1 and 2, the responsibilities of the Tribunal shall include the following:

a) Minor repairs of buildings, installations and fittings

The Tribunal shall be responsible for minor repairs of the premises including installations and fittings as provided in article 4, paragraph 1. For the purpose of determining the responsibilities of the Tribunal for minor repairs and of the host country for major repairs the following shall apply:

- in case of a necessary repair measure in respect of buildings, installations and fittings, the Tribunal shall be responsible for covering the costs up to an amount of 1,000 Euro. In case the cost of such a single repair measure exceeds the amount of 1,000 Euro, the host country shall reimburse the Tribunal for the amount in excess. Such reimbursement of repair costs incurred during a calendar year shall be executed by 30 June of the following calendar year. The total responsibility of the Tribunal in respect of such repairs shall not exceed 50,000 Euro per year. The host country shall reimburse the Tribunal for any costs of such repairs which have been paid by the Tribunal and which exceed the overall cost ceiling of 50,000 Euro in any given calendar year;
- in any case where the cost of a single repair measure is assessed to be in excess of the amount of 2,500 Euro, the Tribunal shall seek the prior approval of the *Oberfinanzdirektion* before any repairs are carried out. In such case, the *Oberfinanzdirektion* shall carry out the necessary repairs or authorize the Tribunal in writing to do so on its behalf and at its expense. No reimbursement by the host country of costs exceeding the amount of 1,000 Euro for a single repair measure to the Tribunal shall be made if the total costs for this measure exceed the amount of 2,500 Euro unless such prior written authorization has been given by the *Oberfinanzdirektion*. In any case where the Tribunal notifies the *Oberfinanzdirektion* that such repair measure is urgent, the *Oberfinanzdirektion* shall take the necessary steps to carry out the repair work or provide an authorization, within one month from the date of notification unless the circumstances require earlier action. The Tribunal may proceed with the repair if no response is provided within that timelimit;
- the cost ceilings of 1,000 Euro, 2,500 Euro and 50,000 Euro do not apply to any repairs or replacements of buildings or parts of buildings, installations and fittings which become necessary as a result of faulty operation or inadequate maintenance. In such a case, the Tribunal shall be responsible for covering the full costs of replacement or repair.

b) Operation and maintenance of the premises

The Tribunal shall be responsible as provided in article 4, paragraph 1, for the following:

- operation and maintenance, including inspection and servicing, of installations and fittings;
- disposal of sewage and garbage, including hazardous waste;
- utility costs such as electricity, gas or diesel fuel, and water;
- gardening;
- janitorial services;
- cleaning of buildings and grounds including cleaning of pavements adjacent to the premises on the streets “Am Internationalen Seegerichtshof” and “Elbchaussee”;
- security;
- snow and ice removal including cleaning of pavements adjacent to the premises on the streets “Am Internationalen Seegerichtshof” and “Elbchaussee”;
- maintenance of telecommunication equipment.

c) Upkeep of buildings and care of the grounds

The Tribunal shall be responsible for the upkeep of the buildings and care of the grounds as provided in article 4, paragraph 1. This responsibility includes all cosmetic repairs on the inside and outside of the buildings which are necessary to keep the appearance of the buildings in a good and tenantable condition.

(B) EXCHANGE OF LETTERS

I. Letter from the Director General of Legal Affairs, Foreign Office, Berlin, to the Registrar of the International Tribunal for the Law of the Sea

(Courtesy translation)

Berlin, 18 October 2000

Mr. Registrar,

I have the honour, on behalf of the Government of the Federal Republic of Germany, to refer to the Agreement between the Government of the Federal Republic of Germany and the International Tribunal for the Law of the Sea on the Occupancy and Use of the Premises of the International Tribunal for the Law of the Sea in the Free and Hanseatic City of Hamburg (hereinafter "Additional Agreement"), which was signed today, and to confirm the following understandings:

1. The Government of the Federal Republic of Germany and the International Tribunal for the Law of the Sea have agreed to sign the Additional Agreement, in order to enable the Tribunal to move into the new premises, although negotiations with regard to the Agreement between the Federal Republic of Germany and the International Tribunal for the Law of the Sea regarding the Headquarters of the Tribunal (hereinafter "Headquarters Agreement") have not been concluded.
2. With regard to references in the Additional Agreement to provisions of the Headquarters Agreement, the parties have agreed that these references are to the draft Headquarters Agreement which is under negotiation between them (relevant excerpts of the draft Headquarters Agreement are annexed herewith and the passage of the text set out in the excerpts is not to be treated as definitive for the purposes of the Headquarters Agreement).
3. Upon signature of the Headquarters Agreement, corrections, if any, made in the citations of specific articles of the Headquarters Agreement and deletion of square brackets around such articles in the Additional Agreement shall not constitute formal amendments to the Additional Agreement and would not, therefore, attract the procedure for amendment under article 11, paragraph 1, of the Additional Agreement. Such corrections, if any, and deletions shall be made on the basis of an exchange of letters between the parties immediately following signature of the Headquarters Agreement.
4. The duty of the Tribunal under article 4, paragraph 1, of the Additional Agreement to maintain the premises "in good repair and tenantable condition" shall be interpreted to include the Tribunal's responsibility to keep the premises in a safe condition. This corresponds to the Government's responsibility under article 3, paragraph 6, to make the premises available to the Tribunal safe, fit and ready for use and occupancy. With respect to articles 7 and 8 of the Additional Agreement, the term "other causes" contained in the expression "the elements, fire or other causes" shall mean other similar causes such as *force majeure*.

5. The temporary premises of the Tribunal, located at Wexstrasse 4, Hamburg, shall be available to the Tribunal for a period of 30 days after the date of occupation of the new premises by the Tribunal. The transfer of possession of the new premises to the Tribunal will take place, as agreed between the parties, on 6 November 2000.

Please accept, Mr. Registrar, the assurance of my highest consideration.

(Signed)
G. Westdickenberg

II. Letter from the Registrar of the International Tribunal for the Law of the Sea to the Director General of Legal Affairs, Foreign Office, Berlin

18 October 2000

Mr. Director General,

I have the honour to acknowledge receipt of your letter of 18 October 2000 in which you confirm, on behalf of the Government of the Federal Republic of Germany, the understandings concerning the Agreement between the International Tribunal for the Law of the Sea and the Government of the Federal Republic of Germany on the Occupancy and Use of the Premises of the International Tribunal for the Law of the Sea in the Free and Hanseatic City of Hamburg (hereinafter "Additional Agreement") which reads as follows:

[See letter I]

I confirm that the understandings set out in your letter correspond to those of the International Tribunal for the Law of the Sea.

Please accept, Sir, the assurances of my highest consideration.

(Signed)
Gritakumar E. Chitty
Registrar

ANNEX VII

LIST OF JUDGMENTS AND ORDERS OF THE TRIBUNAL

1997

Case No. 1: The M/V "SAIGA" Case (Saint Vincent and the Grenadines *v.* Guinea), Prompt Release

- Order of 21 November 1997
- Order of 27 November 1997
- Judgment of 4 December 1997

1998

Case No. 2: The M/V "SAIGA" (No. 2) Case (Saint Vincent and the Grenadines *v.* Guinea)

- Order of 20 January 1998 (Provisional Measures)
- Order of 20 February 1998
- Order of 23 February 1998
- Order of 11 March 1998 (Provisional Measures)
- Order of 16 September 1998
- Order of 6 October 1998

1999

Case No. 2: The M/V "SAIGA" (No. 2) Case (Saint Vincent and the Grenadines *v.* Guinea)

- Order of 18 January 1999
- Judgment of 1 July 1999

Cases Nos. 3 and 4: Southern Bluefin Tuna Cases (New Zealand *v.* Japan; Australia *v.* Japan), Provisional Measures

- Order of 3 August 1999 (New Zealand *v.* Japan)
- Order of 3 August 1999 (Australia *v.* Japan)
- Order of 16 August 1999
- Order of 27 August 1999

2000

Case No. 5: The "Camouco" Case (Panama *v.* France), Prompt Release

- Order of 17 January 2000
- Judgment of 7 February 2000

Case No. 6: The "Monte Confurco" Case (Seychelles *v.* France), Prompt Release

- Order of 27 November 2000
- Judgment of 18 December 2000

Case No. 7: Case concerning the Conservation and Sustainable Exploitation of Swordfish Stocks in the South-Eastern Pacific Ocean (Chile/European Community)

- Order of 20 December 2000

ANNEX VIII

SELECTED COMMUNICATIONS FROM PARTIES ON MATTERS OF IMPLEMENTATION OF JUDGMENTS AND ORDERS

This annex includes information received by the Registry on matters concerning action taken pursuant to the decisions of the Tribunal. The Registry publishes it without comment and can accept no responsibility in connection with it.

1. *The M/V "SAIGA" (No. 2) Case*

On 17 July 2000 the Registry received by facsimile copy of a communication dated 14 July 2000, from the Agent of Saint Vincent and the Grenadines sent to the Government of Guinea through its Ambassador in France. The relevant extracts of the communication read as follows:

> …
> I am writing to you with regard to the outstanding Judgment of the International Tribunal for the Law of the Sea in the above matter.
> …
> You will be aware that under paragraph (12) the Tribunal:
>
> "*Decides* that Guinea shall pay compensation to Saint Vincent and the Grenadines in the sum of US$ 2,123,357 (United States Dollars Two Million One Hundred and Twenty-Three Thousand Three Hundred and Fifty-Seven) with interest, as indicated in paragraph 175."
> …
> The interests I represent are troubled to note that Guinea has failed to comply with the Judgment and the provisions of Article 296(1) of the Convention for over a year now.
> …
> Honourable Ambassador, in the light of the above St. Vincent & the Grenadines now cordially invites Guinea's proposals to settle the Judgment debt, including the additional interest earned over the last year or so, within the next fourteen days.

Subsequently, the Registry received a facsimile copy of a letter dated 21 September 2000, addressed to the Secretary-General of the United Nations, from the Prime Minister of Saint Vincent and the Grenadines, Sir James Mitchell. The contents of this letter read as follows:

> In your speech on the inauguration of the permanent headquarters of the International Tribunal for the Law of the Sea on 3rd July this year you described it as "the keystone of the United Nations Law of the Sea Convention, which in turn is one of the United Nations' greatest achievements". You added that:
>
> > "the Tribunal's decisions, once given, are put into effect. States, and other parties, recognize its authority and accept the objectivity of its interpretations and decisions, which are coming to form the core of international jurisprudence in the Law of the Sea."

We share your enthusiasm for the success of the Tribunal and your desire to secure respect for its decisions. It is therefore with regret that we must draw your attention to the fact that its first judgment on the merits of a case – hitherto its only such judgment – remains unsatisfied, more than one year after it was delivered.

On 1st July 1999 the Tribunal decided, by 18 votes to 2, in the case between *Saint Vincent and the Grenadines v Republic of Guinea, The MV Saiga*:

> "that Guinea violated the rights of Saint Vincent and the Grenadines under the Convention in arresting the *Saiga*, and in detaining the *Saiga* and members of its crew, in prosecuting and convicting its Master and in seizing the *Saiga* and confiscating its cargo;
>
> "that in arresting the *Saiga* Guinea acted in contravention of the provisions of the Convention on the exercise of the right of hot pursuit and thereby violated the rights of Saint Vincent and the Grenadines;
>
> "that while stopping and arresting the *Saiga* Guinea used excessive force contrary to international law and thereby violated the rights of Saint Vincent and the Grenadines; and
>
> "that Guinea shall pay compensation to Saint Vincent and the Grenadines in the sum of US$ 2,123,357 (United States Dollars Two Million One Hundred and Twenty-Three Thousand Three Hundred and Fifty-Seven) with interest."

Saint Vincent & The Grenadines has yet to receive any sum in satisfaction of that judgment or any response to its notes on the subject to the Guinean authorities. Those acting for the individuals and interests concerned have also received no response to their communications to the Guinean authorities. Copies of the most relevant of these communications are attached.

On the facts of the case, this is a particular cause of concern, since the damages assessed by the Tribunal were designed to provide reparation for individuals who had suffered material loss, including serious personal injuries. Moreover the Republic of Guinea did not challenge the assertion, made to the Tribunal, that they had realized more then $3,000,000 by the forced sale of the cargo. The outstanding damages are therefore less than the sum realized by the Guinean authorities, in violation, as the Tribunal has held, of the rights of Saint Vincent and the Grenadines.

Our concerns, however, go beyond the facts of the case. Along with other maritime countries, having neither the resources nor the desire to deploy substantial armed force on the oceans, Saint Vincent and the Grenadines relies on respect for the rules of international law. We take the view that if Contracting States can, without adverse consequences, fail to comply with judgments of the Tribunal, grave damage will be done to the authority of the Tribunal itself and to the law that it interprets and enforces. Contracting Parties are bound, by Article 33 of Annex VI to the Convention, to respect the finality and binding force of decisions of the International Tribunal. That engagement, solemnly undertaken by the Contracting Parties, must not become a dead letter.

> We regard it as particularly reprehensible that Guinea continues to receive funding from United Nations organs such as the World Bank and the International Monetary Fund in these circumstances. However inadvertently it may be, this can only result in creating the perception that the international community is condoning Guinea's conduct in failing to honour this long outstanding Judgment.
>
> For these reasons Saint Vincent & The Grenadines request you to use your good offices and authority with the Republic of Guinea, to secure prompt satisfaction of the judgment debt. A copy of this letter is sent to the President of the Tribunal, in the belief that all of its members must share our concern for the damage that may be done to its authority if the present situation is permitted to persist. My Government and its mission in New York remain at your disposal, or at the disposal of the Tribunal, to assist in the resolution of this matter.

2. *Southern Bluefin Tuna Cases*

In accordance with the Order of the Tribunal dated 27 August 1999, the parties, on 6 October 1999, submitted initial reports informing the Registry as to the steps taken or to be taken in order to assure prompt compliance with the provisional measures prescribed pursuant to article 95 of the Rules. Subsequently, the Registry received further information on this matter by a facsimile dated 9 March 2000 from the Agent of New Zealand. The relevant extracts of this communication read as follows:

> I am writing to inform you that the New Zealand Ministry of Fisheries has discovered that the level of New Zealand's catch of Southern Bluefin Tuna for the 1998/99 fishing year has exceeded the level prescribed in paragraph 90.1(c), of the Tribunal's Order of 27 August 1999. Although the New Zealand Government had informed the Tribunal in the *Joint Report by Australia and New Zealand on Compliance with the Provisional Measures* of 6 October 1999 that New Zealand's catch would not exceed its 420 tonne allocation (paragraph 6 of that report), it has since become apparent that the actual catch was in excess of that allocation by 37 tonnes.
>
> An annual catch limit of 420 tonnes on the taking of Southern Bluefin Tuna is prescribed in New Zealand law. A monitoring system which in previous seasons has ensured that actual catch does not exceed the legal catch limit (indeed that catch has often fallen short of the limit) has proven inadequate in the most recent season.
>
> ...
>
> Immediate steps have been taken to amend the catch monitoring system so that this situation does not arise in the future. In addition, New Zealand will reduce its catch for the 1999/2000 season by the amount of excess catch and legislative steps are underway to amend the legal catch limit accordingly. This is a measure of New Zealand's concern about the overall health of the SBT stock and New Zealand's continuing respect for the orders of the Tribunal. The New Zealand Embassy in Tokyo and the High Commission in Canberra have been instructed to inform the Governments of Japan and Australia of this regrettable, albeit unintentional, overcatch.

By facsimile letter dated 10 March 2000, the Agent of Australia transmitted comments on the information submitted by New Zealand to the Registry. Extracts from this communication read as follows:

> Obviously, Australia is disappointed that such over catch, although unintentional, has occurred. Nevertheless, we welcome the prompt remedial action taken by New Zealand and its continuing assurances concerning the Orders made by the Tribunal.

3. *The "Camouco" Case*

Several facsimiles from the Agent of Panama during the month of March 2000 provided information to the Registry on developments regarding proceedings pending before the domestic court for the release of the vessel *Camouco* and its Master.

By a communication dated 10 March 2000, and received on 13 March 2000, the Registry was informed that, regarding the vessel, the bank guarantee had been constituted on 24 February 2000.

On 23 March 2000 the Registry was informed by a facsimile of the same date from the Agent of Panama that:

> On the 21 [M]arch 2000, the judgement of the Court of Appeal [h]as concluded that the pleadings of Mercepesca should be accepted and has ordered to the French authorities to free the vessel. This liberation was effective the 22 march 2000.

Copies of the orders of the domestic court were also transmitted to the Tribunal (see Appendices A and B).

On 24 March 2000 a facsimile of the same date from the Agent of Panama was received informing the Registry that:

> I have just learned that the "Tribunal correctionel" of Saint Denis has just accepted to "free" the master of the "CAMOUCO" by giving him back his Spanish passport. He will be soon in a position to leave the island and to go back to Spain.
> …
> As far as the vessel is concerned, it is now in a Mauritian shipyard for repair works.

4. *The "Monte Confurco" Case*

On 19 and 29 December 2000, the Registry received two facsimiles from the Agent of the Seychelles, which provided information on the developments regarding proceedings pending before the domestic court for the release of the vessel Monte Confurco and its Master.

Appendices

The following documents were attached to a communication from the Agent of Panama to the Registrar of the International Tribunal for the Law of the Sea dated 23 March 2000.

Appendix A

Judgment of the Court of Appeal of Saint Denis of 21 March 2000 (Appellant Mr. José Ramon Hombre Sobrido)

[Translation from French]

*[Stamp: Extract of minutes of the
Registry of the Court of Appeal of
Saint Denis (Reunion)
French Republic
In the name of the French People]*

JUDGMENT No. 266/2000
PG: 99/02715

HOMBRE SOBRIDO

v.

THE FRENCH STATE

COURT OF APPEAL OF SAINT DENIS
CIVIL CHAMBER
JUDGMENT OF 21 MARCH 2000

Appeal from a decision of the *Tribunal d'Instance de Saint Paul* of 14 December 1999, pursuant to the notice of appeal dated 23 December 1999.

APPELLANT:

Mr. José Ramón HOMBRE SOBRIDO
ABOARD THE VESSEL CAMOUCO
Pointe des Galets
97420 LE PORT
counsel: Dominique LAW-WAI, *Avocat*, Bar of SAINT-DENIS

RESPONDENT:

THE FRENCH STATE
represented by the REGIONAL AND DEPARTMENTAL DIRECTORATE OF MARITIME AFFAIRS *[Direction Régionale et Départementale des Affaires Maritimes]*
11 Rue de la Compagnie
97400 SAINT-DENIS
counsel: SCP BELOT-AKHOUN-CREGUT-HAMEROUX, *Avocats*, Bar of SAINT DENIS

CLOSURE: 14/03/2000
COMPOSITION OF THE COURT

At the public hearing of 17 March 2000 before Mr. DAROLLE, President of the Chamber, who heard the parties and their arguments, the said parties and their counsel having raised no objection, judgment was entered on this day, upon report to the Court composed as follows:

Mr. Bertrand DAROLLE, President of the Chamber
Mr. Gérard GROS, Judge
Mrs. Nadia BERGOUNIOU, Judge

who deliberated thereupon in accordance with the law,

Delivered by Mr. Bertrand DAROLLE, President of the Chamber,
CLERK OF THE COURT: Mrs. Marie-José SERY (during argument and delivery of the judgment)

*
* *

By a statement filed with the Clerk of the Court on 23 December 1999, Mr. José Ramón HOMBRE SOBRIDO interposed an appeal against the FRENCH STATE represented by the REGIONAL AND DEPARTMENTAL DIRECTORATE OF MARITIME AFFAIRS *[Direction Régionale et Départementale des Affaires Maritimes]* from the order given on 14 December 1999 by the *Tribunal d'Instance de Saint-Paul*, which:

In view of Act No. 83-582 of 5 July 1983, as amended, regarding the arrest regime;

In view of articles 85 *et seq.* and 114 *et seq.* of the Code of Criminal Procedure;

In view of the fact that the owner of the vessel did not bring indemnification proceedings [*se constituer partie civile*] in the proceedings brought against the Master of the vessel;

declared the request of the Merce-Pesca Company inadmissible;

dismissed the requests of Mr. Hombre Sobrido for release and ruled that there were no grounds for reducing the amount of the bond;

ordered the Merce-Pesca company and Mr. Hombre Sobrido to pay to the French State compensation of 10,000.00 francs, i.e. 1,524.49 Euros;

ordered the Merce-Pesca Company and Mr. Hombre Sobrido to pay full costs.

By submissions filed with the Clerk of the Court on 14 March 2000, the appellant, in view of the Judgment of 7 February 2000 of the International Tribunal for the Law of the Sea and the bank guarantee of 8,000,000 francs remitted to the Maritime Administration [*Administration des Affaires Maritimes*] on 1 March 2000, requested the Court:

- to set aside the order appealed from;
- to declare and adjudge that the security shall be set at 8,000,000 F and that it can be given in the form of a bank guarantee;

- to take notice that the guarantee as hereinabove described had already been transmitted to the respondent;

- to order, accordingly, the immediate release from detention of the vessel *Camouco*;

By submissions received by the Clerk of the Court on 14 March 2000, the FRENCH STATE, represented by the REGIONAL AND DEPARTMENTAL DIRECTORATE OF MARITIME AFFAIRS *[Direction Régionale et Départementale des Affaires Maritimes]*, requested that notice be taken that it did not object to the granting of release from detention of the vessel *Camouco*;

The case was communicated, at his request, to the public prosecutor [*Procureur Général*], who was advised of the date of the hearing and gave his approval, on 14 March 2000, "without objection provided that the terms of the Judgment of 7 February 2000 are satisfied".

The order of closure was given on 14 March 2000.

WHEREFORE

CONSIDERING that the facts of the case, the procedure and the initial claims of the parties were set out by the Judge below in statements to which the Court refers; that it suffices to recall that, by an order of 8 October 1999, the *Tribunal d'Instance de Saint Paul* upheld the arrest of the *Camouco* and ruled that release would be subject to payment of a bond of 20 million francs;

CONSIDERING that FRANCE has ratified the United Nations Convention on the Law of the Sea of 10 December 1982, which entered into force under domestic law on 11 May 1996, article 292 of which provides that, "Upon the posting of the bond or other financial security determined by the court or tribunal (referred to in paragraph 1), the authorities of the detaining State shall comply promptly with the decision of the court or tribunal concerning the release of the vessel";

CONSIDERING that in the present case a decision of 7 February 2000 by the International Tribunal for the Law of the Sea, in particular:

"ordered that FRANCE shall promptly release the Camouco (...) upon the posting of a bond;

"determined that the bond shall be eight million French Francs (8,000,000 FF) to be deposited with FRANCE;

"determined that the bond shall be in the form of a bank guarantee or, if agreed by the parties, in any other form";

CONSIDERING that the appellant has produced the bank guarantee, issued by the *Banque Nationale de Paris Intercontinentale* on 1 March 2000, in the amount of eight million francs "in order to permit the release from preventive attachment of the vessel *Camouco*";

NOTING that the FRENCH STATE, "acknowledging that the obligations incumbent upon the appellant under the Judgment of 7 February 2000 have been satisfied, does not object to release being granted";

CONSIDERING, therefore, that the appeal of the appellant, as representative of the ship owner, must be deemed to be well-founded and that the costs of the appeal should be borne by the Public Treasury, pursuant to article 696 of the New Code of Civil Procedure;

FOR THESE REASONS

The Court, sitting in public *inter partes* civil proceedings at last instance,

DECLARES that the appeal of Mr. José Ramón HOMBRE SOBRIDO is admissible;

Considering the Judgment of the International Tribunal for the Law of the Sea of 7 February 2000 and the bank guarantee of 1 March 2000,

SETS ASIDE the order appealed from insofar as it dismisses the claims of Mr. HOMBRE SOBRIDO;

Ruling *de novo*:

TAKES NOTICE that the bond of eight million francs (8,000,000 F) determined by the aforementioned Judgment of the International Tribunal for the Law of the Sea has the form of a bank guarantee given by the *Banque Nationale de Paris Intercontinentale* (BNPI) on 1 March 2000;

ORDERS, therefore, that the vessel *Camouco* be immediately released;

RULES that costs shall be borne by the Public Treasury.

The minutes of the present judgment have been signed by the President and the Clerk of the Court.

[*Stamp, signatures*]

Appendix B

Judgment of the Court of Appeal of Saint Denis of 21 March 2000 (Appellant Merce-Pesca SA)

[Translation from French]

[Stamp: Extract of minutes of the
Registry of the Court of Appeal of
Saint Denis (Reunion)
French Republic
In the name of the French People]

JUDGMENT No. 267/2000
PG: 99/02727
1999 – 0932
14 December 1999

MERCE PESCA COMPANY

v.

THE FRENCH STATE

COURT OF APPEAL OF SAINT DENIS
CIVIL CHAMBER
JUDGMENT OF 21 MARCH 2000

Appeal from a decision of the *Tribunal d'Instance de Saint Paul* of 14 December 1999, pursuant to the notice of appeal dated 27 December 1999.

APPELLANT:

MERCE PESCA S.A.
16 Panama City 5
REPUBLIC OF PANAMA
counsel: Jean-Jacques MOREL, *Avocat*, Bar of SAINT-DENIS

RESPONDENT:

THE FRENCH STATE
represented by the REGIONAL AND DEPARTMENTAL DIRECTORATE OF MARITIME AFFAIRS *[Direction Régionale et Départementale des Affaires Maritimes]*
11 Rue de la Compagnie
97400 SAINT-DENIS
counsel: SCP BELOT-AKHOUN-CREGUT-HAMEROUX, *Avocats*, Bar of SAINT DENIS

CLOSURE: 14/03/2000
COMPOSITION OF THE COURT

At the public hearing of 17 March 2000 before Mr. DAROLLE, President of the Chamber, who heard the parties and their arguments, the said parties and their counsel having raised no objection, judgment was entered on this day, upon report to the Court composed as follows:

Mr. Bertrand DAROLLE, President of the Chamber
Mr. Gérard GROS, Judge
Mrs. Nadia BERGOUNIOU, Judge

who deliberated thereupon in accordance with the law,

Delivered by Mr. Bertrand DAROLLE, President of the Chamber,
CLERK OF THE COURT: Mrs. Marie-José SERY (during argument and delivery of the judgment)

*
* *

By a statement filed with the Clerk of the Court on 27 December 1999, MERCE PESCA S.A. interposed an appeal against the FRENCH STATE represented by the REGIONAL AND DEPARTMENTAL DIRECTORATE OF MARITIME AFFAIRS *[Direction Régionale et Départementale des Affaires Maritimes]* from the order given on 14 December 1999 by the *Tribunal d'Instance de Saint-Paul*, which:

In view of Act No. 83-582 of 5 July 1983, as amended, regarding the arrest regime;

In view of articles 85 *et seq*. and 114 *et seq*. of the Code of Criminal Procedure;

In view of the fact that the owner of the vessel did not bring indemnification proceedings [*se constituer partie civile*] in the proceedings brought against the Master of the vessel;

declared the request of the Merce-Pesca Company inadmissible;

dismissed the requests of Mr. HOMBRE SOBRIDO for release and ruled that there were no grounds for reducing the amount of the bond;

ordered the Merce-Pesca company and Mr. HOMBRE SOBRIDO to pay to the FRENCH STATE compensation of 10,000.00 francs, i.e. 1,524.49 Euros (one thousand five hundred twenty-four Euros and forty-nine cents);

ordered the Merce-Pesca Company and Mr. HOMBRE SOBRIDO to pay full costs.

By submissions filed with the Clerk of the Court on 10 March 2000, the appellant corporation, in view of the Judgment of 7 February 2000 of the International Tribunal for the Law of the Sea and the bank guarantee of 8,000,000 francs remitted to the MARITIME ADMINISTRATION [*Administration des Affaires Maritimes*] on 1 March 2000, requested the Court:

- to set aside the order appealed from;

- to declare and adjudge that the security shall be set at 8,000,000 F and that it can be given in the form of a bank guarantee;

- to take notice that the guarantee as hereinabove described had already been transmitted to the respondent;

- to order, accordingly, the immediate release from detention of the vessel *Camouco*;

- to make an appropriate order as to costs.

By submissions received by the Clerk of the Court on 14 March 2000, the FRENCH STATE, represented by the REGIONAL AND DEPARTMENTAL DIRECTORATE OF MARITIME AFFAIRS *[Direction Régionale et Départementale des Affaires Maritimes]*, requested that notice be taken that it did not object to the granting of release from detention of the vessel *Camouco*;

The case was communicated, at his request, to the public prosecutor [*Procureur Général*], who was advised of the date of the hearing and gave his approval, on 14 March 2000, "without objection provided that the terms of the Judgment of 7 February 2000 are satisfied".

The order of closure was given on 14 March 2000.

WHEREFORE

CONSIDERING that the facts of the case, the procedure and the initial claims of the parties were set out by the Judge below in statements to which the Court refers; that it suffices to recall that, by an order of 8 October 1999, the *Tribunal d'Instance de Saint Paul* upheld the arrest of the *Camouco* and ruled that release would be subject to payment of a bond of 20 million francs;

CONSIDERING that the Judge below declared inadmissible the claim in chief of the ship owner, MERCE PESCA, for the release of the vessel and its subsidiary claim for reduction of the amount of the bond, by reason of the fact that it did not bring indemnification proceedings [*se constituer partie civile*] in the inquiry proceedings brought against the Master of the vessel;

CONSIDERING, however, that the latter, while he may be personally liable for violations of the laws on maritime fishing, is merely the representative of the ship owner with respect to the arrest of the vessel, so that the claims of ship owner, who manifestly has a legitimate interest to adduce, are admissible;

THAT the decision taken should therefore be set aside insofar as it declared the claims of MERCE PESCA inadmissible;

CONSIDERING that FRANCE has ratified the United Nations Convention on the Law of the Sea of 10 December 1982, which entered into force under domestic law on 11 May 1996, article 292 of which provides that, "Upon the posting of the bond or other financial security determined by the court or tribunal (referred to in paragraph 1), the authorities of the detaining State shall comply promptly with the decision of the court or tribunal concerning the release of the vessel";

CONSIDERING that in the present case a decision of 7 February 2000 by the International Tribunal for the Law of the Sea, in particular:

"ordered that FRANCE shall promptly release the Camouco (...) upon the posting of a bond;

"determined that the bond shall be eight million French Francs (8,000,000 FF) to be deposited with FRANCE;

"determined that the bond shall be in the form of a bank guarantee or, if agreed by the parties, in any other form";

CONSIDERING that the appellant has produced the bank guarantee, issued by the *Banque Nationale de Paris Intercontinentale* on 1 March 2000, in the amount of eight million francs "in order to permit the release from preventive attachment of the vessel *Camouco*";

NOTING that the FRENCH STATE, "acknowledging that the obligations incumbent upon the appellant under the Judgment of 7 February 2000 have been satisfied, does not object to release being granted";

CONSIDERING, therefore, that the appeal of the appellant must be deemed to be well-founded and that the costs of the appeal should be borne by the Public Treasury, pursuant to article 696 of the New Code of Civil Procedure;

FOR THESE REASONS

The Court, sitting in public *inter partes* civil proceedings at last instance,

DECLARES that the appeal of the MERCE PESCA COMPANY is admissible;

Considering the Judgment of the International Tribunal for the Law of the Sea of 7 February 2000 and the bank guarantee of 1 March 2000,

SETS ASIDE the order appealed from insofar as it declares inadmissible the claims of the MERCE PESCA COMPANY;

Ruling *de novo:*

TAKES NOTICE that the bond of eight million francs (8,000,000 F) determined by the aforementioned Judgment of the International Tribunal for the Law of the Sea has the form of a bank guarantee given by the *Banque Nationale de Paris Intercontinentale* (BNPI) on 1 March 2000;

ORDERS, therefore, that the vessel *Camouco* be immediately released;

RULES that costs shall be borne by the Public Treasury.

The minutes of the present judgment have been signed by the President and the Clerk of the Court.

[*Stamp, signatures*]

ANNEX IX

LIST OF DONORS TO THE LIBRARY OF THE INTERNATIONAL TRIBUNAL FOR THE LAW OF THE SEA DURING 2000*

American Society of International Law, Washington, D.C., United States of America

Professor Takashi Aoki, Seiwa University, Faculty of Law, Chiba, Japan

Asociación Argentina de Derecho Internacional, Córdoba, Argentina

Mr. Vincent P. Bantz, Graduate Institute of International Studies, Geneva, Switzerland

Bundesamt für Seeschiffahrt und Hydrographie, Hamburg, Germany

Center for Oceans Law and Policy, University of Virginia School of Law, Charlottesville, United States of America

Centre d'Etudes et de Recherche de Droit International, Université de Paris I Panthéon-Sorbonne, Paris, France

Comité Maritime International, Antwerp, Belgium

Economic Court of Commonwealth of Independent States, Minsk, Russia

Food and Agriculture Organization of the United Nations, Development Law Service, Legal Office, Rome, Italy

Fundación Pedro Barrié de la Maza, La Coruña, Spain

Professor Dr. Hartmut Goethe, Deutsche Gesellschaft für Schiffahrts- und Marinegeschichte, Düsseldorf, Germany

Germanischer Lloyd, Hamburg, Germany

Institute of International Public Law and International Relations, Thessaloniki, Greece

* This list of donors does not take into account donations from members of the Tribunal and staff of the Registry.

Inter-Parliamentary Union, New York, United States of America

International Criminal Tribunal for the Former Yugoslavia, The Hague, Netherlands

International Maritime Organization, London, United Kingdom

IUCN – The World Conservation Union, Bonn, Germany

International Whaling Commission, Cambridge, United Kingdom

Professor Barbara Kwiatkowska, The Netherlands Institute for the Law of the Sea, Utrecht, The Netherlands

Professor Dr. Rainer Lagoni, Institut für Seerecht und Seehandelsrecht der Universität Hamburg, Hamburg, Germany

Mare, Die Zeitschrift der Meere, Hamburg, Germany

Max-Planck-Institut für ausländisches öffentliches Recht und Völkerrecht, Heidelberg, Germany

Dr. Erik Jaap Molenaar, The Netherlands Institute for the Law of the Sea, Utrecht, The Netherlands

Mr. Ibrahim Najjar, Cabinet d'avocats, Beirut, Lebanon

Naval War College, Newport, United States of America

Oceana Publications, Dobbs Ferry, United States of America

Permanent Court of Arbitration, The Hague, The Netherlands

Professor Adela Rey Aneiros, Facultade de Direito, Universidade da Coruña, La Coruña, Spain

RAMOGE Agreement, Secretariat, Monaco

Alexander Roth, Stalfort & Partner, Berlin, Germany

Dr. Chua Thia-Eng, Director of the Regional Programme for the Prevention and Management of Marine Pollution in the East Asian Seas, Quezon City, Philippines

Professor Daniel Vignes, Paris, France

Professeur Philippe Weckel, Cagnes sur Mer, France

Werner Simon, United Nations Library, Geneva, Switzerland

Walther-Schücking-Institut für Internationales Recht an der Universität Kiel, Kiel, Germany

ANNEX X

STATEMENTS DELIVERED AT THE JOINT CEREMONY OF THE TRIBUNAL, THE GOVERNMENT OF THE FEDERAL REPUBLIC OF GERMANY AND THE SENATE OF THE FREE AND HANSEATIC CITY OF HAMBURG FOR THE OFFICIAL OPENING OF THE HEADQUARTERS BUILDING OF THE TRIBUNAL ON 3 JULY 2000

(A) STATEMENT BY THE REGISTRAR OF THE INTERNATIONAL TRIBUNAL FOR THE LAW OF THE SEA, MR. GRITAKUMAR E. CHITTY

Today, the International Tribunal for the Law of the Sea, the Government of the Federal Republic of Germany, and the Senate of the Free and Hanseatic City of Hamburg jointly celebrate the opening of the Headquarters building of the International Tribunal for the Law of the Sea.

A few moments ago, the Headquarters building was handed over to the Tribunal with the symbolic handing over of the keys of the building to the President of the Tribunal, who entrusted them to my custody as the Registrar.

This marks the final step of a process, the start of which goes back more than 20 years. The Government of the Federal Republic of Germany had then submitted the candidature of the Free and Hanseatic City of Hamburg for the seat of the Tribunal to the Third United Nations Conference on the Law of the Sea, which subsequently voted in favour of Germany and the Free and Hanseatic City of Hamburg.

Today's festivity takes place in the presence and with the participation of His Excellency Mr. Kofi Annan, the Secretary-General of the United Nations, who is the depository of the United Nations Convention on the Law of the Sea; with the participation of Her Excellency Mrs. Herta Däubler-Gmelin, the Federal Minister of Justice of the Federal Republic of Germany, representing the host country, His Excellency Mr. Ortwin Runde, the First Mayor of the Free and Hanseatic City of Hamburg, representing the host city, His Excellency Mr. Peter Donigi, the President of the Meeting of States Parties to the United Nations Convention on the Law of the Sea, and other prominent representatives of governments and of the host country who are gathered here today, and also in the presence of the specially invited guests and the representatives of the media.

I wish to convey to the meeting the regrets communicated by three Judges of the Tribunal, Judge Lihai Zhao, Judge Choon-Ho Park and Judge Vicente Marotta Rangel, who are unable to attend today's event. They have asked me to convey their good wishes and to felicitate all participants in this celebration.

On 18 October 1996 the Tribunal met for the first time in open session and the Judges took their oath of office in the City Hall of Hamburg. The foundation stone for this building was laid the same day.

...

The President of the Tribunal will now address this august gathering.

(B) STATEMENT BY THE PRESIDENT OF THE INTERNATIONAL TRIBUNAL FOR THE LAW OF THE SEA, MR. P. CHANDRASEKHARA RAO

We have gathered here today to celebrate the official opening of the building into which the International Tribunal for the Law of the Sea will move soon. On behalf of the Tribunal, I extend a warm welcome to all the persons participating in this opening ceremony. To the representatives of French-speaking countries: *je vous souhaite la bienvenue*. We are indeed privileged to have the Secretary-General of the United Nations, His Excellency Mr. Kofi Annan, in our midst on this important occasion in the life of the Tribunal. We are particularly thankful to the Minister of Justice of the Federal Republic of Germany, Her Excellency Dr. Herta Däubler-Gmelin, the First Mayor of the Free and Hanseatic City of Hamburg, Mr. Ortwin Runde, the President of the Meeting of States Parties to the Law of the Sea Convention, His Excellency Mr. Peter Donigi, and the Legal Counsel of the United Nations, His Excellency Mr. Hans Corell, for their participation in today's ceremony. We are also honoured by the presence of the Acting Foreign Minister of Afghanistan, the Minister of State from Syria, representatives of the International Court of Justice and the European Court of Justice, diplomatic and consular representatives, senior German government officials, officers of other national and international courts, legal advisers of Foreign Offices, senior officials of UN organizations, distinguished academics, representatives of trade and commerce and other distinguished participants.

We in the Tribunal, like others, are struck by the silent grandeur of this building. It is ideally suited for judicial work. We wish to convey our appreciation to the firm of Baron Alexander and Baroness Emanuela von Branca, the architects of this building, for their design. The international community should be especially grateful to the Federal Republic of Germany and the Free and Hanseatic City of Hamburg for their joint efforts in erecting this building in such a delightful setting on the banks of the River Elbe at considerable expense.

I must place on record our appreciation to the Government of the Federal Republic of Germany and the Senate of the Free and Hanseatic City of Hamburg for the excellent support the Tribunal received from them at all stages of its work. At the local level, both the present First Mayor of Hamburg, Mr. Ortwin Runde, and his predecessor in office, Mr. Henning Voscherau, have been a source of strength to us. We are also thankful to Ambassador Kastrup, Permanent Representative of Germany to the United Nations, and his predecessor, for the help extended to us.

I am very happy to announce that the Tribunal and the Federal Republic of Germany have been able to make good progress in negotiations concerning the Headquarters Agreement and the Agreement on the Occupancy and Use of the Premises of the Tribunal in a spirit of goodwill and cooperation. It is our hope that we would soon reach agreement in these matters.

The official inauguration of the Tribunal took place in the City Hall of Hamburg on 16 October 1996. Since then, the Tribunal functioned from its temporary premises, provided to it by the Government of the Federal Republic of Germany. The foundation stone for the Headquarters building here was laid on 18 October 1996 in the presence of, among others, Dr. Boutros Boutros Ghali, the then Secretary-General of the United Nations.

The Tribunal is happy that its seat is in the Free and Hanseatic City of Hamburg, which is a well-known port city reputed for its long tradition in international shipping and maritime trade. As the former Secretary-General put it at the inaugural session of the Tribunal, I quote: "this great city symbolizes humankind's eternal relationship with the sea – as a source of life, as a means of commerce, as the common heritage of all the peoples of the globe" – unquote.

We are thankful to the people of Hamburg for extending to the judges and officers of the Tribunal courtesies that make living in Hamburg a pleasurable experience. On behalf of the Tribunal, I assure the people of Hamburg that it shall be our constant endeavour to blend in well with the natural fabric of life in Hamburg. We propose to make the building accessible to the public on days to be specified soon.

The Tribunal does not enjoy an organic link with the United Nations. Nevertheless, it owes its existence to the efforts of the United Nations towards establishing a new legal order for ocean space. In recognition of its special relationship with the United Nations, the Tribunal and the United Nations concluded in 1997 an Agreement on Cooperation and Relationship. The Tribunal has been participating in all UN meetings of relevance to the Tribunal. The Secretary-General of the United Nations, the Legal Counsel to the United Nations and the Division for Ocean Affairs and the Law of the Sea have all helped us on appropriate occasions. The Tribunal looks forward to cementing its links with the United Nations.

The United Nations Convention on the Law of the Sea established the Tribunal to serve as a world court and play a central role in the resolution of law of the sea disputes. The Convention does not provide a single body for adjudicating law of the sea disputes; it provides for a number of alternative mechanisms for the settlement of disputes. Nevertheless, the Tribunal, composed as it is of persons of "recognized competence in the field of the law of the sea", is accorded, by the Convention, a prominent position in the matter of settlement of law of the sea disputes. The Tribunal is given a special competence to hear applications for the prompt release of vessels and crews under article 292 and to deal with requests for provisional measures under article 290, paragraph 5, of the Convention. The Seabed Disputes Chamber of the Tribunal also enjoys exclusive jurisdiction in respect of certain disputes referred to in the Convention. As underlined by the General Assembly in its resolution 54/31 of 16 November 1999, the Tribunal has an "important role and authority concerning the interpretation or application" of the United Nations Convention.

There is no conflict between the Tribunal and other bodies competent to adjudicate under the United Nations Convention. When providing for more than one universal court, the makers of the Convention did not see any danger to the unity of international law. These bodies are intended to complement each other in the global system for the peaceful settlement of disputes. They fulfil complementary needs. They are not in any hierarchical relationship. It is to be hoped that each international tribunal or court, though autonomous in itself, will not ignore precedents of other bodies, thus ensuring the harmonious development of the law of the sea. For its part, where appropriate, the Tribunal, in its Judgments, relied upon or referred to the precedents set by other international courts and tribunals. It is in the interests of sound legal jurisprudence that adjudicatory bodies show mutual respect to each other's decisions.

It is now just over three years since the Tribunal was inaugurated in October 1996. During this short period, much has been achieved. The Tribunal adopted its Rules for carrying out its functions, the Resolution on the Internal Judicial Practice of the Tribunal and the Guidelines concerning the Preparation and Presentation of Cases before the Tribunal. Most importantly, the Tribunal has become a functioning judicial institution. It heard five cases and was able to deliver its Orders and Judgments in these cases within reasonably short periods. This should remain a matter of special satisfaction to litigants. Though the Tribunal is a standing body, it meets in Hamburg only when the business so demands. Judges assemble in Hamburg on very short notice and oftentimes work without breaks, thus promoting dispute settlement without unnecessary delay or expense. The Tribunal has made every effort to be user-friendly. We are happy that the UN General Assembly noted with satisfaction what it called the continued contribution of the Tribunal to the peaceful settlement of disputes in accordance with the Convention.

Of the 133 States Parties to the Convention, 25 States Parties have so far filed declarations under article 287 of the Convention with regard to choice of procedure for the settlement of disputes. It may be that, in the early years of the Tribunal, there was some hesitation in accepting the jurisdiction of the Tribunal on an exclusive or preferential basis. Now that the Tribunal has established itself as an active and effective body in deciding law of the sea disputes, it would be opportune for States to consider again the choices open to them in the matter of dispute settlement mechanisms.

Our Library is in its early stages of development. On this occasion, I would like to express our gratitude to the individuals, research institutions and organizations that have donated publications to our Library in the past. I wish to acknowledge in particular the significant contribution of the Korea Foundation that enabled us to complete our holdings for many journals essential to the work of the Tribunal. The Tribunal would welcome further expressions of support as we endeavour to create a reference library to serve our present and future requirements.

The United Nations Convention on the Law of the Sea is of fundamental importance for the maintenance and strengthening of international peace and security, as well as for the sustainable use and development of the seas and oceans and their resources. The Convention on the Law of the Sea is not, however, an end in itself; its successful working depends on, among other things, the conclusion of detailed agreements on promotion of cooperation at the regional and international levels, as well as enactments of national law in States Parties to the Convention.

There are also major challenges facing the international community in the field of the law of the sea: over-exploitation of marine living resources, degradation of the marine environment, dumping of nuclear waste and toxic substances into the sea, piracy and armed robbery at sea, threats to international peace and security from disputed maritime boundaries, etc. The Report of the United Nations Secretary-General of 20 March 2000 documents these issues in full. The Secretary-General's efforts in support of the Convention and in its effective implementation deserve full support.

The United Nations General Assembly has taken a timely initiative to establish an open-ended informal consultative process to achieve better integration on ocean affairs. This initiative reflects, at the turn of the millennium, the importance of the oceans and seas to mankind. The first meeting of the UN Open-ended Informal Consultative Process on Oceans and the Law of the Sea, held from 30 May to 2 June 2000 in New York, underlined in a conscious manner the current priorities that need urgent attention. The outcome of this process will have a bearing on the application of the Convention and is thus of interest to all of us. It is heartening to note the decision of the recent Meeting of States Parties to the United Nations Convention on the Law of the Sea to request the UN General Assembly to establish a Trust Fund to assist deserving developing countries in the cases before the Tribunal.

There is nothing abnormal in States having differences of opinion with regard to the interpretation or application of the Convention. All are subject to the rule of law as enshrined in the Convention and are required to compose their differences by having recourse to the systems incorporated in the Convention for settlement of disputes. Threats to the Convention arise when States pursue unilateral action *de hors* the Convention. It shall be the constant endeavour of the Tribunal to serve as the upholder of the Convention.

The Tribunal has demonstrated its ability to deal efficiently with cases submitted to it. It is ready to deal with future cases with the same efficiency. I am confident that this splendid new building will assist the Tribunal in carrying out its important tasks. On behalf of the Tribunal, may I say how grateful we are to the Federal Republic of Germany, the Senate of the Free and Hanseatic City of Hamburg and the people of Germany for dedicating this building in the service of the cause of settlement of law of the sea disputes by peaceful means. To them, I say: *der Seegerichtshof und ich danken Ihnen recht herzlich*.

(C) WELCOMING ADDRESS BY THE MINISTER OF JUSTICE OF THE FEDERAL REPUBLIC OF GERMANY, MRS. HERTA DÄUBLER-GMELIN

Mr. Secretary-General, dear Mrs. Annan,
Mr. President of the International Tribunal for the Law of the Sea,
Mr. President of the Senate of the Free and Hanseatic City of Hamburg and First Mayor,
Judges, Excellencies,
Ladies and Gentlemen,

My best greetings to the International Tribunal for the Law of the Sea, its friends and its guests!

It is a great honour and a special pleasure for me to welcome you here today in the Tribunal's permanent building and to convey to you the best wishes and greetings of the Chancellor of the Federal Republic of Germany, Gerhard Schröder, and the whole Federal Government.

We wish you all the best for your forthcoming move to this really beautiful court building on the impressive and equally beautiful Hamburg Elbchaussee.

We all are particularly delighted – and proud – that you, Secretary-General, are here today to attend this opening ceremony. Your presence underlines the special importance of the International Tribunal as an essential factor for the peaceful use of the seas which is, as we all know, guaranteed by the United Nations. And – of course – your presence,

Secretary-General, gives you the opportunity to see for yourself that we, the Federal Government, have kept to our special obligations after the decision in favour of Hamburg as the seat of this important Tribunal. As President Rao has rightly pointed out, we actively supported this decision from the very beginning of negotiations in the Preparatory Commission.

We all are aware of the great importance of the United Nations Convention on the Law of the Sea, which contains, for the first time, a global maritime regime that is really accepted on a universal basis. The International Tribunal for the Law of the Sea applies the rules of this convention as a central body for dispute resolution, as a permanent court with its own powers, where States, and – in relation to seabed mining – also other legal entities can initiate proceedings.

And we all are equally aware that this tribunal enjoys the best of all reputations. It is well accepted and appreciated – though it has only been in existence for a relatively short time. You, President Rao, were absolutely right when you pointed out, in your speech to the 54th United Nations General Assembly on 22 November 1999, that the International Tribunal has well succeeded in consolidating its worldwide special position.

Three and a half years ago, when the Tribunal started its work, sceptical observers could, indeed, be heard, anxious that there would not be many cases where States would turn to the Tribunal, since – as we well know – contracting States are free to have recourse for dispute resolution to institutions other than the International Tribunal, such as the International Court of Justice in The Hague or an arbitration tribunal.

Today we observe that these fears were unjustified. Of those States making a declaration, under article 287 of the UN Convention, on the choice of means for the settlement of disputes, two-thirds have decided to choose the International Tribunal for the Law of the Sea. Most of these States have even given the International Tribunal their first preference.

Just two weeks after the adoption of the Tribunal's Rules, the first case came up: the *Saiga* case.

You remember: *Saiga*, a ship owned by a Cypriot shipping company and managed by a Scottish one, was seized by Guinea in its exclusive economic zone – a truly international case. At the time of the incident in dispute, it had been chartered by a Swiss company and was sailing under the flag of Saint Vincent and the Grenadines. The crew came from Ukraine; other workers were Senegalese citizens, and the cargo was owned by yet another Swiss company.

This case was also complicated from the legal point of view: questions of vessel registration, of arrest, of hot pursuit, of the use of force and of compensation had to be clarified – problems calling in each case for new solutions and approaches.

Not only did this first case demonstrate the special and difficult questions the International Tribunal has to deal with in its daily work, but also the following ones, be it the interesting *Southern Bluefin Tuna Cases* or the *Camouco Case*. Others will follow.

I am confident that the International Tribunal for the Law of the Sea will successfully continue to intensify its activities in the settlement of disputes and in the development of the law.

This will be ensured by the judges who, as the most prominent and knowledgeable personalities and experts of the world's major legal systems and of the law of the sea, are not only excellently qualified for their function, but are also genuine custodians of the international law of the sea.

That is why the United Nations General Assembly, at its 54th session last year, took special note of the important contribution being made by the International Tribunal towards the peaceful settlement of disputes and it expressed its respect and appreciation for the Tribunal and its work. I think we all agree with this assessment.

Ladies and gentlemen, this important international tribunal, of course, needs appropriate accommodation.

For this reason, in the spring of 1989, the Federal Republic of Germany organized an international competition. The winners, the architects Alexander and Emanuela von Branca, have built this wonderful and really impressive building. Mrs. von Branca, fortunately, can be with us today. A warm welcome to you!

At the first jury meeting UN Under-Secretary Nandan expressed what he imagined an ideal court building to be: it would have to express harmony and an atmosphere of peace and justice for the high seas. Really a great challenge.

Today, President Rao, Secretary-General Annan, ladies and gentlemen, we know and we can see that with their creation the architects have met that challenge. Thank you for this, Mrs. von Branca, and thanks to all – the managers, the workers, the craftsmen – who successfully took part in building and giving shape and form to the initial vision.

We all do wish that you, President Rao, esteemed members of the Tribunal and all members of your staff will enjoy working in this wonderful building. I am convinced that the specific and renowned Hanseatic working environment will inspire decisions that underscore the excellent reputation and importance of the International Tribunal for the Law of the Sea.

I wish you all the best – that the spirit of liveliness, peace and hope which the children down in the hall, singing the "Nienstedten Song", have expressed so nicely, will live on in this building.

(D) STATEMENT BY THE FIRST MAYOR OF HAMBURG, MR. ORTWIN RUNDE

Mr. President,
Secretary-General,
Madam Minister,
Ladies and Gentlemen,

it is now almost 20 years since the day – it was 21st August 1981 – that Hamburg was designated the new seat of the International Tribunal for the Law of the Sea.

Nearly two decades, filled with plans, preparations and make-shift solutions.

Today, this phase has now finally come to an end.

Hamburg is delighted about that and we welcome all those who have come to celebrate this significant day with us.

Another reason to call this an important day is that the city has been enriched with a most attractive example of the architect's craft.

My thanks to all those who were and are involved in this project. In order not to leave anyone out – neither planners nor implementers – I shall not single out anyone at all for special mention. Thank you, each and every one of you.

The building's location is itself full of symbolism. From here – up above the Elbe, directly overlooking one of the world's major shipping lanes – the International Tribunal for the Law of the Sea keeps watch on international shipping. And judgments will be handed down in this room.

The Town Hall of Hamburg may, however, claim the honour of being the place where the very first ruling was made.

On 4th December 1997, in the Great Salon of the Town Hall, the judges passed their first verdict. The fact that the Town Hall was used for this purpose is, I believe, an especially apt way to emphasize the fact that maritime law has always played an important role in Hamburg and continues to do so.

Ever since 1189 – when Emperor Barbarossa granted the city the privilege of free access to the seas – maritime law has been an integral part of the jurisdiction of our City State. And in the past it was not unusual for the Senate of Hamburg to be asked to act as arbitrator in legal disputes involving maritime matters.

It is only logical that in this day and age the law of the sea is especially important for a world port and trading city such as Hamburg. All in all, Hamburg was the candidate that seemed especially predestined to be chosen as the right place to establish the International Tribunal for the Law of the Sea.

Of course, we first had, literally, to convince "the rest of the world" of this. But – as one can see – we succeeded in this task. We are gratified that the signatory States to the Convention on the Law of the Sea felt Hamburg provided a worthy setting for the Tribunal. And I may assure you: we count it an honour to host this court of law. Hamburg will live up to the high expectations that are placed in the host of such an institution.

The International Tribunal has the judges, it has a building – what it needs now is general acceptance.

We cannot expect this to happen overnight and it will take time to grow. But it will come, we know that from the experience of other international courts.

With every new case that is brought before the Tribunal on the Law of the Sea, the community of nations will take more and more notice of the court's work.

And since the oceans of the world will become much more important in the 21st century – whether as transportation routes or reservoirs of natural resources – many legal questions will need to be clarified. The forecasts are that the Tribunal will not be able to complain about lack of work!

I congratulate the International Tribunal for the Law of the Sea on its new home.

I hope that all those who use these rooms will find them pleasant and that the building provides a good setting for people to work in.

This institution will stimulate new ideas. It will be a stimulus that helps create a new culture of maritime law – which will then be associated with the name of our city. And so there will be further confirmation: that Hamburg was the right place for the International Tribunal on the Law of the Sea to cast anchor.

(E) STATEMENT BY THE SECRETARY-GENERAL OF THE UNITED NATIONS, MR. KOFI ANNAN

Mr. President,
Madam Minister,
Mr. Mayor,
Ladies and Gentlemen,

I am honoured and delighted to join you for this solemn and yet very happy event, in this beautiful City which is proud to call itself "Free and Hanseatic".

Those titles evoke a great history and form in themselves an eloquent manifesto. The Hanse, that great league of north European trading cities to which Hamburg once belonged, was almost a forerunner of the United Nations. It brought together, for mutual assistance and defence, communities whose way of life was founded on seaborne commerce, freely transacted by free men under agreed rules.

For them, as for all of us in today's global economy, the Law of the Sea was no luxury but essential to their survival. What more fitting location could there be, then, for the permanent seat of the International Tribunal for the Law of the Sea? And what a pleasure it is, today, to celebrate the installation of the Tribunal in that permanent seat!

I think we all knew, when the Law of the Sea Conference decided 20 years ago to accept Germany's offer to host the Tribunal, that we would get something pretty impressive. But we could hardly have imagined an edifice quite so splendid, or so appropriate to the theme of peace and justice in the oceans.

Having just completed a tour of the premises, I can assure you that the building, besides being meticulously crafted to serve the specialized needs of this institution, is a work of art in its own right. It has a timeless quality, which no doubt it owes in part to the tranquil parkland setting, but in larger part to the genius of the architects. They have achieved a remarkable harmony between the ancient trees so carefully preserved, the renovated villa in all its glory, and the glass, metal and stone of the modern structure they have added.

We must all feel particular gratitude to the City, and indeed to the German people. By establishing the Tribunal in Hamburg, and generously endowing this magnificent new Headquarters Building, they have shown once again their strong commitment to promoting the rule of international law and preventing armed conflict. They have shown that they understand how much world peace depends on the existence of robust mechanisms for the peaceful settlement of disputes.

The Tribunal, dedicated to the peaceful resolution of international disputes relating to the oceans, is such a mechanism. It is the keystone of the United Nations Law of the Sea Convention, which in turn is one of the UN's greatest achievements. And, like the International Court of Justice, it is central to the regime of international peace and security that has evolved since the United Nations Charter was adopted.

The Law of the Sea Convention, now almost universally accepted, provides the essential framework for the rule of law in the marine sphere, governing the uses of the sea and access to its resources, and regulating inter-State relations. It is sometimes called the Constitution for the Oceans.

Under that Constitution, the Tribunal plays a key role in the uniquely binding dispute settlement procedure. It is the central forum available – to States, to certain international organizations, and even to some corporations – for resolving disputes about how the Convention should be interpreted and applied.

When the Convention was adopted, the Secretary-General was entrusted with the task of starting up the Tribunal. The United Nations lent its staff to the new institution to assure it a successful start.

I myself, like my predecessors, have maintained a keen interest in developments relating to the Convention and its institutions. I am delighted to note that in its first four years the Tribunal has already built a reputation among international lawyers as a modern court that can respond quickly.

In large part this is due to the outstanding quality of the judges, who have carried out their work in an expeditious, responsible and efficient manner. The Tribunal is indeed fortunate to have secured the services of members so eminent, and so learned in the law of the sea.

On a personal note, I take particular pride in the work of my countryman, Judge Thomas Mensah, who served as President of the Tribunal for its first three years. But I have no doubt at all, Mr. President, that under your able leadership the Tribunal will maintain the same record of success.

Credit is also due, of course, to the dedication and hard work of the Registrar, Mr. Gritakumar Chitty, his deputy, M. Philippe Gautier, and all their staff.

Naturally, recourse to international dispute resolution depends on the parties being ready to submit their differences for judicial decision. It is very encouraging that this Tribunal had more cases submitted to it in its first three years than any previous international court. It has dealt with a wide variety of cases, from both developing and developed countries, involving such matters as the prompt release of vessels and crew, the prescription of legally binding provisional measures, and more substantive issues concerning the rights and obligations of States under the Convention.

The record already shows that the Tribunal's decisions, once given, are put into effect. States, and other parties, recognize its authority and accept the objectivity of its interpretations and decisions, which are coming to form the core of international jurisprudence in the law of the sea.

I hope that more and more parties will be encouraged to make use of the Tribunal in settling their disputes, and also that States will support it – notably by giving it the financial security it needs. And I am glad to note the recommendation of the Meeting of States Parties to the Convention, that a voluntary Trust Fund be established to assist States which have difficulty in meeting the costs of bringing a case before the Tribunal. It is indeed vital that the Tribunal be fully accessible to all.

The Judges of the Tribunal, as well as the staff of the Registry, reflect the cultural and geographical diversity of the human family. That reminds us that societies and cultures can coexist, blossom and flourish only when international law, firmly rooted in global values, is fully implemented and enforced. The Tribunal is there to help us implement an important aspect of international law, and so put those global values into practice.

Long may it continue to do so!

ANNEX XI

STATEMENT BY THE PRESIDENT OF THE TRIBUNAL, MR. P. CHANDRASEKHARA RAO, ON AGENDA ITEM 34 (a): "OCEANS AND THE LAW OF THE SEA" AT THE 44TH PLENARY MEETING OF THE FIFTY-FIFTH SESSION OF THE UNITED NATIONS GENERAL ASSEMBLY, 30 OCTOBER 2000

Mr. President and distinguished delegates:

It is an honour to address the Millennium General Assembly in connection with the discussion of the item "Oceans and the Law of the Sea". I extend to you, Mr. President, our congratulations on your election as the President of the General Assembly.

I regret to inform you of the death, in Beijing, on 10 October 2000, of Judge Lihai Zhao. Judge Zhao had been a member of our Tribunal since October 1996. His term was due to expire in September 2002. Steps are being taken to fill the vacancy created by his death in accordance with the Statute of the Tribunal.

I am glad to report to you that the official opening of the headquarters building of the Tribunal in the Free and Hanseatic City of Hamburg took place on 3 July 2000, in the presence of several high dignitaries, including His Excellency Mr. Kofi Annan, the Secretary-General of the United Nations. The Tribunal is grateful to the Federal Republic of Germany and the Free and Hanseatic City of Hamburg for their efforts in erecting this magnificent new headquarters building.

It is a matter of special satisfaction that the Federal Republic of Germany and the Tribunal have, on 18 October 2000, concluded an Agreement on the Occupancy and Use of the Premises of the Tribunal. We hope to operate from the new building very soon. However, negotiations with regard to the Headquarters Agreement have not been concluded. It is our hope that we would soon reach agreement in this matter also.

During this year, the Tribunal heard the "*Camouco*" *Case* between Panama and France. Panama brought the case to the Tribunal on 17 January 2000 and the Tribunal was able to deliver the judgment within a period of three weeks thereafter. This case has once again demonstrated the Tribunal's ability to bring about dispute settlement without unnecessary delay or expense.

Speaking on the occasion of the official opening of the headquarters building of the Tribunal, the Secretary-General, Mr. Kofi Annan, observed that the Tribunal is "the keystone" of the Convention, that it is "the central forum available – to States, to certain international organizations, and even to some corporations – resolving disputes about how the Convention should be interpreted and applied", and that it has "already built a reputation among international lawyers as a modern court that can respond quickly". We are thankful to the Secretary-General for his support of the Tribunal. It is also very encouraging to note that the draft resolution under consideration (doc. A/55/L.10) underlines the Tribunal's important role and authority concerning the interpretation and application of the Convention.

I wish to bring to your attention that under the Convention the Tribunal could offer flexible mechanisms for settlement of disputes. Parties may choose between having a dispute heard by the full Tribunal, which includes all its judges, and having a dispute heard by one of its special chambers. The Tribunal formed the following special chambers for dealing with particular categories of disputes: Chamber of Summary Procedure; Chamber for Fisheries Disputes; Chamber for Marine Environment Disputes. It may form other special chambers, depending upon the need.

The Tribunal is also required to form an *ad hoc* chamber for dealing with a particular dispute submitted to it if the parties so request. The composition of such an *ad hoc* chamber is required to be determined by the Tribunal with the approval of the parties. This option would be of particular interest to parties who are considering arbitration. The costs of an *ad hoc* chamber are met from the general budget of the Tribunal and are not borne by the parties to the case. Parties also have the option of choosing *ad hoc* judges on their behalf. And a judgment given by any of the special chambers of the Tribunal shall be considered as rendered by the Tribunal. Some States have shown interest in *ad hoc* chambers.

The rule of law in international relations cannot be maintained unless international disputes are resolved by peaceful means. It is equally important that judgments rendered by international courts or tribunals are implemented in good faith and in time by States and other parties to international adjudication. It is encouraging to note that the United Nations Millennium Declaration found it appropriate to call upon Member States of the United Nations to "ensure compliance" with the decisions of the International Court of Justice, in compliance with the Charter of the United Nations, in cases to which they are parties. This exhortation is equally relevant in respect of decisions of all international courts or tribunals, whether within the framework of the United Nations system or outside. We are very happy to see that the draft resolution notes the obligation of parties to cases before a court or a tribunal referred to in article 287 of the Convention to ensure prompt compliance with the decisions rendered by such court or tribunal.

Not many States Parties to the Convention have filed declarations as regards choice of compulsory procedures for the settlement of disputes under article 287 of the Convention. Only 25 States Parties have filed such declarations. It is satisfying to note that the draft resolution under consideration calls upon States Parties to the Convention to consider making a written declaration choosing from the means for the settlement of disputes set out in article 287 of the Convention.

The establishment of new tribunals in recent years is indeed a positive development since such bodies fulfil complementary needs. The United Nations Convention on the Law of the Sea offers States a wide choice among several procedures for dispute settlement entailing binding decisions. These forums are of equal standing. The effect of more tribunals being available to the litigants is that more disputes have come to be resolved by parties by means of their choice. There is also the additional but in no way less important factor that several of the newly created tribunals are also accessible to non-State entities.

The financial situation of the Tribunal remains far from satisfactory. As of 9 October 2000, there was an unpaid balance of assessed contributions to the overall budget of the Tribunal in the amount of $ 1,791,009. I regret to inform you that as many as 35 States Parties to the Convention have never paid their assessed contributions. Timely payments of contributions have an important bearing on the ability of our Tribunal to discharge its functions effectively. I thank the sponsors of the draft resolution under consideration for inviting the General Assembly to make an appeal to States Parties to the Convention to pay their assessed contributions to the Tribunal, in full and on time.

Establishment of trust funds with a view to providing financial assistance to States for costs incurred in connection with disputes before international adjudicative forums is not a new concept. The availability of such funds would serve as a device to overcome financial impediments to the judicial settlement of disputes and promote peaceful settlement of disputes. We welcome in this regard the decision of the Tenth Meeting of States Parties to the Convention to recommend to the General Assembly the establishment of a trust fund, to be financed through voluntary contributions, for the purpose of providing financial assistance to States in order to help them in proceedings before our Tribunal. I wish to thank again the co-sponsors of the draft resolution for inviting the Assembly to request the Secretary-General to establish such a voluntary fund. I convey my appreciation to the delegations which announced contributions to the proposed Fund.

There has not been much progress in the matter of ratification of the Agreement on the Privileges and Immunities of the International Tribunal for the Law of the Sea. Since I spoke to you on 22 November 1999, only two more States have ratified the Agreement, making the total number of ratifications four. As you are aware, for the Agreement to enter into force, at least ten instruments of ratification or accession need to be deposited with the Secretary-General of the United Nations. Here, too, we welcome the provision in the draft resolution calling upon States that have not done so to consider ratifying or acceding to the Agreement.

ANNEX XII

RESOLUTION 55/7 ON "OCEANS AND THE LAW OF THE SEA"

Adopted on 30 October 2000 by the United Nations General Assembly.

TEXT: UN document A/RES/55/7 of 2 May 2001.

Resolution adopted by the General Assembly
[without reference to a Main Committee (A/55/L.10 and Corr.1 and Add.1)]

55/7. Oceans and the law of the sea

The General Assembly,

Recalling its resolutions 49/28 of 6 December 1994, 52/26 of 26 November 1997, 54/31 and 54/33 of 24 November 1999 and other relevant resolutions adopted subsequent to the entry into force of the United Nations Convention on the Law of the Sea ("the Convention")[1] on 16 November 1994,

Recalling also its resolution 2749 (XXV) of 17 December 1970, and considering that the Convention, together with the Agreement relating to the Implementation of Part XI of the United Nations Convention on the Law of the Sea of 10 December 1982 ("the Agreement"),[2] provides the regime to be applied to the Area and its resources as defined in the Convention,

Emphasizing the universal and unified character of the Convention and its fundamental importance for the maintenance and strengthening of international peace and security, as well as for the sustainable use and development of the seas and oceans and their resources,

Reaffirming that the Convention sets out the legal framework within which all activities in the oceans and seas must be carried out and is of strategic importance as the basis for national, regional and global action in the marine sector, and that its integrity needs to be maintained, as recognized also by the United Nations Conference on Environment and Development in chapter 17 of Agenda 21,[3]

Conscious of the importance of increasing the number of States parties to the Convention and the Agreement in order to achieve the goal of universal participation,

Conscious also that the problems of ocean space are closely interrelated and need to be considered as a whole,

Convinced of the need, building on arrangements established in accordance with the Convention, to improve coordination at the national level and cooperation and coordination at both intergovernmental and inter-agency levels, in order to address all aspects of oceans and seas in an integrated manner,

Recognizing the important role that the competent international organizations have in relation to ocean affairs, in implementing the Convention and in promoting sustainable development of the oceans and seas and their resources,

Taking note of the report of the Secretary-General,[4] and reaffirming the importance of the annual consideration and review of developments relating to ocean affairs and the law of the sea by the General Assembly as the global institution having the competence to undertake such a review,

---

[1] United Nations publication, Sales No. E.97.V.10.

[2] Resolution 48/263, annex.

[3] *Report of the United Nations Conference on Environment and Development, Rio de Janeiro, 3–14 June 1992* United Nations publication, Sales No. E.93.I.8 and corrigenda, vol. I: *Resolutions adopted by the Conference*, resolution 1, annex II.

[4] A/55/61.

Taking note also of the outcome of the first meeting of the United Nations open-ended informal consultative process ("the Consultative Process"),[5] established by the General Assembly in its resolution 54/33 in order to facilitate the annual review by the Assembly of developments in ocean affairs,

Mindful of the importance of the oceans and seas for the earth's ecosystem and for providing the vital resources for food security and for sustaining economic prosperity and the well-being of present and future generations,

Bearing in mind the contribution that major groups, as identified in Agenda 21, can make to raising awareness of the goal of the sustainable development of the oceans and seas and their resources,

Underlining the essential need for capacity-building to ensure that all States, especially developing countries, in particular least developed countries and small island developing States, are able both to implement the Convention and to benefit from the sustainable development of their marine resources, as well as to participate fully in global and regional forums and processes dealing with oceans and law of the sea issues,

Expressing serious concern at the increase in illegal, unreported and unregulated fishing, and recognizing the importance of strengthening cooperation to combat such activities, particularly through the relevant regional fisheries management organizations and arrangements,

Recalling that the role of international cooperation and coordination on a bilateral basis and, where applicable, within a subregional, interregional, regional or global framework is to support and supplement the national efforts of coastal States to promote the integrated management and sustainable development of coastal and marine areas,

Expressing its deep concern at the degradation of the marine environment, particularly from land-based activities, and emphasizing the need for international cooperation and for a coordinated approach at the national level to this problem, bringing together the many different economic sectors involved and protecting the ecosystems, and in this context reaffirming the importance of ensuring full implementation of the Global Programme of Action for the Protection of the Marine Environment from Land-based Activities,[6]

Reiterating its concern at the degradation of the marine environment as a result of pollution from ships, in particular through the illegal release of oil and other harmful substances, and as a result of pollution by dumping of hazardous waste, including radioactive materials, nuclear waste and dangerous chemicals,

Recalling the importance of marine science in promoting the sustainable management of the oceans and seas, including in the assessment, conservation, management and sustainable use of fish stocks,

---

[5] See A/55/274.

[6] A/51/116, annex II.

Emphasizing the need to ensure access of decision makers to advice and information on marine science and technology, as well as to the transfer of technology and support for the production and diffusion of factual information and knowledge for end-users, as appropriate,

Expressing concern once again at the continuing threat from piracy and armed robbery at sea, and in this context noting the letter from the Secretary-General of the International Maritime Organization to the Secretary-General of the United Nations drawing attention to the increasing number and seriousness of incidents of piracy and armed robbery at sea,[7]

Reaffirming the importance of enhancing the safety of navigation, as well as the necessity for cooperation in this regard,

Emphasizing the importance of the protection of the underwater cultural heritage, and recalling in this context the provisions of article 303 of the Convention,

Noting the responsibilities of the Secretary-General under the Convention and related resolutions of the General Assembly, in particular resolutions 49/28 and 52/26, and in this context the expected increase in responsibilities of the Division for Ocean Affairs and the Law of the Sea of the Office of Legal Affairs of the Secretariat in view of the progress in the work of the Commission on the Limits of the Continental Shelf ("the Commission") and the anticipated receipt of submissions from States,

1. *Calls upon* all States that have not done so, in order to achieve the goal of universal participation, to become parties to the Convention and the Agreement;

2. *Reaffirms* the unified character of the Convention;

3. *Calls upon* States to harmonize, as a matter of priority, their national legislation with the provisions of the Convention, to ensure the consistent application of those provisions and to ensure also that any declarations or statements that they have made or make when signing, ratifying or acceding to the Convention are in conformity therewith and, otherwise, to withdraw any of their declarations or statements that are not in conformity;

4. *Encourages* States parties to the Convention to deposit with the Secretary-General charts and lists of geographical coordinates, as provided for in the Convention;

5. *Urges* the international community to assist, as appropriate, developing countries, in particular least developed countries and small island developing States, in the acquisition of data and the preparation of charts or lists of geographical coordinates for publication under articles 16, 22, 47, 75 and 84 of the Convention and in the preparation of information under article 76 and annex II to the Convention;

---

[7] A/55/311, annex.

6. *Requests* the Secretary-General to convene the eleventh Meeting of States Parties to the Convention in New York from 14 to 18 May 2001 and to provide the services required;

7. *Notes with satisfaction* the continued contribution of the International Tribunal for the Law of the Sea ("the Tribunal") to the peaceful settlement of disputes in accordance with Part XV of the Convention, underlines its important role and authority concerning the interpretation or application of the Convention and the Agreement, encourages States parties to the Convention to consider making a written declaration choosing from the means set out in article 287 for the settlement of disputes concerning the interpretation or application of the Convention and the Agreement, and invites States to note the provisions of annexes V, VI, VII and VIII to the Convention concerning, respectively, conciliation, the Tribunal, arbitration and special arbitration;

8. *Recalls* the obligations of parties to cases before a court or a tribunal referred to in article 287 of the Convention to ensure prompt compliance with the decisions rendered by such court or tribunal;

9. *Requests* the Secretary-General to establish a voluntary trust fund to assist States in the settlement of disputes through the Tribunal, and to report annually to the Meeting of States Parties to the Convention on the status of the fund;[8]

10. *Invites* States, intergovernmental organizations, national institutions, non-governmental organizations, as well as natural and juridical persons, to make voluntary financial contributions to the fund;

11. *Encourages* States that have not yet done so to nominate conciliators and arbitrators in accordance with annexes V and VII to the Convention, and requests the Secretary-General to continue to update and circulate lists of these conciliators and arbitrators on a regular basis;

12. *Welcomes* the adoption of the Regulations on Prospecting and Exploration for Polymetallic Nodules in the Area by the Assembly of the International Seabed Authority ("the Authority") on 13 July 2000,[9] and notes with satisfaction that the Authority is now in a position to proceed to issue contracts to the registered pioneer investors in accordance with the Convention, the Agreement and those Regulations;

13. *Appeals* to all States parties to the Convention to pay their assessed contributions to the Authority and the Tribunal in full and on time, and appeals also to all former provisional members of the Authority to pay any outstanding contributions;

---

[8] Terms of reference are annexed to the present resolution (see annex I).

[9] ISBA/6/A/18, annex.

14. *Calls upon* States that have not done so to consider ratifying or acceding to the Agreement on the Privileges and Immunities of the Tribunal[10] and to the Protocol on the Privileges and Immunities of the Authority;[11]

15. *Notes* the continuing progress in the work of the Commission, including the successful open meeting on 1 May 2000[12] aimed at assisting States in implementing the provisions of the Convention related to the establishment of the outer limits of the continental shelf beyond 200 nautical miles and facilitating the preparation of submissions to the Commission by coastal States regarding the outer limits of their continental shelf;

16. *Also notes* that the Commission has issued a basic flow chart on the preparation of submissions[13] and has adopted an outline for a five-day training course on the delineation of the outer limits of the continental shelf beyond 200 nautical miles and for the preparation of submissions,[14] and encourages concerned States and relevant international organizations and institutions to consider developing and making available such training courses;

17. *Recalls* that under article 4 of annex II to the Convention, a State intending to establish the outer limits of its continental shelf beyond 200 nautical miles is to submit particulars of such limits to the Commission within ten years of the entry into force of the Convention for that State;

18. *Requests* the Secretary-General to establish a voluntary trust fund to provide training for technical and administrative staff, and technical and scientific advice, as well as personnel, to assist developing States, in particular the least developed countries and small island developing States, for the purpose of desktop studies and project planning, and preparing and submitting information under article 76 and annex II to the Convention in accordance with the procedures of the Scientific and Technical Guidelines of the Commission on the Limits of the Continental Shelf, and to report annually to the General Assembly on the status of the fund;[15]

19. *Invites* States, intergovernmental organizations and agencies, national institutions, non-governmental organizations and international financial institutions as well as natural and juridical persons to make voluntary financial or other contributions to the fund;

20. *Requests* the Secretary-General to establish a voluntary trust fund for the purpose of defraying the cost of participation of the members of the Commission from developing States in the meetings of the Commission,[16] and invites States to contribute to the fund;

21. *Approves* the convening by the Secretary-General of the ninth session of the Commission in New York from 21 to 25 May 2001 and a tenth session, if necessary, starting

---

[10] SPLOS/25.

[11] ISBA/4/A/8, annex.

[12] See CLCS/21.

[13] CLCS/22.

[14] CLCS/24.

[15] Terms of reference are annexed to the present resolution (see annex II).

[16] Covering both travel expenses and daily subsistence allowance.

on 27 August 2001 of a duration of three weeks in the event of a submission being filed, or of one week, depending on the workload of the Commission;

22. *Calls upon* bilateral and multilateral donor agencies to keep their programmes under review to ensure the availability in all States, particularly in developing States, of the economic, legal, navigational, scientific and technical capacities and skills necessary for the full implementation of the Convention and the sustainable development of the oceans and seas and their resources nationally, regionally and globally, and in so doing to bear in mind the rights of landlocked developing States;

23. *Requests* the Secretary-General, in cooperation with the competent international organizations and programmes, including the Food and Agriculture Organization of the United Nations, the International Labour Organization, the International Hydrographic Organization, the International Maritime Organization, the United Nations Development Programme, the United Nations Industrial Development Organization, the Intergovernmental Oceanographic Commission of the United Nations Educational, Scientific and Cultural Organization, the United Nations Environment Programme, the United Nations Conference on Trade and Development, the World Meteorological Organization and the World Bank, as well as representatives of regional development banks and the donor community, to review the efforts being made to build capacity as well as to identify the duplications that need to be avoided and the gaps that may need to be filled for ensuring consistent approaches, both nationally and regionally, with a view to implementing the Convention, and to include a section on this subject in his annual report on oceans and the law of the sea;

24. *Urges* States to continue the development of an international plan of action on illegal, unregulated and unreported fishing for the Food and Agriculture Organization of the United Nations, as a matter of priority, and in this context recognizes the central role that regional and subregional fisheries organizations and arrangements will have in addressing this issue;[17]

25. *Emphasizes* the importance of the implementation of Part XII of the Convention in order to protect and preserve the marine environment, including coastal areas, and its living marine resources against pollution and physical degradation;

26. *Acknowledges* the need to build national capacity for the integrated management of the coastal zone and for the protection of its ecosystem, and invites relevant parts of the United Nations system to promote these aims, including through the provision of the training and institutional support needed to achieve them;

27. *Calls upon* States to prioritize action on marine pollution from land-based sources as part of their national sustainable development strategies and local Agenda 21 programmes, in an integrated and inclusive manner, as a means of enhancing their support for the Global Programme of Action for the Protection of the Marine Environment from

[17] See resolution 55/8.

Land-based Activities, and calls for their active collaboration to ensure that the 2001 intergovernmental review will enhance the implementation of the Global Programme of Action;

28. *Calls upon* United Nations agencies and programmes identified in General Assembly resolution 51/189 of 16 December 1996 to fulfil their roles in support of the Global Programme of Action and to provide information to Governments for their consideration at the 2001 intergovernmental review of the Global Programme of Action and to the Secretary-General for his annual report on oceans and the law of the sea on their action in this regard and on other steps which could be taken to protect the marine environment;

29. *Invites* the United Nations Environment Programme and the World Bank, as part of the preparations for the 2001 review of the Global Programme of Action, to consult with Governments, representatives of the private sector, financial institutions and bilateral and multilateral donor agencies to review their involvement in the implementation of the Global Programme of Action and to consider, inter alia, what international support is needed to help overcome the obstacles to the preparation and implementation of national and local action programmes and how they can participate actively in partnership-building with developing countries for the transfer of the requisite technology in accordance with the Convention and taking into account the relevant parts of Agenda 21, capacity-building and funding for the implementation of the Global Programme of Action;

30. *Emphasizes* the importance of ensuring that adverse impacts on the marine environment are taken into account when assessing and evaluating development programmes and projects;

31. *Urges* States to take all practicable steps, in accordance with the International Convention for the Prevention of Pollution from Ships, 1973, as modified by the Protocol of 1978 relating thereto, to prevent pollution of the marine environment from ships and, in accordance with the 1972 Convention on the Prevention of Marine Pollution by Dumping of Wastes and Other Matter,[18] to prevent pollution of the marine environment by dumping, and further calls upon States to become parties to and to implement the 1996 Protocol to the 1972 Convention;[19]

32. *Stresses* the need to consider as a matter of priority the issues of marine science and technology and to focus on how best to implement the many obligations of States and competent international organizations under Parts XIII and XIV of the Convention, and calls upon States to adopt, as appropriate and in accordance with international law, the necessary national laws, regulations, policies and procedures to promote and facilitate marine scientific research and cooperation;

33. *Urges* all States, in particular coastal States, in affected regions to take all necessary and appropriate measures to prevent and combat incidents of piracy and armed robbery at sea, including through regional cooperation, and to investigate or cooperate in the

---

[18] United Nations, *Treaty Series*, vol. 1046, No. 15749.

[19] IMO/LC.2/Circ.380.

investigation of such incidents wherever they occur and bring the alleged perpetrators to justice, in accordance with international law;

34. *Calls upon* States, in this context, to cooperate fully with the International Maritime Organization, including by submitting reports on incidents to the organization and by implementing its guidelines on preventing attacks of piracy and armed robbery;

35. *Urges* States to become parties to the Convention for the Suppression of Unlawful Acts against the Safety of Maritime Navigation and its Protocol,[20] and to ensure its effective implementation;

36. *Notes* the continued work of the United Nations Educational, Scientific and Cultural Organization towards a convention for the implementation of the provisions of the Convention, relating to the protection of the underwater cultural heritage, and re-emphasizes the importance of ensuring that the instrument to be elaborated is in full conformity with the relevant provisions of the Convention;

37. *Invites* Member States and others in a position to do so to contribute to the further development of the Hamilton Shirley Amerasinghe Memorial Fellowship Programme on the Law of the Sea established by the General Assembly in resolution 35/116 of 10 December 1980 and to support the training activities under the TRAIN-SEA-COAST Programme of the Division for Ocean Affairs and the Law of the Sea of the Office of Legal Affairs of the Secretariat;

38. *Expresses its appreciation* to the Secretary-General for the annual comprehensive report on oceans and the law of the sea, prepared by the Division for Ocean Affairs and the Law of the Sea, as well as for the other activities of the Division, in accordance with the provisions of the Convention and the mandate set forth in resolutions 49/28, 52/26 and 54/33;

39. *Requests* the Secretary-General to continue to carry out the responsibilities entrusted to him in the Convention and related resolutions of the General Assembly, including resolutions 49/28 and 52/26, and to ensure that appropriate resources are made available to the Division for Ocean Affairs and the Law of the Sea for the performance of such responsibilities under the approved budget for the Organization;

40. *Reaffirms* its decision to undertake an annual review and evaluation of the implementation of the Convention and other developments relating to ocean affairs and the law of the sea, taking into account resolution 54/33 establishing the consultative process to facilitate the review of developments in ocean affairs, and requests the Secretary-General to convene the second meeting of the Consultative Process in New York from 7 to 11 May 2001;

41. *Recommends* that, in its deliberations on the report of the Secretary-General on oceans and the law of the sea at its second meeting, the Consultative Process organize its discussions around the following areas:

---

[20] International Maritime Organization publication, Sales No. 462.88.12E.

(a) Marine science and the development and transfer of marine technology as mutually agreed, including capacity-building in this regard;
(b) Coordination and cooperation in combating piracy and armed robbery at sea;

42. *Requests* the Secretary-General to ensure more effective collaboration and coordination between the relevant parts of the Secretariat of the United Nations and the United Nations as a whole, in particular in ensuring the effectiveness, transparency and responsiveness of the Subcommittee on Oceans and Coastal Areas of the Administrative Committee on Coordination, and also requests the Secretary-General to include in his report suggestions on initiatives to improve coordination, in accordance with resolution 54/33, and encourages all United Nations bodies to help this process by drawing to the attention of the Secretariat and the Subcommittee those areas of their work which may, directly or indirectly, affect the work of other United Nations bodies;

43. *Also requests* the Secretary-General to bring the present resolution to the attention of heads of intergovernmental organizations, the specialized agencies and funds and programmes of the United Nations engaged in activities relating to ocean affairs and the law of the sea, and the Subcommittee on Oceans and Coastal Areas of the Administrative Committee on Coordination, drawing their attention to paragraphs of particular relevance to them, and underlines the importance of their input for the report of the Secretary-General on oceans and the law of the sea and of their participation in relevant meetings and processes;

44. *Invites* the competent international organizations, as well as funding institutions, to take specific account of the present resolution in their programmes and activities, and to contribute to the preparation of the comprehensive report of the Secretary-General on oceans and the law of the sea;

45. *Requests* the Secretary-General to establish a voluntary trust fund for the purpose of assisting developing countries, in particular least developed countries, small island developing States and landlocked developing States, in attending the meetings of the Consultative Process, and invites States to contribute to this fund;

46. *Also requests* the Secretary-General to report to the General Assembly at its fifty-sixth session on the implementation of the present resolution, including other developments and issues relating to ocean affairs and the law of the sea, in connection with his annual comprehensive report on oceans and the law of the sea, and to provide the report in accordance with the modalities set out in resolution 54/33;

47. *Decides* to include in the provisional agenda of its fifty-sixth session the item entitled "Oceans and the law of the sea".

44th plenary meeting
30 October 2000

Annex I

International Tribunal for the Law of the Sea Trust Fund

Terms of reference

Reasons for establishing the Trust Fund

1. Part XV of the United Nations Convention on the Law of the Sea ("the Convention") provides for the settlement of disputes. In particular, article 287 specifies that States are free to choose one or more of the following means:

(a) The International Tribunal for the Law of the Sea;

(b) The International Court of Justice;

(c) An arbitral tribunal;

(d) A special arbitral tribunal.

2. The Secretary-General already operates a Trust Fund for the International Court of Justice (see A/47/444). The Permanent Court of Arbitration has established a Financial Assistance Fund. The burden of costs should not be a factor for States, in making the choices under article 287, in deciding whether a dispute should be submitted to the Tribunal or in deciding upon the response to an application made to the Tribunal by others. For these reasons, it was decided to create a Trust Fund for the International Tribunal for the Law of the Sea ("the Tribunal").

Object and purpose of the Trust Fund

3. This Trust Fund ("the Fund") is established by the Secretary-General in accordance with General Assembly resolution 55/7 and pursuant to the Agreement on Cooperation and Relationship between the United Nations and the Tribunal of 18 December 1997 (resolution 52/251, annex).

4. The purpose of the Fund is to provide financial assistance to States parties to the Convention for expenses incurred in connection with cases submitted, or to be submitted, to the Tribunal, including its Seabed Disputes Chamber and any other Chamber.

5. Assistance, which will be provided in accordance with the following terms and conditions, should only be provided in appropriate cases, principally those proceeding to the merits where jurisdiction is not an issue, but in exceptional circumstances may be provided for any phase of the proceedings.

Contributions to the Fund

6. The Secretary-General invites States, intergovernmental organizations, national institutions, non-governmental organizations, as well as natural and juridical persons, to make voluntary financial contributions to the Fund.

Application for assistance

7. An application for assistance from the Fund may be submitted by any State party to the Convention. The application should describe the nature of the case which is to be, or has been, brought by or against the State concerned and should provide an estimate of the costs for which financial assistance is requested. The application should contain a commitment to supply a final statement of account of the expenditures made from approved amounts, to be certified by an auditor acceptable to the United Nations.

Panel of experts

8. The Secretary-General will establish a panel of experts, normally three persons of the highest professional standing, to make recommendations on each request. The task of each panel is to examine the application and to recommend to the Secretary-General the amount of the financial assistance to be given, the phase or phases of the proceedings in respect of which assistance is to be given and the types of expenses for which the assistance may be used.

Granting of assistance

9. The Secretary-General will provide financial assistance from the Fund on the basis of the recommendations of the panel of experts. Payments will be made against receipts showing expenditures made in respect of approved costs. The latter may include:

(a) Preparing the application and the written pleadings;

(b) Professional fees of counsel and advocates for written and oral pleadings;

(c) Travel and expenses of legal representation in Hamburg during the various phases of a case;

(d) Execution of an Order of Judgment of the Tribunal, such as marking a boundary in the territorial sea.

Application of the Financial Regulations and Rules of the United Nations

10. The Financial Regulations and Rules of the United Nations will apply to the administration of the Fund, including the procedures for audit.

Reporting

11. An annual report on the activities of the Fund, including details of the contributions to and disbursements from the Fund, will be made to the Meeting of States Parties to the Convention.

Implementing office

12. The Division for Ocean Affairs and the Law of the Sea of the Office of Legal Affairs is the implementing office for this Fund and provides the services for the operation of the Fund.

Offers of professional assistance

13. The implementing office also maintains a list of offers of professional assistance which may be made on a reduced fee basis by suitably qualified persons or bodies. If an applicant for assistance so requests, the implementing office will make the list of offers available to it for its consideration and decision; both financial and other assistance may be extended in respect of the same case or phase thereof.

Revision

14. The General Assembly may revise the above if circumstances so require.

Annex II

Trust fund for the purpose of facilitating the preparation of submissions to the Commission on the Limits of the Continental Shelf for developing States, in particular the least developed countries and small island developing States, and compliance with article 76 of the United Nations Convention on the Law of the Sea

Terms of reference, guidelines and rules

1. Reasons for establishing the Trust Fund

1. Promoting and developing the marine scientific and technological capacity of developing States, in particular the least developed countries and small island States, with a view to accelerating their social and economic development, is essential for the effective implementation of the United Nations Convention on the Law of the Sea of 10 December 1982 ("the Convention").

2. Coastal States intending to establish the outer limits of their continental shelf beyond 200 nautical miles from the baseline from which the breadth of their territorial sea is measured are required by article 76 of the Convention to submit the relevant data and information to the Commission on the Limits of the Continental Shelf ("the Commission"). In accordance with article 4 of annex II to the Convention, the particulars of such limits should be submitted to the Commission within ten years of the entry into force of the Convention for that State. For some States a submission should be made by 16 November 2004.

3. Developing States, in particular the least developed countries and small island developing States, may face difficulties in complying with the time limit for submissions to the Commission. The Trust Fund is intended to assist these States in complying with the requirements relating to a submission to the Commission.

4. Under article 3, paragraph 1 (b), of annex II to the Convention, the Commission may provide scientific and technical advice, if requested by the coastal States concerned, during the preparation of the data to be submitted in accordance with article 76.

5. The Commission has adopted an outline for a five-day training course in order to facilitate the preparation of submissions in accordance with its Scientific and Technical

Guidelines. The course is to be developed and delivered by interested Governments, international organizations and institutions which possess the necessary expertise and facilities. The Commission has likewise prepared a basic flow chart illustrating the preparation of submissions by coastal States.

6. The delineation of the continental shelf of a coastal State in accordance with article 76 and annex II to the Convention and annex II to the Final Act of the Third United Nations Conference on the Law of the Sea ("the Final Act") requires a programme for hydrographic and geoscientific surveying and mapping of the continental margin. The complexity and scale, and hence the costs involved, of such a programme will vary greatly from State to State according to the different geographical and geophysical circumstances. A first approach will always involve an assessment of the particular case at hand, followed by planning of appropriate projects for further data acquisition. Such projects require the contracting of high-level scientific/technical expertise and modern technology. By nature, the costs involved in such data acquisition projects are substantial. In addition to contributing to the Voluntary Fund herein established, the international community should make every effort to facilitate the full implementation of article 76 both financially and in any other possible way or capacity.

7. The initial assessment and the project planning itself will require qualifications in hydrography and geosciences in addition to a full understanding of the relevant provisions of the Convention. The final preparation of a submission to the Commission also requires high-level expertise in geosciences and hydrography.

8. The United Nations has extensive experience in providing assistance to countries for their industrial and economic development. This experience could be extended and utilized to assist States in implementing their rights and obligations under article 76 of the Convention.

2. Objects and purpose of the Trust Fund

9. The Secretary-General, under the Financial Regulations and Rules of the United Nations, establishes the present Trust Fund ("the Fund"). The object of the Fund is to enable developing States, in particular the least developed coastal countries and small island developing States, to make an initial assessment of their particular case, make appropriate plans for further investigations and data acquisition, and to prepare the final submission documents when the necessary data have been acquired.

10. The data acquisition campaigns themselves are not the object of the Fund.

11. An initial assessment of the nature of the continental shelf of a coastal State is often made in the form of a desktop study, which is a review and compilation of all existing data and information. Decisions for further action and/or planning for further data acquisition and mapping projects will be based on such a study.

12. The purpose of the Fund is to provide, in accordance with the terms and conditions specified in the Financial Regulations and Rules of the United Nations:

(a) Training to the appropriate technical and administrative staff of the coastal State in question, in order to enable them to perform initial desktop studies and project planning, or at least to take full part in these activities;

(b) Funds for such studies and planning activities, including funds for advisory/consultancy assistance if needed.

13. The preparation of the final submission documents will have to meet the requirements of article 76 and annex II to the Convention (and for some States, annex II to the Final Act) and the Scientific and Technical Guidelines of the Commission. The training should take this into account and aim at enabling the State's personnel also to prepare most of these documents themselves. The preparation of the submission may induce costs that may be met by funds from the Fund (e.g. software and hardware equipment, technical assistance, etc.).

3. Contributions to the Fund

14. The Secretary-General invites States, intergovernmental organizations and agencies, national institutions, non-governmental organizations and international financial institutions as well as natural and juridical persons to make voluntary financial or other contributions to the Fund.

4. Application for financial assistance

15. An application for financial assistance from the Fund may be submitted by any developing State, in particular the least developed countries and small island developing States, who are Members of the United Nations and party to the Convention.

16. The purpose of the financial assistance applied for should be specified. Financial assistance may be sought for the following purposes:

(a) Training of technical and administrative staff;

(b) Desktop study or other means to make an initial assessment of the nature of the continental shelf and its limits;

(c) Working out of plans for the acquisition of necessary additional data and mapping projects;

(d) Preparation of final submission documents;

(e) Advisory/consultancy assistance related to the above points.

17. Detailed information under each of these purposes should be provided as follows:

(a) *Training of technical and administrative staff*

The application shall be accompanied by:

(i) A specification of the goal of the training and which positions the trainees are intended to fill afterwards;

(ii) Information on the training institute(s) in question;

(iii) A copy of the training course(s);

(iv) The curricula vitae of the trainees;

(v) An itemized statement of the estimated costs for which assistance is requested.

(b) *Desktop study or other means to make an assessment of the nature of the continental shelf and its limits*

The application shall be accompanied by:

(i) A short description of the aim of the study;

(ii) An overview map of the area in question;

(iii) An overview, as complete as possible, of the database already available to the State;

(iv) An outline of how the work will be done and what tools are available (software and hardware);

(v) A specification of what will be done by the State's own staff, and what will be contracted for;

(vi) An itemized statement of the estimated costs for which assistance is requested.

(c) *Working out of plans for the acquisition of necessary additional data and mapping projects*

The application shall be accompanied by:

(i) A summary of the status of knowledge of the continental margin, preferably based on a previous desktop study;

(ii) A preliminary assessment of the needs for specific additional data and/or information in accordance with the requirements of article 76 and annex II to the Convention, and annex II to the Final Act;

(iii) An itemized statement of the estimated costs for which assistance is requested.

(d) *Preparation of final submission documents*

The application shall be accompanied by:

(i) A specification of what kind of assistance is needed;

(ii) An itemized statement of the estimated costs for which assistance is requested.

(e) *Advisory/consultancy assistance related to the above points*

The application shall be accompanied by:

(i) A copy of the contract between the Government and the technical or scientific expert in question;

(ii) An itemized statement of the costs for which assistance is requested.

18. In all these cases the application shall be accompanied by an undertaking that the requesting State shall supply a final statement of account providing details of the expenditures made from the approved amounts, to be certified by an auditor acceptable to the United Nations.

5. Consideration of applications

19. Each request for financial assistance shall be considered by the Division for Ocean Affairs and the Law of the Sea of the Office of Legal Affairs ("the Division"), which acts as the secretariat of the Commission.

20. The Division may engage an independent panel of experts of the highest moral standing to assist in the examination of applications on the basis of section 4 above and to recommend the amount of financial assistance to be given. However, no sitting Commission member should serve on this panel of experts. The Division shall prepare and circulate to Member States a list of prospective members of the panel of experts. Any member of the expert panel opposed by a Member State should not be included in the panel. The Division shall on an annual basis provide a list of the panel of experts as an annex to the annual report of the Secretary-General.

21. In considering the application, the Division shall be guided solely by the financial needs of the requesting developing State and availability of funds, with priority given to least developed countries and small island developing States, taking into account the imminence of pending deadlines.

22. Travel expenses and subsistence allowance are payable to independent experts engaged by the Division to consider applications.

6. Granting of assistance

23. The Secretary-General will provide financial assistance from the Fund on the basis of the evaluation and recommendations of the Division. Payments will be made against receipts evidencing actual expenditures for approved costs.

7. Application of article 5 of annex II to the Convention

24. Nationals of the coastal State making the submission who are members of the Commission and any Commission member who has assisted a coastal State by providing scientific and technical advice with respect to the delineation shall not be a member of the subcommission dealing with that submission but have the right to participate as a member in the proceedings of the Commission concerning the said submission. In an effort to promote transparency and to give full effect to article 5 of annex II to the Convention there should be full disclosure by Commission members, Trust Fund recipients and training sponsors to the Division of any pre-submission contacts.

8. Reporting requirements for full disclosure

25. Interested Governments, international organizations and institutions who provide any training for which any costs are reimbursed by this Fund are strongly encouraged to provide the complete list of participants to the Division.

26. Commission members who participate in any activities pursuant to this Fund shall disclose this information to the Division.

27. Upon submission to the Commission of its information on the limits of its continental shelf pursuant to article 76 of the Convention, a coastal State that has received assistance from this Fund shall disclose this information, including the involvement of any Commission members.

9. Application of the Financial Regulations and Rules of the United Nations

28. The Financial Regulations and Rules of the United Nations shall apply to the administration of the Fund. The Fund shall be subject to the auditing procedures provided therein.

10. Reporting to the General Assembly

29. An annual report on the activities of the Fund, including details of the contributions to and disbursements from the Fund, will be made to the General Assembly.

11. Implementing office

30. The Division for Ocean Affairs and the Law of the Sea of the Office of Legal Affairs is the implementing office for the Fund and will provide the services required for the operation of the Fund.

12. Revision

31. The General Assembly may revise the above if circumstances so require.